MEMOIRS OF AN OXFORD DON

Mark Pattison was born in 1813 and grew up in the rectory at Hauxwell in Yorkshire. As a student at Oriel College, Oxford, he knew Newman and Pusey and was influenced by their ideas for religious reform. In 1839 Pattison was elected to a fellowship at Lincoln College, where he worked hard to improve the college's academic standing. He was principal tutor, bursar and subrector, but his failure in 1851 to be elected Rector was a personal crisis from which he never really recovered, despite success at a subsequent election.

In the eyes of his contemporaries, Pattison was the archetypal abrasive scholar and he has been identified with the character of Dr Casaubon in George Eliot's *Middlemarch*. But his *Memoirs*, remarkable at the time for their frankness, reveal a sensitive, introspective nature and a fine and independent mind, critical of many of the values of his day.

Pattison died in 1884. *Memoirs* were published in 1885.

Dr Vivian H. Green, editor of this edition of the *Memoirs*, was also Rector of Lincoln College. His other books include *Oxford Common Room* (Edward Arnold, 1957), *The Commonwealth of Lincoln College 1427 – 1977* (Oxford University Press, 1979) and *Love in a Cool Climate: Letters of Mark Pattison and Meta Bradley* (Oxford University Press, 1985).

CASSELL BIOGRAPHIES

MEMOIRS OF AN OXFORD DON

Mark Pattison
Late Rector of Lincoln College, Oxford

Edited with an Introduction and Notes by
Vivian H. H. Green
Honorary Fellow, formerly Rector, of Lincoln College, Oxford

CASSELL

Cassell Publishers Limited
Artillery House, Artillery Row
London SW1P 1RT

Introduction and Notes © V H H Green 1988

First published by Macmillan in 1885
Published in Cassell Biographies 1988

British Library Cataloguing in Publication Data
Pattison, Mark, *1813 – 1884*
[Memoirs]. Memoirs of an Oxford don. —
(Cassell biographies).
1. Oxfordshire. Oxford. Universities.
Colleges. Lincoln College. Pattison, Mark,
1813 – 1884. Biographies
I. [Memoirs] II. Title III. Green,
Vivian H.
378.425'74

ISBN 0-304-32219-9

Printed and bound in Great Britain
by Biddles Ltd, Guildford & King's Lynn

Contents

INTRODUCTION

by V. H. H. Green

MARK PATTISON'S *Memoirs*, though autobiographical in character, is not strictly speaking an autobiography. While it paints a fascinating picture of early and mid-nineteenth-century Oxford, the book is essentially an intellectual history. Prima facie, Mark Pattison's life was uneventful and even prosaic: that of an Oxford don dedicated to study and teaching, refreshed by gossip and dessert after dinner at the high table in the college hall. His *Memoirs* do not so much tell the story of this everyday life as disclose the slow liberation of a mind from the shackles and trammels of outmoded religious and intellectual prejudice. Not devoid of passion, the story is very personal, subtle, precise, clear, cool and sensitive. Even if it encapsulates a long-forgotten world, the drama is still sufficient to move us.

Mark Pattison was born on 10 October 1813, the first son of a Yorkshire clergyman, also called Mark, and his wife, Jane, the daughter of a Richmond jeweller. Since 1825 the elder Mark had been Rector of the small village of Hauxwell, near Catterick, on the fringes of beautiful Wensleydale. Life at Hauxwell in Mark's boyhood was isolated and, in some respects, idyllic. He never lost his love of country pursuits: riding on the moors, fishing in the rushing waters of the Rivers Ure and Swale, walking on the springy turf, listening to the song of the birds and breathing in the pure moorland air – enchantments which he continued to cherish throughout his life. They were still to form a consolation in illness and old age. Yet it was a restricted world in which Mark spent his boyhood, shrill with the childish voices of his sisters – there were to be ten in all. (His only brother, Frank, was twenty-one years younger than him.) His mother, rarely free from the pangs of childbirth, was a pious, placid woman, over-subservient to her strong-willed husband.

Mark's father, as the *Memoirs* make plain, dominated his son's early years, at first benevolently, ultimately diabolically. He had been at Brasenose College, Oxford, and was sufficiently acquainted with classical literature to educate Mark himself and later to coach him for entrance to the university. Yet he was not a cultured man, nor a man of wide intellectual interests. In the *Memoirs*, Pattison complained bitterly of the narrow and patchy instruction that he received from his father. His father was ambitious for his son, wanting him to go to Oxford and to win a fellowship at one of the colleges.

At first, relations between father and son were intimate and amicable. Mark won a place at Oriel College, then one of the most prestigious of Oxford's colleges, and he enjoyed returning home in the vacations. His sisters, full of admiration for their clever brother, listened intently to his tales of Oxford life. Then, in 1834, his father had a severe nervous breakdown and, for a time, was confined to a mental home at Acomb, near York. 'How to convey to you a correct idea of your father's mind I know not,' his mother told Mark. However his father seemed to recover and returned to the parish where he was to remain rector until his death, some thirty years later. In reality, his mental balance was irretrievably damaged. He became irascible and tyrannical, neglecting his parish and venting his spite on his unfortunate wife and daughters, who had no means of protecting themselves against the manifestations of his malevolence.

Mark, who hardly refers to the terrible situation that was developing at home in the *Memoirs*, was himself a target of his father's rage. A dry-as-dust Evangelical by conviction, Mark's father, his mind in a state of angry ferment, took umbrage when he learned that his son was becoming deeply involved in the Oxford Movement, or Tractarianism, so alien to his own religious views.

Pattison draws a very vivid picture of his years at Oriel. When he became an undergraduate, Oxford was already in the throes of a reform movement designed to remove the archaic features which had become characteristic of the university's life in the eighteenth century, but the movement was dilatory and only very slowly percolated through the colleges. Even at Oriel, generally regarded as the most academically advanced college, Pattison felt that the teaching was largely a matter of rote and old-fashioned in substance. Inadequately taught at Oxford, and suffering still from the defects of his earlier education at home, he graduated with only a second-class degree, to his acute disappointment.

After graduation, he stayed on at Oxford, hoping that, in spite of his unimpressive degree, he would stand a chance of being elected to a vacant fellowship at one or other of the colleges. He had gone up to Oxford a very gauche youth, socially unsure of himself. He was always to remain lacking in the social graces, but at least Oxford had eliminated the gaucheries characteristic of his first year. He had found congenial friends in Oriel with whom he walked and played cards and went to debates at the Oxford Union. Yet the feeling of inadequacy, which had so depressed him when he failed to get a first-class degree, was never far absent, reinforced by his failure to get the fellowships for which he had applied.

At the time, Oxford was in the midst of an upheaval much more controversial than the one which was so slowly reforming its conservative studies and system of government. This was the religious revival known familiarly as the Oxford Movement or, from the tracts by which their views were circulated, as Tractarianism. A group of Oxford dons, made up of John Keble, E. B. Pusey, Hurrell Froude and John Henry Newman, most of whom were associated with Oriel College, thought the established Church of England had lost its way by shedding its apostolic foundations and catholic teaching. In their eyes, it had now become too identified with the State, a theme which John Keble had elaborated in his famous Assize Sermon delivered at the university church, St Mary's, in July 1833. If, they concluded, the Church was truly to fulfil its divine mission, then it must recover its freedom and its catholicity. These views were popular neither with the ecclesiastical establishment nor with the majority of Oxford dons. Controversy raged, in which the undergraduate Pattison initially appeared to take only a passing interest. However, he became deeply involved in it after graduation.

As a member of the senior common room at Oriel, he came into contact with its leading lights, Pusey and Newman, and soon fell under the latter's spell. Until then, his only contact with Newman had been in a decanal role. Newman was now to become a sort of father-figure whom Pattison regarded with the deepest veneration, as he did the religious views of the Tractarians, the gospel by which he tried to live. Pattison became a regular worshipper at St Mary's Church, where Newman was the vicar until 1843. He also went eagerly to the gatherings of the semi-monastic community which Newman had set up at Littlemore, just outside Oxford, the activities of which he describes in great detail in the *Memoirs*, culled from the daily diary that he kept. At Newman's request, he wrote two books for the series of the lives of the saints which Newman was editing. These were short studies of the thirteenth-century archbishops of Canterbury, Stephen Langton and Edmund of Abingdon. E. B. Pusey, once a fellow of Oriel and then the Regius Professor of Hebrew and canon of Christ Church, was the doyen of the movement. He was very learned and pious but a narrow and reserved man who never fully enjoyed Pattison's confidence. However, he entrusted Pattison with the task of editing some patristic writings, and for a time Pattison lived in a small community which Pusey and Newman had set up in St Aldate's. He left it shortly before his election, in 1839, to a fellowship at Lincoln College.

If Oriel was one of the most advanced colleges in Oxford, Lincoln was certainly one of the more fossilised and conservative, if not patently reactionary, ones. If its fellows had known of Pattison's close association with the Tractarians, whom most of them regarded with suspicion, if not with hostility, they would never have elected him; but it was not only Pattison's religious enthusiasm which they soon grew to dislike. A natural student, he proved to be a very conscientious tutor whose pupils grew to regard him with real affection. One of them, A. J. Church, was later to comment that 'no one came away from his lectures without the feeling of roused enquiry, rather than that satisfied sense of acquisition which is so conducive to success ... he taught us to enter into the real minds of Aristotle and Plato, rather than to furnish assertions with well-founded theories.' However, Pattison's colleagues were unsympathetic towards his zeal for scholarship and his desire to improve the college's academic standing: both of which represented an implied criticism of their own slovenly standards. They also resented his unsocial nature. He had little time for drinking and cards, which his colleagues indulged in after dinner (which still took place at 4 or 5 p.m.), and he rarely dined in hall. Yet they could not ignore his ability and in

1842 he became one of the college's principal tutors, serving his turn, too, as bursar and subrector. His influence in college may have grown more by chance than by design, but it resulted in the occasional election to fellowships of men who sympathised with his academic aspirations and in some cases were strong supporters of his religious views. Nevertheless, the 'old gang' managed to reinforce their own views with elections which brought men like Metcalfe and Washbourne West into the governing body, who proved to be uncongenial colleagues for Pattison.

In these years, Pattison was a vigorous and even uncritical disciple of Newman and his associates – something that is borne out in the *Memoirs*. Although he did not openly proselytise in college, young men, who were attracted by the religious revival, sought his guidance and advice. 'I have got three of our own men,' he told his sisters at Hauxwell, 'a B.A. and two undergrads, who come every day to say Vespers with me – their own proposition you may be sure – I cannot express the joy with which I received it or the consolation it has been to me. I can see very plainly too they are all making efforts to keep the (Lenten) fast.' Some young men under his lead even formed a small brotherhood to foster devotion, to promote abstinence and charity in their own lives, to take the sacrament of Communion as frequently as possible and to set aside a part of their income for charitable purposes.

His election to a fellowship at Lincoln had been warmly greeted by the family at Hauxwell; but his father had taken strongly against the Oxford Movement. On the other hand, his sisters, reacting against the dry religious regime sponsored by their father, embraced Mark's religious views with great enthusiasm. They perused all the current literature, the sermons of Newman and Pusey, which their brother sent to them and endeavoured to put their teachings into practice. In the isolated Yorkshire rectory, the results were horrific. Pattison's father stormed, raged, forbade the practices and even preached against his family in the local church. 'Will you join the Papists in the dining room,' he once asked a visitor sarcastically, 'or be content to partake the fare of the poor solitary persecuted Protestant here?' In truth, though, he was the persecutor, not the persecuted. 'I imagine,' Fanny Pattison told her brother on 20 December 1842, 'the name of Christmas is almost forbid at Hauxwell, the termination of it being so dreadfully papistical . . . I cannot bear to give it the name of home, sweet place as it is in itself, yet anything more like home I never beheld.' 'He heard us shut the front door,' another sister, Eleanor, wrote on 6 January 1843, 'and flew out in so awful a rage after us into the lane, he cursed me, spit in my face, several times, and used most horrid language . . .' 'Our books,' she told Mark three days later, 'are threatened with destruction. Our united voices as we read the Psalms . . . were heard in the day time and listened to on the top of the stairs and this produced the uproar.' 'This poor, ill-fated parish before it is done with,' Mary Pattison reflected on 4 January 1844, 'every remnant of good such as may be found in such retired country places will be entirely eradicated.' The anguish of Hauxwell, which can hardly be glimpsed in the *Memoirs*, helps in part to explain the mental and spiritual crisis which Mark was to experience.

In Oxford, Mark was remote from his father's disapproval, but he could not be unaffected by his family's unhappiness – an unhappiness to which he had contributed by the propagation of his religious convictions. He found the atmosphere so fraught that, to the obvious distress of his sisters, his visits to Hauxwell became fleeting and infrequent. What made the situation even more harrowing was that, by the late 1840s, the faith which he had embraced with such enthusiasm was itself beginning to wane.

The *Memoirs* describes clearly, and even dispassionately, the emergence from what he was later to describe as a nightmare. He had become so identified with the fortunes of the right wing of the Tractarians that he had seriously considered joining the Roman Catholic Church. When, at the end of 1844, the heads of houses (that is the Oxford colleges) considered imposing a test which would have required a strictly Protestant interpretation of the Thirty-nine Articles of the *Book of Common Prayer*, Pattison came reluctantly to the conclusion that if this proposal were to become a law of the university, he would have no option but to become a Roman Catholic. The proposal was, however, given up. When Newman became a Roman Catholic, it was widely supposed by Pattison's friends that he would follow suit. 'We expected him', Pusey said, 'to become a Roman Catholic earliest of all.' It was then rumoured, as Meta Bradley reminded him many years later, 'that you had made up your mind to become a R.C. but that you

6

lost a particular train and next day you'd changed your mind.' 'I don't believe,' she added truly enough, 'that you would long have remained a Catholic, my own idea is that religion would never have suited your character.' To have become a Roman Catholic would have necessarily entailed the loss of his fellowship, which he cherished not simply as a means of livelihood, but as giving him the opportunity to follow a life of scholarship.

In fact, deep down, Pattison may never have been as completely committed as he makes out in the *Memoirs*. The seeds of scepticism fertilising in his fine, critical mind may have remained dormant, but they were not dead. He admitted that he did not find it easy to keep strictly to the rules of a spiritual life; fasting did not always suit the nervous digestion from which he always suffered. 'Altogether', he wrote in November 1843, 'I seem to be broken from my moorings and to have lost sight altogether of all that I thought I saw and felt so deeply and strongly.' So he shed slowly the doctrines of a faith which he came more and more to regard as irrational and illiberal, and turned his attention to what seemed to him a more urgent and pressing task – the reform of the university and an improvement in academic standards. In the late 1840s, he concentrated increasingly on these matters. His sisters at Hauxwell, still strongly committed to the views that he was now shedding, were much disturbed by this about turn, as were many of his former pupils at Lincoln.

As he dropped his Tractarian ideas in favour of a broad churchmanship, which was to move slowly but inexorably towards radical liberalism and ultimately agnosticism, so his reputation as a man of learning grew. Although still regarded with distaste by the old-timers at Lincoln, he had a sufficiently strong following among the fellows to warrant the supposition that when the Rector, John Radford, died in the autumn of 1851, he stood a good chance of being elected his successor. In the *Memoirs*, he describes the story of the election vividly but not wholly accurately.† At length, he realised that, as a result of the backstepping of one of the fellows who had promised to support him, he would lose the election. Although he and his followers could not save their cause, they managed to frustrate the election of the rival

† See Appendix: The Lincoln College Election of 1851.

candidate by putting forward, at the last minute, the name of a third party, James Thompson, of whom few of the fellows really approved but who was elected Rector by the requisite number of votes.

For Pattison, personally, the sequel was devastating. It is impossible to read his account of the aftermath without sensing the depth of his despair. It seemed as if all his hopes had collapsed, all his expectations extinguished, all his work for the college brought to nought. It bit so deep into his soul that the anguish of that night and day was never to leave him.

The election also attracted the attention of the media, for it coincided with the sittings of the Royal Commission which had been set up by the government to investigate the state of the universities with a view to recommending much-needed reforms in their constitutions and teaching. So the Lincoln election attracted far more attention than it probably deserved, exemplifying the type of abuse characteristic of unreformed institutions. There was a war of pamphlets; lawsuits were threatened. Inevitably the college's reputation suffered, and the number of entries declined.

Pattison himself withdrew into his shell, carrying out his duties so perfunctorily that the new Rector, exasperated by his conduct, found it necessary to require his resignation as a tutor. 'So ends my 13 years service to the College,' Pattison wrote, 'They have been of that sort that could only be paid by ingratitude. Oh, God, why has it come to this? This is the finishing stroke!' Pattison's reaction, as on so many other occasions, was over-dramatised. In 1858 he went abroad for three months as *The Times*'s correspondent in Berlin, and was then invited by the Duke of Newcastle to become a member of a commission to investigate education in Switzerland and Germany. Yet, even in the dejection of these years, he continued to study, to read and to write.

In 1861 the record was put straight in a further Rectorial election. This time his chief rival was his old enemy, Richard Michell, disqualified as a candidate in 1851 but eligible again under the new statutes. Pattison was elected Rector (actually by his own vote). 'Justice,' as J. H. Newman wrote, 'is at length done to your merits ... What wonderful changes on all sides of us! I cannot bring myself to lament that the reign of such men, as I suppose Thompson to have been, is gone out.' All the omens seemed to point to a notable Rectorship. Pattison married a talented and beautiful woman, Francis Strong, twenty-seven years his junior. He was closely identified with the reform party in the university and the liberal party in the Church and so, though regarded with suspicion and dislike by the university clericals, seemingly in the van of progress. His work as a scholar was highly esteemed.

Yet none of these hopes was ever fulfilled in his twenty-three years as Rector. There was an element of Greek tragedy in Pattison's life; the more so since he often seemed the victim who brought disaster upon himself. He became convinced that the reforms which he had once championed, the work of the Royal Commission of 1854, were inadequate, but he had little confidence in the recommendations of a new commission set up in 1872. What was happening in the academic life of Oxford filled him with acute misgiving, to which he gave voice in a masterly and far-sighted book, *Suggestions on Academical Organization*, published in 1868. His Churchmanship became increasingly heterodox. His association with the book *Essays and Reviews*, published in 1860, to which he had contributed a stimulating article on 'Tendencies of Religious Thought, 1688–1750', had led to his being regarded with grave suspicion by orthodox Churchmen. In the intervening years, though he continued outwardly to play the part of an Anglican clergyman, celebrating the Holy Communion and attending college chapel, his faith faded to an amorphous agnosticism. In Lincoln itself, he found the majority of the undergraduates unrewarding and he made little attempt to win their regard; while his relations with the fellows of the college, with a few notable exceptions, were distant and in some cases downright hostile.

Even his marriage turned sour. In later years, his wife, ostensibly for reasons of health, wintered in the south of France. In 1881, Pattison met a Miss Meta Bradley, forty years younger than himself, a naïve, earnest seeker after truth who came to admire him as a great scholar and used him as a father-confessor. Her relations with her own father were difficult and she felt that she had found in Pattison a kindred spirit. He, too, believed that Meta alone really understood him. But what might have blossomed into an intimate love-affair withered in the face of Oxford's censure and the joint disapproval of his wife and Meta's father. What started off as a romance ended as a correspondence course.

Pattison had become the archetypal abrasive scholar. No wonder that he was identified, probably justifiably, with the character of Dr Casaubon in George Eliot's *Middlemarch*. He was certainly cruelly satirised in Rhoda Broughton's *Belinda*, though she had some reason, or thought she had, for being vindictive, and he appeared with more justice as Squire Wendover in Mrs Humphry Ward's *Robert Elsmere*, published four years after his death. A Lincoln undergraduate, Washington Ray, caught the mood of his young contemporaries when he wrote:

> *Cross the quad the Rector goes*
> *With a dew-drop at his nose.*
> *His chilly hands those black gloves enfold*
> *Irresistibly, I fear,*
> *Suggesting the idea*
> *Of a dissipated lizard with a cold.*

> *In a voice serene and calm*
> *Pours Robarts [the college chaplain] the mellow psalm*
> *At a pace for which he's often been maligned,*
> *While the Rector, who's no notion*
> *Of such expedite devotion,*
> *Slowly snarls at the Almighty far behind.*

In a life, which was in so many respects frustrating, lonely and unrewarding, in which he had to pay lip-service to conventions in which he no longer believed, Pattison remained utterly loyal to scholarship, his true religion. He was to publish only one book of fundamental importance, *Casaubon*, in 1875, a study of the Renaissance scholar; but to the very end he was an omnivorous reader, with the reputation, whether justified or not, of being the most learned man in Oxford. He never deviated from his dedication to the life of the mind.

The *Memoirs* constitute, in his opinion, the story of his mind's growth and development. They were penned in the bitterness and disappointment of old age and in the rapid onset of what was to prove a terminal illness. They can only be properly understood if his life is seen in the round. In some ways, they give a jaundiced and unfair view of his experiences, but they were an honest attempt to describe events as he saw them, the evidence drawn from the diaries which he had kept throughout his life. He wrote with a frankness which his Victorian contemporaries found disturbing. Yet, in its sensitive self-portrayal, in its clear and polished style, *Memoirs* remains a minor literary classic, ageless in its appeal.

Mark Pattison had kept a daily journal throughout his life. The first entry was dated 1 June 1831, when he was a young man of 17, and the last on 13 June 1884, only a few weeks before his death. In it he noted the chief events of his daily life, whom he had met and what he had read. Like the man himself, it is terse and only rarely self-revelatory. Yet there are moments of self-confession, especially in earlier years, when, like other diarists, the celebration of his birthday or the beginnings of a new year culled from him painful post-mortems of past failings and resolutions to do better.

Introspective by nature, from time to time he would fish out his old diaries and re-read them, living once again the traumatic, sometimes agonising moments of his past. He told Meta Bradley:

> I found my diary in Norris St [London, where he kept a room at a Mrs Lynn's], I was surprised to find it so interesting. I suspect you were too much occupied with your home troubles to have leisure to read it properly. The two things which seem to me most surprising about those years in looking back are: 1. My own industry – while I seem to myself to be doing nothing and I see what a mass of reading I got through, doing a little every day – and the other what mental suffering my wife's selfish egoism caused me.

Generally speaking, the journals were kept in a tin box in the lodgings, away from prying eyes, especially those of Mrs Pattison.

When Meta Bradley came to stay at the Rector's Lodgings in the winter of 1880, winning his confidence and affection, he evidently allowed her to read some of the volumes. Pattison told her that it was his intention to bequeath his journals, together with other papers, to the Bodleian Library in Oxford, with instructions that the material should not be read for ten or twenty years after his death. Meta expressed her dismay that the story of his life should be screened from the public for so long. 'I do wish,' she had written to him in February 1881, 'I could have known you when you were a youth ... I wish you would really try to give an account of your real inner self, think how intensely interesting it would be.'

The seed seems to have taken root. Egocentric and narcissistic, Pattison did not find the idea of describing his early life and mental development wholly unattractive. It was not to be an apologia as much as an exposition of truth, a demonstration of spiritual integrity. He had been reading Renan's *Souvenirs de Jeunesse*, finding that it was 'highly interesting, bien q'un peu babillard' [though rather a chatterbox]. 'I know,' Meta Bradley wrote to him in August 1881, 'you've often thought of an auto-biography but I do wish you'd begin your history of a mind.' It was only as illness made its dreaded inroad that the idea which had been merely simmering in his mind began to take shape. 'My illness,' he told Meta on 27 October 1883, 'is getting serious ... Thinking my time would be but short now, I wrote all the morning at reminiscences of my life.' He had written some seventy-five pages by early November. His niece, Jeannie Stirke, who was looking after him in Oxford, was badgered into dragging out boxes of letters, which she then read to him; later he dictated his *Memoirs* to her.

He found the composition burdensome but, aware that his time was rationed, he soldiered on. 'I read next to nothing, and if it were not for the desire to complete my Memoirs I should have the blank of nothing to live for.' By early December 1883 he had reached his days at Oriel, and by Christmas Eve the manuscript was virtually complete. 'It only comes down to 1861,' he told his friend Mrs Hertz, 'the time of my Rectorship is too recent and people still living makes it too dangerous ground.'

The manuscript finished, Pattison then set about trying to make preparations for its publication, whether for private circulation or for a more public audience. Provisionally, he came to an agreement with Macmillan's. He was, however, apprehensive that the manuscript might be tampered with after his death, presumably fearing that his wife might make alterations. 'I cannot allow them to be corrected or altered in one tit(t)le from the text as I leave it, and I have no friend whom I can trust to print them as they stand.' This was an odd comment, since there was Meta Bradley who had shown a constant interest in what he was doing. She had even offered to supervise the publication. 'I should deeply value this opportunity of doing something for you. I don't see how my doing it could do you any harm as only the publisher need know.' Fond as he was of Meta, Pattison was aware of her intellectual limitations, and so was hesitant about giving her the responsibility, especially as he knew how furious his wife would be if she learned of what he had done. Although he must have feared that his wife might tamper with the manuscript, in the closing months of his life he became dependent upon her.

So, when he died in July 1884, his wife rather than Meta Bradley, whom he had originally intended, became his literary executor. A few days before he died, his wife commented that he had been much 'interested ... in dictating directions as to the editing of his Memoirs which he wishes to be done wholly by myself.' Mrs Pattison had been horrified to learn that her husband had not merely left Meta Bradley £5,000 in a codicil to his will, which she thought she had persuaded him to delete, but that his relationship with Meta was stronger and more intimate, though how intimate it is impossible to say, than she had supposed. Such was her anger, that, with the complicity of Mark's younger brother, Frank, she either cut out or obliterated every reference to Meta, however innocuous, in the journals.

Since, however, the text of the *Memoirs* left Pattison in 1861, before his marriage, it required only minor modifications: a few passages deleted, a few names of those still living omitted. It is plain that at one time Pattison had had every intention of dedicating the *Memoirs* to Meta Bradley. 'The *Memoirs*,' he told her on 9 December 1883, '... are addressed to you so that whether they are printed or not, you will see them.' This was something which Mrs Pattison could not stomach. She explained in the preface that the *Memoirs*

were originally entitled by the writer 'Recollections of my Life', but when he gave his last direction concerning them he directed that they should be called *Memoirs*. He was asked whether they were dedicated to an old and valued friend of his early life, and replied 'They are not dedicated to anyone: you will see for yourself, when you come to read them, that they are not fit to be dedicated to anyone.' A provisional dedication, which was found in the MS has been withdrawn by the same authority as that whereby the title has been changed.

The explanation was as disingenuous and even palpably dishonest as in the circumstances it was understandable.

When *Memoirs* was published, it met with a mixed reception. This was not because of the style, 'ice-flavoured' as one reviewer called it, or because of the manner of composition, but because of its contents. These seemed to strike at many of the sacred cows of Victorian society. Pattison's account of Oxford in his day eroded the traditional and religious values essential to the maintenance of an ordered and religious society. His criticism of the Oxford tutorial system, of the university's disinclination to endow research, its rigidity, its suspicion of science, his attack on the Oxford Movement and his implied criticism of religion itself, smelt of subversion.

Moreover, his own self-portrait appeared too stark, almost indecent. The emperor had no clothes; the don had doffed his gown, and the clergyman had unfrocked himself. Reviewers, aware of Pattison's well-known angularities, wrote sadly of the author's lamentable failure of character. 'The book,' as a writer in the *Spectator* wrote, 'is like the story of a wreck told without the reader being aware that in a wreck it is to end.' It made for needlessly embarrassing reading

not only for its picture of the pettinesses and spites of collegiate life at Oxford, but for the impression it leaves upon us that Mr Pattison, in throwing off also the moral restraints of all pure theology over the inner life, gave himself up to the indolent melancholy and the vivid moroseness which the disappointment of legitimate hopes had engendered in him, without making even the slightest moral struggle to turn his own wounded feelings into the sources of a nobler life than any he had lived before.

'The shadows indeed prevail,' so the *Oxford Magazine* commented, 'like its writer's face, it seldom brightens into gaiety, and is always keen, deliberate, self-possessed.'

Even the politician and writer, John Morley, an old member of Lincoln, sympathetic to Pattison's liberalism, felt that in the end there was a fatal flaw in his character. 'There was,' he admitted, 'nobody on whom one might so surely count in the course of an hour's talk for some stroke of irony or pungent suggestion, or, at the worse, some significant, admonitory, and almost luminous manifestation of the great *ars tacendi*.' Yet 'the stamp of moral defaillance was set upon his brow from the beginning.' The book was an 'instructive account of a curious character.'

Morley's friend and master, W. E. Gladstone, who can have had little sympathy with Pattison's religious convictions, more correctly described the work as 'among the most tragic and memorable books of the nineteenth century'. It was, however, the reviewer in *Pall Mall* (6 March 1885) who should have the last word.

> Brief and fragmentary and uneven as these *Memoirs* are . . .
> they yet depict as distinctly as, perhaps more distinctly
> than, a fuller and more elaborate record might have done an
> intellect and temperament as extraordinary, and a life as
> unique in single-minded devotion to wisdom, as any that
> has been lived in our day.

The reviewer concluded that they recorded

> the development of a mind almost beyond comparison
> clear, subtle and well-balanced, and the trials and sufferings
> of a character remarkably solitary and yet intensely sensi-
> tive of the opinions and judgment of others.

PREFACE TO THE FIRST EDITION

THESE *Memoirs* were originally entitled by the writer *Recollections of my Life*, but when he gave his last directions concerning them he directed that they should be called *Memoirs*. He was asked whether they were dedicated to an old and valued friend of his early life, and replied, 'They are not dedicated to any one; you will see for yourself, when you come to read them, that they are not fit to be dedicated to any one.' A provisional dedication, therefore, which was found in the MS., has been withdrawn by the same authority as that whereby the title has been changed. One or two paragraphs at the beginning, which he considered of 'too egotistical a character', have also been cancelled by his express directions and indications.

As regards the rest of the MS. the writer expressly forbade the alteration of a word, especially in reference to his estimates of persons, which he thought the editor might be tempted to soften. 'If you are attacked on this score,' he added, 'you must shelter yourself by saying you are bound to fulfil the wishes of the dead. As to the rest,' he went on, 'I give you full editorial powers.'

On these indications the editor of this volume has scrupulously acted. Not a line, not a word of the MS. has been changed or destroyed. The exercise of the editorial powers, which the writer conferred, has been strictly limited to the incorporation of certain dictated matter at points clearly indicated, and to the omission from the present edition of a few passages, the publication of which would have been likely to wound the feelings of the living. Whenever such an omission has been made the fact has been carefully indicated by asterisks in the text.

CHAPTER 1

As LIFE may not be granted me to write out all I can remember, I shall begin with my coming up to Oxford in the year 1832, leaving my boyish years for a later book of reminiscences. For I have really no history but a mental history. When I read other persons' autobiographies I feel that they were justified in writing them by the variety of experiences they have gone through, and the number of interesting persons they have known. Harriet Martineau, e.g., or Leigh Hunt, were in the way of seeing historic names, and can tell one much about them.[1] I have seen no one, known none of the celebrities of my own time intimately, or at all, and have only an inaccurate memory for what I hear. All my energy was directed upon one end – to improve myself, to form my own mind, to sound things thoroughly, to free myself from the bondage of unreason, and the traditional prejudices which, when I began first to think, constituted the whole of my intellectual fabric. I have nothing beyond trivial personalities to tell in the way of incident. If there is anything of interest in my story, it is as a story of mental development.

Mozley, in the *Reminiscences*, says 'People may perhaps remember what they saw and heard forty years ago, but they cannot so easily remember what they were themselves' (ii, 270).[2] But if I cannot remember of myself the hidebound and contracted intellect, with which I entered upon life, and something of the steps by which I emerged from that frozen condition, I have nothing else worth recording to write. A reviewer says of George Sand that 'no part of her *Memoirs* is more interesting than her description of the development of her own genius. To remember the dreams and confusions of childhood, never to lose the recollection of the curiosity and simplicity of that age, is one of the gifts of the poetic character'[3] (*Quart. Rev.*, Ap. 1877).

My father was one of those who are receptive of very vivid impressions from outward events, though not exact in the reproduction of their impressions.[4] The imagination is too powerful, and infuses itself into the fact. Sister Dora had his habit of embroidering and glorifying.[5] My father used to tell many occurrences of his school-life with great force and picturesque effect; but of all his early life, nothing had taken so much hold of his memory and imagination as his three years at the University. He had been a commoner of B. N. C., taking his degree of B.A. in 1809.[6] His tutor was Frodsham Hodson.[7] I will only set down one of his many anecdotes of this college celebrity, for whom my father had a high respect. Returning to college, after one Long Vacation, Hodson drove the last stage into Oxford, with post-horses. The reason he gave for this piece of ostentation was, 'That it should not be said that the first tutor of the first college of the first university of the world entered it with a pair.' This was perhaps only a common-room story, made to fit the character somewhat γαῦρος of Hodson. The story is symbolical of the high place B. N. C. held in the University at the time, in which, however, intellectual eminence entered far less than the fact that it numbered among its members many gentlemen commoners of wealthy and noble families.[8] Among these was Lord George Gordon, afterwards known as concerned in the Greek War of Independence.[9] * * * *

In those days, and especially in such a society, scholars – at B. N. C. they mostly came from Manchester – were looked down upon as an inferior caste. Ashhurst T. Gilbert, who was a first class in 1808, and became Principal of the College in 1822, and in 1842 was made Bishop of Chichester by Sir Robert Peel, who had been in the same class with him, was always spoken of by my father with disdain, as associating with a low set, and having himself low tastes. * * * My father was too proud to be a tuft-hunter,[10] but he liked, and appreciated the advantages of 'worshipful company'. But his 'set' at college was not that of the gentlemen commoners, nor that of the reading men. I suppose he was excluded from the first by want of means, and from the latter by his want of literary cultivation. For some reading men certainly were in the college in 1805, when my father went into residence, seeing that the two Hebers, Reginald and Richard, had only recently passed through, and could not have been isolated exceptions in the college.[11] The famous 'Palestine' breakfast in B.

N. C. had only taken place in May 1803. This historical breakfast is on 'record' in Lockhart's *Life of Scott* (ii. 122), when Heber's prize poem was read to Scott, who made the happy suggestion which led to the insertion of the lines: 'No hammer fell, no ponderous axes rung', etc. But of any such society, if such there were in B. N. C., my father had nothing to tell.

His friends were men of moderate means and quiet habits, who read too, but were without that decided intellectual bias which would have admitted them into the best and most cultivated circle, such as that in which the Hebers moved. My father was not acquainted with Tyler, Whately, Peel, Conybeare, Baden Powell, Rolleston, Valpy, all of whom were about contemporary with him.[12] True, they were in different colleges, which, I suppose, constituted a greater barrier to acquaintance than it does now.

My father's friends, of whom he continued to speak with regard twenty years afterwards, were John Le Mesurier, afterwards chaplain to the forces in Malta, and Archdeacon John Blackburne; John Ford; Wheatley, afterwards a Chancery barrister; Thomas Farrer. All these (except Wheatley), as well as my father himself, achieved second classes in Litt. Hum.,[13] which, we should now say, was respectable for commoners, when every one at all capable of getting a first is provided with a scholarship. And I should gather, from what I can remember of my father's talk, that none of the party had greater abilities than himself. In those days a second class required only four books of Aristotle's Ethics, and neither Rhetoric nor Politics. My father never professed any understanding of Aristotle, and had a very faint idea of Logic, as I discovered when he tried to read Aldrich with me.[14] His favourite book was Aristophanes. He was one night caught by Hodson on the back of Cain and Abel,[15] and being asked what he did there, replied, ''Ἀεροβατῶ καὶ περιφρονῶ τὸν ἥλιον.'[16] 'Oh!' cried Hodson, 'it's only Aristophanic Pattison.' * * * *

Many more of my father's stories occur to me, but these I give as showing how he loved to recur to his college days, and how I was made familiar with college life from as early a time as I can remember. Nor was only the social and undergraduate side of the University brought before me. My father, though not a well-read man, had, after leaving Oxford and settling in his curacy, taken some pains to extend his knowledge, and had read some of the best books of English literature. I remember a C. P. B.,[17] in which were notes on several plays of Shakespeare. He was fond of English history, and made me read Hume through;[18] also constitutional law, Blackstone;[19] the history of the last century, Pitt and Fox; all in a desultory way, but with a lively political interest. Though more political than literary, he had a veneration for intellectual eminence. In particular, he looked upon Copleston as the representative man of university culture, and had begun to perceive in a dim way that the light had departed from B. N. C., and that Oriel was now the centre of intelligence.[20]

There never was any question as to my destination. It was assumed from the cradle upwards that I was to go to Oxford, and to be a Fellow of a college. From about 1825 onwards a Fellowship of Oriel was held up to me as the ideal prize to which I was to aspire. I was never diverted or distracted from this goal of ambition by any alternative career being proposed to me. I was to go to Oriel, of course, as a commoner, – there were no scholars in those days, – and then it would depend upon what talents I might give proof of whether a fellowship of Oriel were within my reach or not.

In 1830, when I was not quite seventeen, my father and mother went up to London. It was only the second time since their marriage that they had left Yorkshire. It was a great undertaking, and a costly one. Two hundred and twenty miles of posting had to be done, and you had to sleep two nights at some of the great hotels on the north road. We had an old open barouche of our own. The competition of the posting-houses was such, that pairs of horses and ready-mounted postillions were at the door as you drove up, and in less than five minutes you were off again. Leaving Hauxwell very early we arrived at Camp Hill, near Doncaster, to a late lunch with Lane Fox and Lady Charlotte, daughter of the Duke of Leeds, who were temporarily living there.[21] We went out of the way to see Cambridge, and I think it was only on the fourth day after leaving home that we entered London by gaslight. Many years after, when I came to those lines in *Locksley Hall* –

> *Eager-hearted as a boy when first he leaves his father's field,*
> *And at night along the dusky highway near and nearer drawn,*

20

Sees in heaven the light of London flaring like a dreary dawn,

I started to find one of my own unconsciously received impressions thus objectively brought before me. I was too ignorant to
learn what I might have done from this journey, nor was I helped
by my parents, who themselves saw nothing of London but what
country cousins see. They knew no one but a few methodistical
clergymen, and their chief curiosity was about some preachings,
where the 'Gospel' was to be heard – one Wilkinson, at one of the
city churches; and I think they took me to hear —— at the Scotch
Presbyterian Chapel; but it made no impression on me. I was a
mere raw schoolboy.

One thing was done for me which was of great service to me
then and afterwards. I had complained all the winter of worry and
irritation about the eyes. This was not malingering to get off
books, for I was passionately fond of reading, and should have
regarded it as the direst calamity if the eye-affection had been of a
nature to interfere with the future career of academic life which I
dreamed of for myself. But there was no doubt for the moment
that the irritation was a serious mischief of some sort, and that it
was aggravated by reading; riding, especially fast riding, brought
it on. I was devoted to hunting, and had a black mare on which I
used, when I had a holiday, to go to the meets. One morning
early, riding to join Mr Claridge's pack, which would begin at
6 A.M., the wind meeting me was so painful to my eyes that I was
compelled to turn back and forego my favourite sport. I gave up
reading by candle-light, and learned to net, as occupation for my
hands, while the evening reading was going on. My father, who
read well, and liked doing so, read to us that winter *Paradise Lost*,
and it is a measure of my undeveloped intelligence that it made
slight impression on me. Miss Martineau at seven was more
advanced than I at seventeen, for she got hold of *Paradise Lost*,
and was so profoundly moved by it, that 'my mental destiny was
fixed for the next seven years' (*Autob.*, i. 42).

This eye-affection was an important element in arranging my
future, and the placing me under an oculist had been among the
motives which prompted the London expedition. As there was
one of the most celebrated oculists in the kingdom at that time
practising in Leeds, only fifty miles off, it was not absolutely

necessary to have taken me to London. But the London journey being desired on other accounts, the consultation of the oculist contributed to the sum of motive, and to justify the outlay, which was heavy. I was taken to Alexander in Cork Street, who was then at the head of the profession. It was a critical moment for me, for I felt, stupid as I was, that my whole future destination was at stake. My father must have cared for me then, * * * for when Alexander, having examined me, turned to him and said, 'There is nothing the matter with this boy's eyes!' he burst into tears of excitement. The case was one of lid-inflammation, with which I have had much trouble since on two different occasions; in 1854, when I consulted Lawrence, and again in 1867, when I was almost compelled to abstain from books for some months, and when neither Critchett nor Liebreich could succeed in getting rid of the trouble. What Alexander meant was that the disease was not in the eye, or the optic nerve, but in the lid. It was really what I now call 'gout', non-assimilation of food, the superfluous humour flying to any susceptible or tried part – and the tried part with me was certainly the eye. I read too much, especially at night, and all the Christmas had sate in a close room – my father's 'book-room' we called it – looking into a blazing fire in an open grate. Alexander prescribed leeches, bathing in hot water, and an application which he furnished to the lid, much the same as that which Liebreich afterwards put in. He allowed moderate use of the eyes in reading, but prohibited, for the present, candle-light. There was no reason, he said, why I should not go to the University.

The next thought, therefore, was to get my name entered as a candidate for admission at some college. As we were now within sixty miles – seven hours it was then – of Oxford, it was determined that my father should go down to inquire about a college. He was not loth to get an opportunity of revisiting his loved haunts – the spot which occupied so large a space in his imagination. It was May, and Oxford, not then overbuilt and slummy, looked – as Oxford can look still in May – charming. I was intoxicated with delight, and my father was as pleased as a child. His constant recurrence to his reminiscences of the place had so riveted it in my mind that I had, by aid of an old guide book I found at Hauxwell, mastered the topography by anticipation, and was proud, as we walked about the streets, to show that I knew where to find the colleges. In all other respects I was an ignorant country bumpkin, and incapable of learning from what I now saw for the first time. My father, of course, took me 'on the water' – his own favourite amusement. We were sculled down to Iffley, and he enjoyed paying the overcharge, 'eighteenpence each gentleman as went in the boat, and two shillings the man'; being overcharged made him feel that he was in Oxford, and the dialect, unheard for five-and-twenty years, impressed the same fact through another sense.

But the first thing next morning was to enter my name at some college, and the question was, Which? The retired life which, partly from pride, partly from laziness, it was my father's choice to live, had left him without friends of any consequence or consideration. A few like-minded evangelical clergy of the neighbourhood in Yorkshire were of no use in the University. Even when they were Oxford men, having taken their degree years ago, they were as much strangers to the Oxford of 1830 as my father himself; rather, they knew even less about it than he did, as a diligent study of the Oxford Calendar had kept him *au courant* of the changes in the *personnel* of the colleges, so far as the names went.[22] The Calendar could not teach him the value of each personality.

Of residents in the University, two only offered themselves as possible helps when my father began to look round for friends who might give him information about colleges, or introduction to the head of any one. At this day all information is more widely diffused, or accessible; but even at this day a country squire or rector, on landing with his cub under his wing in Oxford, finds himself much at sea as to the respective advantages or demerits of the various colleges, and has but a very dim notion of those distinctions which are elementary knowledge to ourselves. Where the boy has been at a public school, the father is content to be guided by the advice of the schoolmaster, who, through his connections with his university, which every master is careful to cultivate, keeps himself informed as to the internal condition of each college. Yet, with all his means of information, a master does not always succeed in following the changes in tone, discipline, teaching, vigour, which are incessantly going on within the walls of a college. So rapid are these, that three years are often enough to revolutionise a college in some important characteristic. Everything depends on the *moral* or ascendency of a single tutor; he quits college, and what he has held together falls to pieces, without the public – the public of parents and schoolmasters – becoming aware that anything has occurred. The most permanent stamp of college reputation is the social stamp. This measure of worth often remains stationary under every variety of moral and intellectual change. To what stratum of society the undergraduates of any college belong, what degree of connection they have with the upper ten, what social status they maintain – this is the most patent fact about any college, and one which will never cease to be influential upon the choice of parents in this country, where the vulgar estimate of people by income and position is the universal and only standard of merit. As we judge of families in our neighbourhood, so, when we are placing a boy at the University, do we judge of colleges.

I have said there were only two persons among the residents at all known to my father, to whom he could apply to guide his judgment in making choice of a college for me. One was a senior Fellow of Magdalen, Dr Ellerton; he was a native of Swaledale, being a brother of Ellerton, the principal mercer in the borough of Richmond.[23] His father, I think, was a farmer at Downholme, and there being no school at Downholme, the boy used to ride over to Hauxwell School to get his first lessons in writing and ciphering. He held a Yorkshire fellowship at Magdalen, and was supposed to have saved a sum of money out of his fellowship and college offices. He had been Proctor, and had rather offended my father on one occasion. Being down at Richmond one Long Vacation, and meeting my father in the street, he took him to task for the colour of his greatcoat – proctorised him, my father said. However, to him we went, and I was enchanted with the look of bachelor comfort about his room in the 'new building' at Magdalen, and more than ever confirmed in my ambition to become a Fellow of a college. I don't recollect that Ellerton, though his reception of us was gracious enough, gave any counsel or assistance of any consequence. Having taken his B.A. in 1792 he was now sixty or thereabouts; and living in the seclusion of Magdalen Common-room – such was the dissociated condition of Oxford at that time – he probably knew nothing of the internal efficiency of the various colleges. My father must have known William Glaister, who was then Fellow of University College and tutor.[24] Why we did not call upon him I do not remember. He was kind enough to call upon me when I came into residence, and to ask me to breakfast.

The other friend to whom my father applied for help proved far more useful, and his advice did, in fact, determine my destiny. Lord Conyers Osborne, second son of the Duke of Leeds, had lately gone up to Christ Church, with his private tutor, and was now in residence.[25] My father was chaplain to the Duke, had been at one time very much in his confidence, and went in Hornby Castle by the name of 'the Chancellor', as I shall relate when I come to write the earlier part of these memoirs. I had been playmate of Lord Conyers when he came down from Eton in the holidays; he called me 'Mark', and I humbly waited on his will. When we went to stay at the Castle I always had a bedroom which opened into his. Lord Conyers was a lively, bright, well-mannered, and gracious young man, of popular manners, and the hope of the house; his elder brother, the marquis, being like his father, selfish, egotistical, and reserved. In my ignorant eyes Lord Conyers was a marvel of accomplishments; he could do everything I could do, only ten times better, and write Latin verses fast without a false quantity.

His private tutor, who resided in lodgings in S. Aldate's, was Mr Thomas Paddon, a senior Fellow of Caius, Cambridge. In 1822 Mr Paddon had vacated his fellowship on accepting the college living of Mattishall, Norfolk; but he continued to live in the Duke's household as tutor, and, it was understood, would remain with Lord Conyers till he left Christ Church. Lord Conyers' capacity and attainments were such, that his tutor had at one time indulged a hope of his reading successfully for honours. But any such hope was early dissipated by the demoralising atmosphere of Christ Church; and at the time we arrived in Oxford I found Lord Conyers entirely possessed by the opinion of his set, that it was unworthy of a man of his position to 'sap'. Mr Paddon sorrowfully resigned himself to see his pupil follow the ordinary course of a 'nobleman' at the University, i.e. misspend his time, and acquire nothing.

Mr Paddon was undoubtedly a superior man, and of great

judgment. Indeed, no one could have lived with the (then) Duke of Leeds without being, or becoming, wary and discreet in his walk and talk. To Mr Paddon we went, and we could not have gone to a better counsellor, though, as a Cambridge man, he probably did not know all that an indigenous M.A. would have known about the foul linen of the various colleges. We received every attention from Lord Conyers, and were invited to spend that evening in his rooms in Canterbury quad, he giving up a party to stay at home to play draughts with an awkward rustic booby as I was. Instead of sulking he did it with a grace and obligingness, as if it had been what he most liked doing. Mr Paddon and my father discussed apart what was to be done with me.

My father's views for me, which were to guide his choice of college, were twofold. He really wanted me to learn; to get a good education, not so much with the idea of my making my way in the world, as from the value which he had learned to set upon intellect. Himself a man of vigorous powers, but totally undisciplined, he regretted his own want of thorough education, and in his unselfish hours wished to secure for me what he had missed himself. He was fond of repeating the sentence in the Eton Latin grammar – 'Concessi Cantabrigiam ad capiendum ingenii cultum . . . .' This was the proverb which presided over my whole college life. Though often dimmed, it was never lost sight of, and however much occasion I may have had to hate the grammar on other accounts, I think no other sentence of any book has had so large a share in moulding my mind and character as that one. It was then essential to my father's plans for me that the college to be selected for me should be one where the instruction given was reputed to be good. This requirement negatived his own college, to which he might naturally have turned in the first instance. Brasenose had the reputation of being rowdy and drinking; and though the tutors, Hall, Churton, and Richard Harington, were first class men, yet the tuition was not esteemed good.[26] Hall was getting old and weary of it; Tommy Churton I afterwards came to know as a 'stick'; and Harington was a fine gentleman, who sailed his own pinnace on the river, and dined out much. In the matter of tuition there were two colleges whose repute stood higher than that of any – viz. Oriel and Balliol. 'We call those,' – said Lord

Conyers privately to me, from his undergraduate point of view, – 'the two prison-houses'. I was eager to doom myself to either of the prisons. And it was clear that the choice was restricted to these two.

But there was in my father's mind another sentiment, less creditable to him, than the wish to give me the best education to be had. I mean those social aspirations which he continued to nourish, though by his removal to the remote situation of Hauxwell, and consequent detachment from the Castle, he was no longer able to gratify them. He had the instinct of good society, and liked to live with gentlemen, and to know what was going on in the upper world. His acquaintance with the peerage was accurate; he must have read *Debrett* at that time more than the Bible. Hence, in estimating colleges he was led to take the footman's view, and to prefer one which was frequented by the sons of gentlemen. Now Exeter was genteel, but unintellectual. Our friend David Horndon – now (1883) living, and Squire, etc., of Pencrebar, near Callington – had but recently taken his degree from Exeter;[27] and we knew enough about it from him to set down the tuition of Falconer and Richards as the merest pass '*Schlendrian*'.[28] William Sewell, who, though never a good tutor, did so much soon afterwards to raise the intellectual tone of the college, had been only just elected from Merton.[29] As between Oriel and Balliol there could be no doubt that the 'gentility' all belonged to Oriel. The decision, therefore, was for Oriel, by Mr Paddon's advice, and with his approval. Oriel – i.e. Oriel's repute as it stood in the eyes of the outside world – satisfied both of my father's requirements; both his desire to get me the best education, where his disinterested paternal affection showed itself, as well as his ambition to be able to say that his son was at a fashionable college, the resort of gentlemen of old family, in which he gratified his personal vanity.

So far as the class list was any test of the instruction given in a college, it does not appear that there was at this period so much difference between the two colleges, Oriel and Balliol. Taking the lists for the six years preceding 1830 I find that Balliol has six firsts in classics, while Oriel has only three; for the same period, Balliol has nineteen second classes, and Oriel twenty-one. The total number of students in each of the two colleges must at this date have been nearly equal. Second classes were, in those days, better evidence of efficient tuition than first. The manufacture of firsts was not then understood as it is now. The men who got firsts would have done so equally at any college, and under any disadvantages of college instruction. That was the day of private tutors; it was the 'coach,' and not the college tutor, who worked a man up for his first.[30] The standard of lecturing in the college classroom was far below the level of the examinations for honours.

The class lists then were not a decisive test of the intellectual calibre of a college: the first class not at all, and the second class in a slight measure, and indirectly – that is, the preparation for the honours' examination was not conducted by the official tutors, but by the private tutors. Every one who aimed at honours had his coach, to whom he went three days a week for a fee of £10. The college tutor might in the first year lead up in the way of general scholarship to the special preparation, but his influence in producing a crop of classmen was far more in the indirect impulse he gave to intellectual ambition, and the stir of mind he might excite within the walls of his college.

In 1830, the time of which I am now writing, there could be no question as to which of the two colleges, Oriel or Balliol, had most intellectual life within its walls. I shall come back to this point by and by. At present I wish only to say that, had my father's choice of college had to be decided by intellectual eminence, it would have been rightly determined in favour of Oriel. The Balliol tutors were Ogilvie and Round.[31] Both of these men had carried off the highest honours, but both belonged to the genus 'dry stick'. They were before all things clergymen, with all the prepossessions of orthodox clergymen, and incapable of employing classical antiquity as an instrument of mental culture. At most, they saw in Greek and Latin a medium for establishing 'the truth of Christianity'. Chapman was also tutor of Balliol; he had the reputation of high scholarship.[32] It was of him that the fable circulated in my time, that when examiner for the 'Ireland' he would do the papers himself, and place himself second, or third, or fourth, as the case might be.[33]

The Oriel tutors were Newman,[34] Wilberforce,[35] and Froude (R. H.).[36] I need not make any mention of Dornford, as he belonged to the order of Dons, and had a parochial cure – I think Nuneham Courtney.[37] These three men were of inferior academic lustre to the Balliol tutors; but they were men in whom 'heart and mind were in a continual ferment of emotion and speculation', stirring up all who came in contact with them to think and reason out from first principles. The true revolutionary spirit was already there, though it had not yet taken the precise direction which it afterwards did. They were, however, young men; Newman, the oldest of the three, was thirty, and little known. Neither my father nor his adviser could have any knowledge of the stimulating power which was latent in the Oriel tutors of 1830.

Not, then, for the sake of this triumvirate of tutors, – Newman, Wilberforce, and Froude, – but on the general reputation of the college for two things not always combined, intelligence and gentle blood, was it decided that I was to go to Oriel.

The next thing was to get in. In 1830 the Laudian statute[38] which compelled every student to keep his residence within college walls – 'ne quis in domibus privatis victitet aut hospitetur' – was in force.[39] Consequently, in the colleges upon which there was a run, a candidate for admission might wait years before he could succeed to a vacant room. We were told that at Oriel you must have your name down two or even three years before you could come into residence. This was formidable; I was in my seventeenth year, and it might have been deterrent. Though the modern competitive examinations for rooms were not known, there was also a qualifying entrance examination. But we were placed at ease as to this by being assured that it was very elementary. It was a new thing. If the *Quarterly Review* is right, it had only been started in 1827, and at Oriel and Balliol only. We had recourse to interest; my father was good at making interest, which I have never been able to do. I cannot remember who were called in to work upon the Provost; Manuel Echalaz, a Fellow of Trinity,[40] and an ally of Mr Paddon, was to work upon Henry Jenkyns, a brother of the Master of Balliol, who in his turn was to intercede with his brother head. However, we called on the Provost, Dr Hawkins,[41] who entered my name in his book, but could hold out no hopes of rooms for more than two years; he was full up to October 1832, but would give the offer of any chance vacancy. That was all we could get from him; and with this were compelled to be content and to return to London, leaving Oxford in innocent ignorance of all that was brewing beneath the surface – never having so much as heard the name of Keble, or the *Christian Year*.[42]

And from London I went back to Hauxwell, to get over the interval of two years – infinite space it looked – till I should be free, independent, launched upon the world which I knew nothing of, but which seemed from the glimpse I had of it to be full of promise and charm. A boy's, a child's world, as I pictured it, but my ignorance and inexperience gave a zest to my expectation, like the appetite of a savage. We came home at the end of May, when spring was in its first green on our hillside. The freshness of it after the dust and glare of the streets! Then there were the country delights. I was this season first allowed a gun, and joined the farmers in their sport of rook-shooting in the Hall rookery.[43] There were long days of trout-fishing in Garriston Beck – first essays of fishing, with clumsy tackle, and finding out the art for myself, not having any one at hand to give me the most elementary advice. I bought an Angler's Guide in London, and tried to practise its cockney 'instruction for roach-fishers' upon trout. Worm-fishing, of course; the mystery of fly-fishing seemed a craft unattainable. The very element of bottom-fishing I had to rediscover – that the hook must be wholly hidden by the bait, that the angler must not be seen by the fish; these things I found out, was not told, and the gratification of finding them out was more than compensation for the many days of disaster and disappointment before they were sufficiently apprehended and exactly practised. It was many seasons before the utility of the 'landing-net' dawned on me; I was content to pull them up the bank by main force, losing half the fish in the process. I attribute my after skill in fly-fishing to my having been self-taught over worm-fishing in the little bush-grown beck which bounded our parish on the south.

But even above my passion for the sports of the country was that which took possession of me this summer of 1830 for natural history. This, again, was felt by me in its most childish form. The idea of natural science was far beyond me. I only thought of collecting, first birds, then insects. Lepidoptera I could collect, and learnt from books ways of preserving them. Birds, as I could not find space in my little bed-room for my specimens, I was led to observe. In this way the mere boy's collecting fancy led on to observation. When I had noted a new species I used to come home so excited that my mind refused to attend to anything else. I fell in with Gilbert White's *History of Selborne*, and was riveted by the book.[44] I read it over and over, and knew it by heart. My father, who looked upon my naturalist tastes with small favour, as drawing off my attention from Herodotus and Thucydides, yet bowed before the name of Gilbert White, when he found that he had been 'Fellow of Oriel', though he could not get through ten pages of the *History of Selborne*. He would sit hours reading the 'obituaries' in an old volume of the *Gentleman's Magazine*. Selby's *Ornithology*, Montagu's *Dictionary*, were soon added to my stock.[45] No book, however, took more hold on my interest than three volumes by Rennie[46] on Insects – this revealed to me the world of wonders which lay all around me, quite close, and yet I had not known it. It was not only the curiosity of the insect products in themselves – their architecture, as Rennie called it – but the disclosure of a new world of fact, which existed unsuspected beneath my feet, which kindled my imagination. Wandering over the moor whole days, haunting the skirts of the woods at night, on the look-out for birds and moths, the sense of the country, a delight in rural objects, grew within me, and passed insensibly into the more abstract poetic emotion.

I don't think that it was before two or three years after 1830 that this transition from natural history to poetry proper began to take place in my mind. My removal to college diverted me from the pursuit of natural knowledge; my instinctive tastes were never developed into a science. The love of birds, moths, butterflies, led on to the love of landscape; and altogether, in the course of the next six or seven years, grew and merged into a conscious and declared poetical sentiment, and a devoted reading of the poets. I don't suppose the temperament was more inclined to æsthetic emotion in me than in other youths; but I was highly nervous and delicate, and having never been at school had not had sentiment and delicacy crushed out of me; also, living on the borderland of oak woods, with green lanes before me, and an expanse of wild heather extending into Northumberland behind, I was favourably placed for imbibing a knowledge by contrast of the physical features of England. My eye was formed to take in at a glance, and to receive delight from contemplating, as a whole, a hill and valley formation. Geology did not come in till ten years later to complete the cycle of thought, and to give that intellectual foundation which is required to make the testimony of the eye, roaming over an undulating surface, fruitful and satisfying. When I came in after years to read *The Prelude* I recognised, as if it were my own history which was being told, the steps by which the love of the country boy for his hills and moors grew into poetical susceptibility for all imaginative presentations of beauty in every direction.[47]

I see I am in danger of conveying an idea of myself as more advanced in intelligence, or power of perceiving beauty, than I was. I hasten to say that in these first years of the '30's there was nothing in me that could be called intelligence, nor any manifestation of sensibility of feeling. I remember a vague consciousness of being wronged because I had more affection for my sisters than they had for me; * * * a feeling which grew upon me. But as my affection was manifested partly in a general rudeness of behaviour towards them, partly in acts of absolute selfishness, I can now only wonder that one of them remained (and remains) devoted to me still.[48] There was latent in my nature a vast possibility of fine qualities, but they did not manifest themselves in manners, or behaviour, or words. * * * If I preferred being at Hauxwell to being anywhere else, and always came back, as long as I could, to spend my long vacations there, it was the exterior life, and the studious quiet of my room, which attracted me, though not unmixed with a genuine love of my sisters, as I have said. * * * But I was not spoiled, as a boy is who has been brutalised by a school; I was only rude, unfledged, in a state of nature.

In intellectual matters things were no better with me. I have before me a small paper book containing a 'Diary' for parts of the years 1830, 1831, 1832. Its childishness is astonishing. I had read much more than most boys of my age, but I did not seem to understand anything. This was the want of companionship; I had no one except the sons of the village cottagers to play with. We had a man-servant indoors, and a farming-man out of doors; I was much with them, and learnt much from them; but there was nothing to replace the collision of wit with wit, which takes place between boys. One of these men was a dalesman, native of Hawes, and from him I had stories of the old wild life of the dales, mixed largely with the supernatural, which germinated afterwards into a strong turn for county history, and walks of exploration. I read enormously. Constable's *Miscellany*, Murray's *Family Library*, the publications of the Useful Knowledge Society, were coming out at that time; we took them all, and I read them. I read ten times as much as I remembered; what is more odd, I read far more than I ever took in the sense of as I read it. I think the mechanical act of perusal must have given me a sort of pleasure. Books, as books, irrespective of their contents, were my delight. The arrival of a new book in the house was the event of the week. I took in the *Magazine of Natural History*; the anticipation of the first of the month, and the reception of the parcel from the Richmond bookseller, were an excitement that I can remember to this day. I walked up and down in the lane waiting for the butcher's cart, which acted as carrier for the village, to come, snatched up Bell's parcel, and rushed in with it. I was already marked out for the life of a student, yet little that was in the books I read seemed to find its way into my mind. There was no mind there! My outdoor life, long solitary days' fishing, and long rides across country – in 1831 I had a pony and went hunting – rambles over the moor, were doing more for my education than my incessant reading.

A long illness of my mother – bronchitis – in the winter of 1830–31 became the solicitude and occupation of the house. The summer of 1831 proved much as that of 1830 had done. Something was done by way of preparing me for college by getting me a Cambridge man, Bainbridge of Catherine Hall, to read mathematics with me. I must have had some capacity, as he told my father when he left at the end of two months that if I were to go to Cambridge I should be certain to be a wrangler. But he was most likely a bad judge, as he did not himself get more than a Junior Optime.

In the early part of 1832 we began to get impatient at not hearing from the Provost. I was eighteen on 10th October 1831, and much longer delay was impossible. Even my father, who was very blind to the fact that I was wasting my time at home, must have felt that something must be done with me. He was eager about my going to college, and yet allowed me to waste, or nearly so, those two precious years in loafing about at home, in order that he might be able to say that he had sent me up to college wholly from his own tuition. One Saturday evening, 31st March, the farming-man, having been over to Richmond, brought home a letter. How it got to Richmond I cannot tell, for our post-town was Bedale. It was from the Provost, desiring me to proceed to Oxford on Monday to be matriculated. Here was an upset in a parsonage on the Yorkshire moors. All was joy and astonishment and perturbation. I remember that I was in a remote corner of the garden, where I cultivated a special plot called my garden. It was dusk. My father appeared in the distance, agitated with delight, holding up the letter, which had just been put into his hands with the Oxford postmark, before he opened it.

To proceed to Oxford on Monday, and it was Saturday night when the letter was delivered! Surely the Provost must have known that it was three days' journey from Richmond to Oxford. It was very thoughtless of him. However, on Monday morning my father and I were off; arrived, by the 'Telegraph' coach, at Leeds at five; dined there, and at eight on to Sheffield by the night mail. Slept a few hours, and on to Birmingham, where we again dined, and left by the 'Rocket' at nine for Oxford, a fast coach, which did the distance in seven hours. We were put down at the 'Angel' at 4 A.M. on Wednesday morning. I can recall now the state of excitement in which I was all the way from Woodstock, and the exultation of spirits in which I hailed the lights in St Giles'. Could I have anticipated that Oxford was to be my home for fifty years? We called on the Provost. I was handed to W. J. Copleston to be examined at eight in the evening;[49] wrote a piece of (very bad) Latin prose; construed some Greek and Latin *viva voce*, was passed, and next morning matriculated commoner of Oriel, in bands and a white choker. On Saturday evening, seven o'clock, we were home again. I have the dates, and even hours, of the whole journey noted in that paper book above mentioned.

So there was a month at home of pause to think over the sudden change which was before me, for leave-takings, for preparation of clothes and books, and the other requisites for launching me into the world. In my feeling there was no room for regret of what I was leaving, so absorbed was I by anticipation of what was before me. On the evening of Thursday, 4th May, I was set down by the Birmingham coach at the Angel Inn in the High Street – the Examination Schools now stand on the site of the 'famous inn' – and went off with a porter and my trunks to Oriel. I possess still my earliest book of accounts, and I find that the journey from Hauxwell to Oxford – a journey of three days, sleeping two nights on the road – cost me £4 : 12s. In after years I was pleased at discovering that Gilbert White of Selborne, of whose *Natural History* I was a devotee, had kept a similar exact account of his expenditure. We have it still, and extracts from it are given in Bell's edition of the book. My first item of Oxford expenditure is an entry of 2s. to 'porter for carrying my boxes across the quad', an entry in which lurks indignation at the extortion, and the only expression I dared to give to it, as, if he had demanded 5s., I should not have had courage to resist.

I must have cut a laughably boorish figure that Thursday evening, marching up the High Street in an old brown greatcoat of my father's – that identical snuffy brown for wearing which in Richmond market-place Dr Ellerton had pulled him up, and which had been reduced by a Richmond slop-tailor to fit me. Very serviceable to me on this journey up the ἱματιδάριον [50] was, as it had rained a steady spring rain all the way from Sheffield to Birmingham, and I was outside, proud to be on the box with a friendly coachman, but thinking what a fine fishing-day was going to waste. Had it rained twice as heavily the solid broadcloth of the old coat was impenetrable. There was no one in the street to see; the colleges did not meet till Saturday the 6th, Easter being very late that year – viz. 22nd April. I had come up a day earlier than was necessary, in order to get into rooms. On introducing myself to the porter of the college, I was told that there were no rooms ready for me, but that he would put me up for the night in one of the 'scholars'' rooms. The porter's saying 'scholars' was the first of the many puzzles which offered themselves to me in these first days, as I knew that Oriel at that time had no scholars; and I have never been able to make out how the porter came to use the term of a fellow, for it was a fellow's room, that of John Frederic Christie, into which I found myself inducted. [51] I daresay it was like all college rooms at that time, dirty and shabby enough, but it seemed to me a fairy palace; and the thought of becoming a fellow myself, and living in such luxury, was a vision too remote and too dazzlingly bright to be contemplated.

Next day I had to turn out and to go into lodgings for a fortnight, before a room was vacated for me. Oriel at that time was full to crowding; I, being the junior freshman, had the bell-tower room, immediately under the college bell, which at that time rung for every service a full quarter of an hour. There was just room for four chairs, and barely for four men to sit.

There were some four or five other freshmen beginning residence in this same term, and with these I was at first thrown, being in the same classes, and sitting together in hall. But I soon found them uncongenial, and after the first week or two we hardly spoke, though one of them, Porter by name, used to pay me a visit on Sunday evening, for the purpose of copying my sermon notes.[52] Once only the theft was detected by the theological censor, who, without inquiring which was the thief, imposed us both. I think the imposition was to analyse a printed sermon of Bishop Butler. Etiquette forbade me to explain, but I expected Porter to do so, and it was a shock to my moral sense that he did not. I withdrew, prepared to do my imposition. Porter, however, on reflection, saw what he ought to have done, and went and confessed, on which my penance was remitted.

I should never have done, were I to write down all I can recall about the young men among whom I now found myself, transported from a desert moor where were no inhabitants but Highland 'stots'. I may sum up shortly the general impression which this first contact with my species made upon me. Comradeship was the thing I had most longed for, and what, next to help in my reading, I had most missed in my Hauxwell life. Now, when I seemed in the midst of abundance, I found myself repelled. I found, what I had not been prepared for, that the differences between myself on the one side, and all the rest on the other, were greater than the resemblances; the points of antipathy more numerous than the points of sympathy. Large as was the part which the bodily appetites filled in my nature, in these youths they were still more rampant and imperious. If I was lazy, selfish, greedy, and rapacious, these youths were so to a degree which disgusted me. I wanted associates congenial with the better part of me, not with whom I could indulge the baser propensities. * * *

I had no taste for drinking. My father had great difficulty in getting me to drink a single glass on the occasions when he opened a bottle of his choice port. I was over forty before I even began to like wine, and it was later still in life before it became a daily beverage. In 1832 I had not begun to smoke, and did not desire to. * * * *

I was not all at once made aware of this want of conformity between myself and others of my age; I arrived at the apprehension of it slowly, after many vain experiments and successive failures to establish a good understanding with one after another. At first I ascribed my ill success to something in the individual whom I was trying to cultivate, which prevented *rapprochement*, but at last I was compelled to conclude that the impediment to intimacy was a something common to the genus. What was it? Had I been of a stronger character, or had the ordinary experience of a boy of eighteen, I should have asserted my own right to be what I was; I should have condemned the ways of the others, and been content to say I didn't like them. As it was, my weakness of character was such that I came to the conclusion in the end that the fault or defect, whatever it might be, was in *me*. *They* could not be all wrong, and they seemed to have no difficulty in getting on with each other. My boyish inexperience was such, that I could not understand how it could be that the others, many of whom were below me in attainments, were before me in manliness of character; that they dared to assert themselves as they were, while I was deficient in character, and hid, instead of standing by, the small amount I possessed.

This inability to apprehend the reason of my social ill success had a discouraging consequence upon the growth of my character. I was so convinced that the fault was in me, and not in the others, that I lost anything like firm footing, and succumbed to or imitated any type, or set, with which I was brought in contact, esteeming it better than my own, of which I was too ashamed to stand by it and assert it. Any rough, rude, self-confident fellow, who spoke out what he thought and felt, cowed me, and I yielded to him, and even assented to him, not with that yielding which gives way for peace sake, secretly thinking itself right, but with a surrender of the conscience and convictions to his mode of thinking, as being better than my own, more like men, more like the world. My unlikeness to others alarmed me; I wanted to be rid of it, and tried to be so by conformity to whatever came close to me from time to time. All force impressed and moved me, and having no criterion of good and bad in style and manner, I was ready to adopt any that had success and fashion in its favour. Surely no boy ever reached eighteen so unformed and characterless as I was!

The consequences to me of this relation to others did not end with mutability and chameleon-like readiness to take any shade of colour. The sense of weakness being thus daily and hourly pressed upon me grew internally painful. I felt humiliated and buffeted, and as if I were destined to be the sport and football of my companions. Out of this consciousness grew a general self-consciousness, which gained ground rapidly upon me, and became a canker in my character for years afterwards. I, who had come up to Oxford a mere child of nature, totally devoid of self-consciousness, to such a degree that I had never thought of myself as a subject of observation, developed a self-consciousness so sensitive and watchful, that it came between me and everything I said or did. It became physical nervousness. I thought every one was watching me; I blushed and trembled in company when I spoke or moved, and dared not raise a glass to my lips for fear it should be seen how my hand trembled. Before I said anything I had to think what would So-and-so think *of me* for saying it. A morbid self-consciousness was in a fair way to darken my life, and to paralyse my intellect. But here I have rather anticipated what grew up in a later time. I return to my first term's experiences.

As I had no acquaintance to begin with, my father begged my tutor to introduce me. Accordingly, I was breakfasted by Copleston, and presented to a senior commoner, by name John Belfield, a Devonshire man, and a neighbour of the Coplestons in the country.[53] Belfield godfathered me, introduced me into his set, took me under his wing, and was of infinite use to me, in those ways in which a well-established senior in a college can aid a raw – in this case an incredibly raw – freshman. Belfield's special chum was William Froude, the engineer,[54] brother of Anthony and of Richard Hurrell Froude, at that time Fellow of the College. The opening thus made for me through William Froude to Richard Hurrell's acquaintance might have been of inestimable use to me had I been capable of profiting by it. But I was too childish and ignorant even to apprehend what it was that was thus placed within my reach. I spent one evening in Richard Hurrell's rooms without appreciating him myself, or appearing to him to be worth taking up.

Through Belfield I came to know his set, comprising, besides Froude, William Charles Buller, Arthur Entwistle, Arthur Sheppard, William Phelps, and others.[55] But all the while it was with these only the intimacy of play-fellows.† We were together more or less every day, skiffing, walking, teaing; but I never had with any of these that communion of mind with mind, and soul with soul, for which I was all the while inwardly pining; pining unconsciously, for I did not know exactly what it was that was wanting; pining guiltily almost, for I felt that this vague unsatisfied longing within me must be wrong, since the others gave no sign of feeling anything like it. Had I disclosed this inward dissatisfaction to John Belfield he would have quizzed me unmercifully, told me I was a little fool (as he did often enough), and fisticuffed me round the room for my pains, and I should have believed that he was right. This set with which I lived in my first three terms were well-behaved young men, morally far higher than the horsey and drinking set of the Philpotts and Crawleys, but with no souls, all in their ambition and public aims; some, as was William Froude, of superior intelligence, but, having no inner life, no capacity of being moved by poetry, by natural beauty, who are never haunted by the ideal, or baffled by philosophical perplexities.

Another contrast which staggered me between myself and others was their attitude to the studies of the place. I had come up all eagerness to learn. Having had next to no teaching at home, I exaggerated in imagination what a teacher could do for me. I thought that now at last I should be in the company of an ardent band of fellow-students, only desirous of rivalling each other in the initiation which the tutors were to lead into the mysteries of scholarship, of composition, of rhetoric, logic, and all the arts of

† Compare Quinet's experience of first leaving home for college in 1815: – 'Loin que mes compagnons de captivité fussent une consolation pour moi, j'eus presque autant de peine à m'accoutumer à eux qu'aux choses mêmes.... Nous avions si peu d'idées communes entre nous! ... Combien cette première rencontre avec la société réglée me fut difficile, (et sans doute par ma faute)!' (*Hist. de mes Idées*, p. 194).[56]

literature. Philosophy did not come within my purview. I did not know there was such a thing.

I was soon disillusioned. I found lectures regarded as a joke or a bore, condemned by the more advanced, shirked by the backward; Latin and Greek regarded as useless, except for the purpose of getting a degree; and as for modern literature, the very idea of its existence had never dawned upon these youths, none of whom knew any language but English. Such was my simplicity that I had believed that no one went to college but those who were qualified, and anxious, to study. Nor was the difference between the passman and the honourman a sufficient clearing up of the paradox, for such it seemed to me, that men should flock to a university not to study. It fairly puzzled me to find that even William Froude, whom his elder brother was compelling to read for classical honours, 'hated Sophocles' – so he once told me – and regarded the whole job as a disgusting grind. Here again my fatal weakness betrayed me. I adopted his way of thinking – such a knowing man as William Froude must be right – adopted it with my lips, and in my way of talking, though here I think I made a secret reserve. I was trying with all my might to become like the men with whom I lived, and affected their phrases before I could honestly use them as being the expression of my own real thoughts. I was trying to suppress that which was, all the time, my real self, and to put on the new man – the type by which I was surrounded. The assimilating process, which was not wholly bad, was carried to a certain point, and there arrested, as I shall try to tell in the sequel; and that is the history of my life, and its only interest, so far as it may have any.

It was indeed quite necessary for the common conduct of myself that I should become more like others, and take on something of the current fashion, and something of the ordinary motive. I stood sorely in need of this discipline. At the same time the process, necessary as I see it was, had a baneful influence upon character. I was making a constant effort to appear to be, and thus a habit of acting a part, and considering how I looked in it, grew up in me. It was bad enough that I was always surrendering, or crushing out, my natural judgment in favour of other men's judgment, but it was worse that I was trying to pass myself off for something I was not. For it was of course that my endeavour, from being an endeavour to seem *something* I was not, should slide into an endeavour to seem something *better* than what I was. This gave my whole behaviour an insincerity and affection which, when discovered, extremely displeased myself, but which I found it impossible to shake off, as it was bound up with the attempt to do and think as others do – an attempt which at that time was indispensable to my existence as a member of society. I could not continue the wild boy of Hanover such as I had been sent up to Oxford. This constant personation, and considering how I looked in others' eyes, clung about me till very late in life. Had I been thrown more into an active profession I should have rubbed it off sooner, but living a student's life, and only emerging into the sunlight at intervals, this nervous self-consciousness adhered to me long. When at last got rid of it, it gave way, not to the ordinary social friction, but to the substantial development of the real self, which had been all the while dormant within me, as I shall relate.

Meanwhile, and at my *début*, this sheepishness, and wondering what others were thinking of me, was a source of unspeakable misery to me. I did not know where to put my hands, how to look, how to carry myself. I tried in vain to find out by what secret other men moved about so unembarrassed. I remember as if it were yesterday the first time I met the Provost in the street. When I became aware that he was coming I was seized with such a tremor, that in the thought of how I ought to perform my first act of 'capping', I omitted the ceremony altogether, and passed him in blank confusion. I saw he knew me and smiled, and I tortured myself with conjecture as to what the smile meant – contempt or compassion. A few days afterwards I met him and Mrs Hawkins again in the back lane; he knew me – he knew us all by sight – and good-naturedly supposing that on the previous occasion I had not recognised him, he advanced towards me, holding out his hand, 'Good morning, Mr Pattison'. I was again in a state of nervous collapse, but having prepared myself in imagination for the terrible ordeal, I executed according to the rules 'ad justum intervallum caput aperiendo',[57] but took no notice of the outstretched and ungloved hand proffered me. I remember now the grunt of dissatisfaction which escaped from the Provost as I tore past, discovering my blunder when it was too late to repair it. I think the Provost's aversion for me dated from this gross exhibition of *mal-adresse*; and I am not at all surprised at it. He, however, included me in his freshman's dinner-party the very first term. I went like a victim, and sate the allotted two hours in misery. At ringing of chapel-bell we were dismissed, and this time I managed to execute the *nunc dimittis* handshake; rushed to my room, tore off my white choker and my blue swallow-tail coat, with gilt flat buttons, and felt myself again. Since I became a Don I have never been surprised or alienated from one of our men by any *gaucherie* they may have committed in my presence, remembering that they probably came from less gentle homes than my own, and simply didn't know what they ought to do. But I have gone on the plan of leaving a freshman alone, as far as civilities go, the two or three first terms, till he has rubbed off some of his boorishness. I find what indisposes me to cultivate a pupil is never *mauvaise honte*,[58] for which I have nothing but pity. 'Il faut savoir vaincre la pudeur, et jamais la perdre,'[59] says some one; what sets you against a man is more bad manners than none at all. A fellow from a low school, who is confirmed in vulgar ways, can never be got out of them. If a youth, on being presented to his superior in age or station, or to a lady, offers to shake hands, I have little hope of him.

An ungainly and clownish carriage was not the only disadvantage which I laboured under. I had been turned out upon the world without the most elementary knowledge of the rules of etiquette. I don't think I knew that I ought to take off my hat in the street to a lady, but I didn't know any ladies in Oxford. I didn't know I ought to leave a card after hospitality; I doubt if I had any visiting cards to begin with. Mr Glaister of University civilly left a card for me, as son of a neighbour, soon after my arrival, and asked me to breakfast on a Sunday morning. I did not know that a note of invitation required an answer, and supposed a college tutor, though in another college, was a superior being – a schoolmaster whose invites were commands. I went without answering, and found no breakfast. This was soon provided; but after I left I never called, and wondered I was not asked again. After the Provost's dinner above-mentioned I never dropt a card, as I have no doubt all the horsey and smoking set did.

I suffered humiliation from want of such simple training in the *bienséances*. But this source of annoyance was as nothing in comparison with the yoke of moral tyranny which I fastened round my neck, by the growing anxiety as to what others were thinking of what I said and did. I cannot dwell enough on this, as it became the governing law of my words and actions. How I struggled and prayed against my weakness, but in vain! I cannot help thinking, in looking back, that this dressing the window for the customers was partly an inherited failing. My father had many stories of his own experience to tell, and told them with great dramatic power; but the tendency of all of them was to set himself off. He was not a little *glorieux*, and when once set off did not adhere to fact on this theme. My sister Dorothy took after him in this respect, but with a far more vivid imagination than her father; she spent a faculty of invention, which would have placed her in the first rank as a novelist, in embellishing the everyday occurrences of her own life. A very faint reflection of Dorothy's powers of self-glorification is preserved in Miss Lonsdale's romance, *Sister Dora*. Again, * * * [60] shows the same tendency in another way. She is always personating, with a desire to present herself in a little more favourable light than the circumstances warrant. But having no imagination, and being scrupulously truthful as to the most minute details, * * * does not colour; she tries to produce the heightening effect by suppression of the less flattering tones. Hence the unreality we all feel and regret in our intercourse with a person whom we otherwise have so much occasion to esteem and love.

To return to the studies and instruction of the college. My unlikeness to other boys was no less marked in respect of learning than it was in character and deportment. Gibbon says of himself that he 'arrived at Oxford with a stock of erudition that might have puzzled a doctor, and a degree of ignorance of which a schoolboy would have been ashamed.' I at eighteen had nothing to compare with the historical reading which Gibbon could show at fifteen. As, however, to mere Greek and Latin, I had covered a surface vastly more extensive than even the best of the ordinary sixth form boy. I had read Sallust through, about a dozen speeches of Cicero, twenty books of Livy, Vergil through, Horace through, Juvenal through, Persius through, Cæsar through, Terence through; in Greek, the Gospels and Acts, Xenophon's *Anabasis*, Herodotus, Thucydides, some six or seven Orations of

Demosthenes, Homer's *Iliad*, Pindar, Sophocles, Aeschylus, Porson's four plays of Euripides, seven plays of Aristophanes – all these not in scraps, but through. They had not been well read; I had merely translated them *viva voce*, by aid of the Lexicon (Scapula), my father correcting me by aid of the crib, without which he was lost. None of the niceties of scholarship had ever been whispered to me. I was not well grounded even in the Greek grammar; as to accentuation and metrical law I had everything to learn. But the worst of all was that I had not been shown how to read, and that the general mystery of exact language was hidden from me. The book which had taken most hold of my mind was Thucydides; I had written out translations of all the speeches. The political pregnancy of certain words in these had excited my interest, and served afterwards as a kind of introduction to the study of philosophical terms. But I had no apprehension of the refined beauties of poetical expression, the exquisitely clean-cut wording of Sophocles, and no doubt preferred Horace to Vergil. All that my extensive reading had given me was a mere empirical familiarity with the languages, an enlarged vocabulary, and an idea of various and contrasted styles. I had been practised a good deal in translating back from an English Cicero, and had a general sense of Ciceronian Latin as a type to work to, but was very far from being able easily to compose a Latin theme.

I had a very insufficient consciousness of my defects in Greek and Latin, and no conception at all of the immensity of the knowable in this direction. But in my ignorance of what other boys were like, I went into my first lecture with fear and trembling, expecting to find myself very far behind the rest. A college lecture in those days meant the class construing, in turns, some twenty lines of a classical text to the tutor, who corrected you when you were wrong. Of the value as intellectual gymnastic of this exercise there can be no question; the failure as education lay in the circumstance, that this one exercise was about the whole of what our teachers ever attempted to do for us. I had been inscribed in the lecture list which was suspended in the gateway, in Cicero's *Catilinarians* with Copleston, the *Alcestis* with Denison,[61] and Euclid I with Dornford. With the reading I had brought with me, it did not seem promotion to be put into the *Catilinarians* and the *Alcestis*. However, it was a new play, and

G. A. Denison had a reputation as a scholar. I got Monk's edition, and prepared with great care a couple of hundred lines, which did not take me long. I was delighted with Monk's notes, which were new to me. I had had no one to tell me of any of the newer school-books, and had hammered on with Viger, and Matthiae's Greek Grammar.

When we went in to Denison, some one or two members of the class (a large one) did their piece well; to my flat amazement most of them stumbled over the easiest lines. When we came to the first lyrics, Φοῖβ' ἀδικεῖς αὖ τιμὰς ἐνέρων,[62] etc., the tutor put the question, 'What metre is this?' It went the round, no one had any idea; it came to me, and I remember the trembling excitement with which I answered, 'Anapaestic dimeter.' So much information was not far to fetch, for Monk had a note on the metre of the passage, and most of the class had Monk, but they had not read the Latin note. Denison gave me a look as much as to say, 'Who the devil are you?' He had evidently not been accustomed in his class to meet with such profound learning. I do not remember in the whole course of the term that Denison made a single remark on the two plays, *Alcestis* and *Hippolytus*, that did not come from Monk's notes.

In less than a week I was entirely disillusioned as to what I was to learn in an Oxford lecture room. Copleston was still worse. Denison was a scholar according to the measure of those days, knew his Greek plays, and could let fall a clever thing. Copleston was a veritable dunce, who could teach you nothing. He was the butt of the college, and we used to wonder how he ever became Fellow of Oriel. The explanation was probably in the *name*. I suppose it was a job of his uncle's; for though Edward Copleston had ceased to be Provost at the date of W. J. Copleston's election, his influence must have been still powerful with the electors.

I have before said that when I came up to enter my name in 1830 Oriel still held its place as the first college in the University in academical repute.[63] When I came into residence in 1832, though the outside public, either the University public or the wider English public, were not aware of any change in this respect, yet the tide had just turned, and the causes which led to the decline and fall of Oriel had already begun to operate. It must be observed, that as a college rises into repute and prestige slowly, so it loses what it may have once acquired by equally slow steps. The prestige of a school is like the credit of a firm; it lives on for some time after its capital has been lost. It is not often in the history of a college that it is possible to assign a date at which the decline commences so closely as we can in the history of Oriel. That date is 1830–32.

The distinction of a college in the opinion of the public is made up of three elements – the intellectual calibre of the Head and Fellows; the efficiency of the tuition; and the social rank and behaviour of the students. Any one of these three constituents of eminence may be possessed by a college without the other two; as Christ Church at the present day (1883) is, and always must be, the resort of the aristocracy, while the two other qualifications for ἡγεμονία[64] are conspicuously wanting. (The present dean, whose name is immortalised in the annals of English scholarship by his Lexicon, is the same age as myself, and belongs to the past age.)[65] For about the first thirty years of this century Oriel fulfilled all the three conditions of renown. It contained all there was of original intellect at the time in the University; it was usually tutored by energetic and well-qualified (according to the narrow standard of qualification then known) tutors; and an entrance examination sifted the commoners. An examination did not directly bring in youths from good families; but as soon as it is understood that a college chooses to be 'select', good families are anxious to get their sons into it. And as Oriel could only lodge some sixty men, it very soon became matter of favour and showing cause of preference to get a son in. There was a goodly array of silk gowns – gentlemen-commoners they were invidiously called – at the high table. These being better born, or wealthier than the commoners, kept up a style of living such as is usual in large country houses. Molesworth, Monsell, Hawley, Sykes, Domvile, Cadogan, these lingered on into my time, and were much looked up to by us, as giving the tone, and taking the lead, when there had ceased to be any combination of talent in the society to balance rank.

So much for the undergraduate portion of the college during the earlier years of the century. The distinction here was less one of intelligence than of quality, enhanced by that prestige which any set can acquire which tries to be select. Oriel was under

Copleston eminently a gentlemanly college.

When we turn from the commoners, gentlemen or other, to the Collegium, or corporation itself, then it is that we see the true source of the distinction of Oriel, and of the great name it had in the country at large. It must be remembered in abatement of this renown that Oxford was, at the time I write of, *de facto*, though not *de jure*, a close clerical corporation,[66] and that therefore talent was much scarcer here than it now is, since the secularisation of the University. A very little literature, and a modicum of classical reading, went a long way. Sermons were almost the only public appearance to which the teachers of all the arts and sciences ever committed themselves. Any one then who ventured upon the broad ocean of general literature, and could speak to the intelligence of England so as to be attended to, was a more conspicuous person in the place than he would now be. But even after this deduction made, Copleston remains a very considerable figure in the literary history of the day. He had been the champion of the University against the attacks of the new scientific interest which had grown up outside, and of which the *Edinburgh Review* made itself the mouthpiece. He was a regular contributor to the *Quarterly Review*, and he had selected as his specialty currency and finance, topics of great general interest in those years when the resumption of cash payments was under public discussion. His pamphlets on these questions not only attracted attention as able popular statements, but penetrated to the circle of experts; they were quoted in the House, and their author invited to interviews with Mr Peel, Sir A. Baring, and Mr Huskisson.[67]

Within the University he enjoyed an assured ascendency. This was the more surprising, as in politics he espoused the unpopular, i.e. the Liberal side. But though in a minority on political questions, his personal influence as the man of most power and tact in the place was undisputed by any rival; and it was quite understood that the election of Lord Grenville[68] to the Chancellorship (in spite of the Court and the corrupt Tory borough-mongering system, and with all Lord Eldon's popularity against) had been greatly owing to him.[69] Within his own college he was, of course, all-powerful, a proof of which was given on the vacancy of the Headship in December 1814, when the post of Provost was tendered to him in an address signed by all the fellows. He administered the affairs of the college with the skill and decision of a practical man of business. Estates were not in those days the trouble, anxiety, and source of expense they have become lately (1883);[70] but Oriel was the first college which, under Copleston's management, adopted the plan, since universally approved and followed, of running out leases by not renewing the fines, and borrowing money to make good the dividend.[71] Mozley, who entered the college in 1822, knew Copleston as 'the most substantial and majestic, and if I may say so, richly-coloured character within my knowledge' (*Reminiscences*, i. 80).

It is evident that with a man of this stamina at its head Oriel must have come to the front in the rivalry of colleges. But Copleston's imposing personality was, in fact, but one, and by no means the chief, ingredient in the eminent position which Oriel at this date held in public estimation. 'A great age makes a great man,' said Macaulay; but whether this or the converse be true, we certainly expect some relation between any man of special prominence and his environment. Copleston did not stand alone in his college.

Oriel tradition carries back the rise of the college from vulgar mediocrity to the thirty years' provostship of John Eveleigh, 1781–1814.[72] Of Eveleigh personally I know nothing; he died in the year after I was born. But Copleston's funeral oration or address, which is printed in his life, ascribes to his efforts the reformed scheme of examination for degrees.[73] This system of honours and pass which has, in the course of the century, grown into the one absorbing business of the University, began in a timid and unpretending form in 1802. Eveleigh was the chief promoter of this reform. Like all reforms which have ever been carried in our University, this change was stoutly resisted by the majority, and all sorts of possible mischief anticipated as its consequence. It was not till Eveleigh offered out of his own pocket a benefaction for the purpose of providing rewards for meritorious candidates, that the opposition was overcome. At first the examination was a voluntary one – i.e. the candidates for the B.A. degree *must* pass the ordinary farcical examination, *pro forma*, which was held every term, but those candidates who chose to seek distinction *might* offer themselves for the new examination. The new scheme, once set on foot, recommended itself in a very short time to the sense of the University, so that as early as 1807 its voluntary character was abrogated, and the examination was made compulsory on all candidates for the B.A. degree members of New College excepted.[74]

The efficiency of the instrument which Eveleigh had thus introduced into the University, he had previously tested in the case of his own college.

The co-optation of fellows into the society, or corporation, of a college was, in the last century, done under conditions which left no place for any qualification of learning, even if learning had existed at all in the University. The fellow to be chosen must have been born in a particular district, to which the vacancy was appropriated; he must be in orders, or proceed to take orders as soon as elected; he must be, and remain, unmarried. When the possible candidates had been restricted by these conditions, the choice out of the number was made by vote. Each fellow had a vote, and gave it irresponsibly. Like chose like. A drinking society chose a boon companion. Even those societies which had preserved self-respect enough not to sink into the condition of sots and topers preferred a 'companionable' man to any acquirements or talents. The public opinion of the University approved this principle of selection, and had come to regard a college as a club, into which you should get only clubbable men. Then they dispensed each other from the obligation to study for seven years, and from the performance of those exercises which had been the guarantee of study, so that the original object of the foundation, the promotion of learning, was wholly abrogated. The Visitors of the colleges, mostly bishops, did not interfere to check this abuse, so that the only resource to compel the performance of the trust was to call in the intervention of the sovereign power, the State, which was done at last in 1854.[75]

In breaking through this standing abuse, and in making literary acquirement a qualification for the enjoyment of the benefaction, Oriel was taking the first step towards bringing back the college to the intention of the original foundation. Of this first step Provost Eveleigh was the author and prime mover. But there is no record of the mode in which he brought round a majority of his colleagues to take a view of duty so beyond the range of Oxford morality at the time. The implied censure upon themselves was

49

vigorously resented by the cosy family parties in the other common-rooms, and Oriel men were exposed, as T. Mozley could remember (*Reminiscences*, i. 117), to much banter on the score of their pretensions to superiority – pretensions which we may easily believe tended among the younger members to generate not a little presumption and conceit. However, by the beginning of the century, Provost Eveleigh had succeeded in making Oriel a home for a class of Fellows selected from the University at large, on the ground of intellectual qualification alone. Such a body of men were sure to desire to perpetuate their type, and 'like chooses like' became a principle of election as useful here as it had been mischievous in the sociable and toping colleges.

One thing only was still wanting to give the final crown of distinction to this select society. A majority once obtained, who should agree to award Fellowships to intellectual merit, was it possible to carry the agreement farther so as to adopt a uniform standard of merit? Could a body of men, equal and voting irresponsibly, be brought to adopt a test of intellect – a 'Scrutinium ingeniorum'[76] which should be one true, and founded on real distinctions, and not one governed by the fashion or market-value of the day – a test which should set the solid above the showy, which should be a test of mind and not of knowledge and accomplishments? The fortune of Oriel, rising as it were with the occasion, did not deny this last and rarest favour. For nearly thirty years the examinations for Oriel Fellowships were conducted upon the principle of ascertaining, not what a man had read, but what he was like. The prizes or classes which a candidate might bring with him to the competition were wholly disregarded by the electors, who looked at his papers unbiassed by opinion outside. The verdict of the University Examiners was not only often set aside, but even outraged. If Keble, Hawkins, and Jenkyns were double-firsts, Whately, T. Mozley, Newman, and Hurrell Froude were all men of low classes, and taken against candidates of greater *prima facie* claims. Perhaps the word which best expresses what was looked for in the papers of the candidates for an Oriel Fellowship is originality.

There was doubtless a serious defect in this system. The men thus picked out as men of original minds were apt to have too little respect for the past because they were ignorant of it. A man who does not know what has been thought by those who have gone before him is sure to set an undue value upon his own ideas – ideas which have perhaps been tried and found wanting. As accumulated learning stifles the mental powers, so original thinking has been known to bring about a puffy, unsubstantial mental condition. It was only in the then condition of the University, hidebound in the traditions of narrow clerical prejudice, that the new Oriel school of the Noetics, as they came to be called,[77] could be welcomed as a wholesome invasion of a scurfy pond, stagnant with sameness and custom. The Noetics knew nothing of the philosophical movement which was taking place on the continent; they were imbued neither with Kant nor with Rousseau, yet this knot of Oriel men was distinctly the product of the French Revolution. They called everything in question; they appealed to first principles, and disallowed authority as a judge in intellectual matters. There was a wholesome intellectual ferment constantly maintained in the Oriel common-room, of that kind which was so dreaded by the authorities of the German States in the days of the Terror (1851).

> *Wer auf der Strasse raisonnirt*
> *Wird unverzüglich füsilirt;*
> *Das Raisonniren durch Gebärden*
> *Soll gleichfalls hart bestrafet werden.* [78]
> HEINE, *Werke*, iii. 139 (ed. Tiel)

The mental activity prevailing in the German universities was especially irritating to Dr Pusey,[79] who complains (*Evidence on the Recommendations*, p. 24) of their 'theories which pull to pieces what has been received for *thousands of years*'. It was the men in whom this disposition reigned in Oriel† that gave the college its

† So the Noetics appeared to William Palmer, who has written a history of the Tractarian revival. 'A school arose whose conceit led them to imagine that their wisdom was sufficient to correct and amend the whole world. The Church itself produced some such vain reasoners, who, with boundless freedom, began to investigate all institutions, to search into the basis of religious doctrines, and to put forth each his wild theory or irreverential remark. All was pretended to be for the benefit of free discussion, which was substituted for the claims of truth. This school came from Oriel College.' (*Narrative of Events*, p. 20.)

celebrity in the country. The most known names were, besides Provost Copleston, Whately, Arnold,[80] Hampden,[81] Baden Powell. Blanco White, though only an honorary member of the college, lived much in the common-room.[82]

This little germ of premature 'free enquiry', though ultimately destined to grow into a flourishing tree, was at its first appearance too violently in contrast with the established ways of thinking of the whole University not to provoke a reaction. The reaction came, as was to have been expected, within the same college within which the provocation had been given. But it came with a violence and *éclat* which were so out of all proportion to the scale on which the challenge had been given, that it has well-nigh obliterated the historical relations between the movement and the counter-movement.

The Tractarian movement has become historical, and has had more than one historian. As the starting-point of a great church revival, which is still in vogue, Tractarianism has attracted to itself the attention of the public, as though it were an independent phenomenon which could be known and apprehended without its genealogy being traced; whereas it was only one phase – the indispensable, reactionary, and complementary phase – in the movement of thought which belongs to the nineteenth century.

I shall resume what I have to say on Tractarianism when I come to the year – about 1838 – when I myself began to be drawn into its vortex. At present I am writing of the year 1832, in which I came up to Oriel, and what has been above said has been intended to describe the condition of the college as a place of the higher education.

CHAPTER 2

WHEN I went up in 1830 to enter, I said, Oriel still stood at the head of the colleges in all the signs of life and vigour. In point of tutorial efficiency it had greatly the advantage, so it seemed, of the only college which could be considered to compete with it for the ἡγεμονία, viz. Balliol. The age of the Noetics proper was gone by; the whole *personnel* of the college was changed – Copleston and Whately and Tyler had been taken away by church preferment. The college was officered by new men, but by men whose energy and talent had already attracted the eyes of the University towards them.

The new Provost (1827) was not, indeed, the equal of Keble, either in nobility of character or in literary power. But Hawkins was superior to Keble in some of those more superficial qualities which recommend a man as a head of a college – in ready tact, in aptitude for the small details of administration, and strict attention to the enforcement of college rules. Hawkins was, I suppose, generally the more practical man of the two. His mind, says Dr Burgon, was 'essentially legal in its texture' (*Quart. Rev.*, Oct. 1883), and his own desire had been to go to the bar. But having got a fellowship he naturally took orders, and preached sermons of an indisputably judicious character. His edition of Todd's *Milton* (1824) was a work undertaken for the bookseller, and did not add to his reputation. His own notes are signed E. I have not examined these to see what extent of classical allusion was at Hawkins' command. But if he ever, in his early days, went beyond the very narrow range of an Oxford first-classman's reading in classics he very soon abandoned them for theology, and was drawn into the arena of 'church' controversy. 'You don't know Hawkins as well as I do,' wrote an old Oriel fellow to Newman after the election; 'he will be sure to disappoint you.'† What is

† It is common among those who have written of this election to express surprise

certain is, that within five years of Hawkins' election, Oriel showed symptoms of having begun to decline. But in 1827, on the promotion of Copleston to the bishopric of Llandaff, university opinion pronounced that the headship lay between Keble and Hawkins; and when Hawkins, by Newman's support, obtained the prize, it was not denied that the college had made a proper choice. Up to 1830 there were no visible symptoms of dissatisfaction in the college though every one must have felt the thinness and superficiality of the new Provost's character by contrast with the sterling force and richness of that of his predecessors.

The tutors of the college in 1830 were Newman, Hurrell Froude, Robert Wilberforce – all of them considered to be among the most rising men in the University. They were 'bestowing on their pupils as much time and trouble as is usually only expected from very good private tutors' (Mozley, *Rem*. i. 229), and in return the tutors were rewarded by the enthusiastic following of no inconsiderable band of admiring disciples.

This was apparently the condition of the college when my name was entered on its books in 1830. When I came up to reside in May 1832 the scene was totally changed. The Provost had got rid of the three energetic and successful tutors, and had supplied their places with three inefficients – W. J. Copleston, G. A. Denison, and Dornford (continued on). How this came about might have been explained by the principal agent in the revolution, Provost Hawkins himself. Dr Burgon[1] tells us (*Quart. Rev.*, Oct. 1883) that he regularly kept a diary – a record of the writer's state of mind and the employment of his time. It were much to be wished that this diary could be preserved in the permanent form of type; but Dr Burgon assures us it will never be printed, and so

---

that Newman should, on this occasion, have supported Hawkins against Keble. They think because Keble was afterwards a partner with Newman in the Tractarian movement that Newman must have been always a personal friend of Keble. This was not so. In 1827 Newman did not know Keble who, though a Fellow of the College, was non-resident, and only came up occasionally to attend important meetings. On the other hand Newman had acted with Hawkins, whose good qualities he appreciated, and whose sentiments were not, in 1827, materially different from his own. Hawkins was in those days an effective preacher; in any one of his sermons there was matter enough for two, and his manner in the pulpit was peculiarly impressive. This would be a great point with Newman.

this, like so many more precious documents of our university history, will be sacrificed to the petty susceptibilities of relations. Conington's diary was thus destroyed in my time by the timidity of his executors.[2] The account of the transaction given by T. Mozley is, that the three tutors insisted upon a novel and extensive re-organisation of the course of instruction; that Hawkins received their proposal with dismay, suspecting it aimed at his monopoly of college power. The tutors, he thought, would, under the new scheme, get the tuition, and so the conduct of the college, entirely into their own hands, and thus the Provost would find himself left out of the current of college thought and feeling — would lose touch, as we say now. A minor displacement which may have occurred to him was, that he would be unable to take a share in the terminal examinations called 'Collections'. But Mozley has omitted the material point of the attitude taken up by Newman. Newman insisted upon regarding his relation to his pupils as a pastoral one. Unless he could exercise the function of tutor on this basis he did not think that he, being a priest, could be tutor at all. For this purpose it was necessary that a portion of the undergraduates — a third or a fourth — should be entered under him, and the remainder likewise distributed among the other two — or three — tutors. But the Provost's proposal that all undergraduates should be entered under one common name, and no longer under respective tutors, interfered with Newman's doctrine of the pastoral relation. This was the point which Newman would not give up, and for which he resigned, or rather was turned out. It is clear that, under the system for which Newman contended, a college must have become a mere priestly seminary and not an agent of a university. If it happened as T. Mozley relates, we must infer that a narrow collegiate jealousy on the part of the Head prevailed with him to sacrifice what he saw to be the interest of the college to the maintenance of his own authority. He would not do this consciously; he would be impressed with the view that, the welfare of the college being dependent on the Head, the Head must, before all things, be supreme in all that regards the tuition.

This year, 1831, was the turning-point in the fortunes of Oriel. From this date the college began to go downhill, both in the calibre of the men who obtained fellowships and in the style and tone of the undergraduates. In the race for university honours Balliol rapidly shot ahead, and still (1883) maintains the first place among the colleges. In the distinction of its fellows no college has succeeded to the place of the Oriel of Eveleigh and Copleston, as no college has had the skill to choose its members on the same principle – *propter spem* and not *propter rem*. Since the reform of 1854 what superior talent there has been in Oxford has been pretty equally distributed among the colleges, as elections have been made at haphazard, on no principle, and left to the chances of a vote.[3] The eccentricities of this casual co-option were exhibited in a ludicrous light at the Oriel election of 1846, when J. W. Burgon was taken over the head of Goldwin Smith.[4] Some colleges are (1883) more corroded than others by the canker of ecclesiasticism (e.g. Christ Church and S. John's) which excludes all intelligent interests. In no common-room, so far as I know, is there now maintained a level of serious discussion occupying itself with the great problems of speculation, or with the science or the literature of the day. Young M.A.'s of talent abound, but they are all taken up with the conduct of some wheel in the complex machinery of cram, which grinds down all specific tendencies and tastes into one uniform mediocrity. The men of middle age seem, after they reach thirty-five or forty, to be struck with an intellectual palsy, and betake themselves, no longer to port, but to the frippery work of attending boards and negotiating some phantom of legislation, with all the importance of a cabinet council[5] – *belli simulacra cientes*.[6] Then they give each other dinners, where they assemble again with the comfortable assurance that they have earned their evening relaxation by the fatigues of the morning's committee. These are the leading men of our university, and who give the tone to it – a tone as of a lively municipal borough; all the objects of science and learning, for which a university exists, being put out of sight by the consideration of the material means of endowing them.

There is no difficulty, as has been said already, in fixing as a date the epoch at which the decline of Oriel commenced. It was coincident with the accession of Hawkins to the headship. But was the cause of that decline merely the change of Provost, the substitution of Hawkins for Copleston, and the determination of Hawkins to retain supremacy, even at the cost of dismissing three most zealous and active tutors, and filling their place with dummies? It has been often repeated that it was the circumstance of Newman's being turned out of the tutorship that made him into an ecclesiastical agitator; that a college disappointment gave birth to the 'Tracts'. This is laughable and may be compared to George III's belief that there would have been no Wesleyan secession if ministers would have made Wesley a bishop. Those who have known anything of Newman, either in himself or his writings, will understand the flimsiness of this view. And those who do not know anything of the man may satisfy themselves, by a comparison of dates, that Newman's bent had been decided towards theology even before Hawkins became Provost. Newman – a theologian first, a political leader afterwards – was made a leader, not by loss of college preferment, but by the pressure of public events upon his church sentiments. It was the same, in an unequal measure, with all the three tutors whom Hawkins put out; they were all three clergymen; they all held, or had held, curacies in the city or neighbourhood of Oxford; they took pains with their sermons – were, in short, steeped in parochialism. Not that they were of the modern, fussy, curate genus, incapable of thought or study; these men were also students. But the aim of all their studies was 'divinity'; and they took 'divinity' seriously, as men trained in the old Oriel school could not but do. Theology was not a mere professional outfit; it was to supply the aim and rule of life. Newman and Froude took to church history; Newman wrote an article on Apollonius of Tyana for the *Encyclopædia Metropolitana*, and meditated his *History of the Arians*. In 1826 Froude goes back to Oxford (*Remains*, i. 204) with 'a determination to set to at Hebrew and the early fathers'. What they were interested in themselves they were ready to give out to their pupils, and enthusiasm is contagious. At least they had nothing else to give, for their knowledge of the classics was extremely limited. H. Froude has taste in style, and can read Greek sufficiently to admire the slighter dialogues of Plato (*Ibid.* p. 248), *Gorgias, Apology, Crito, Phædo*, but confesses his inability to grapple with the high problems of the *Timæus* or the *Parmenides*. Yet he will try; spends two or three mornings in the attempt, and renounces it as beyond him. 'I have cut Timæus, which gets duller and duller, and harder and harder' (*Letters to friends*, Aug. 1831).

Hawkins had no higher idea of what was required of a tutor. He offered (1835) a tutorship to Thos. Mozley, who had the moral courage to refuse it with all its emoluments and distinction, on the ground that he did not feel himself equal to it. The college standard of what was required of a tutor did not demand such an act of self-denial on Mozley's part. His own estimate of tutorial fitness is just that which prevailed in Oriel at the time. 'I could certainly keep ahead of my pupils, *which was all that many tutors ever did*. I could come round my class by questions they were not prepared for. I was sure always to hear mistakes which it would be easy to correct. In matter of fact a tutor often did no more than half of the class could have done quite as well. Though the method of instruction was very effectual, yet it was easy sailing' (*Reminisc.* i. 237). The Provost was willing to have taken Mozley on if he would have done no more than this; but Mozley was too honest to scamp the work. He thinks the method of instruction was effectual, so crude was the conception which an Oriel fellow, and one of the ablest, had formed of what it is to teach the classics.

If there were any one in the whole of Oxford who could be supposed capable of attaining to a complete conception of what instruction ought to be, it was the author of *Discourses on the Scope, etc., of University Education*. Newman knew that 'ideas are the life of institutions – social, political, literary'; and the idea which he would place as the basis of a university is the master-idea –

> Imagine a science of sciences, and you have attained the true notion of the scope of a university. . . . A science is not mere knowledge; it is knowledge which has undergone a process of intellectual digestion. . . . We consider that all things mount up to a whole; that there is an order and precedence and harmony in the branches of knowledge one with another, and that to destroy that structure is unphilosophical in a course of education (pp. 142–4).

Nothing can be grander than the development of the idea which follows in the same volume (p. 153). 'All knowledge whatever is taken into account in a university, as being the special seat of that large philosophy which embraces and locates truth of every kind, and every method of attaining it.' Thus thought Newman in 1852. Are we to suppose that this magnificent ideal of a national institute, embracing and representing all knowledge, and making this knowledge its own end, was the wisdom of riper years – a vision which grew up in Newman's mind in the course of the twenty or more years which elapsed between the Oriel tutorship and the Dublin presidency?[7] Perhaps so; it required much time and mental enlargement for any of us, who were brought up under the old eight-book system of an Oxford college of 1830, to rise to the idea of a university in which every science should have its proper and appointed place. Newman may have been no exception. At any rate, during the time of his Oriel tutorship, there is no sign that he had any loftier conception of the duties of a tutor than his friends H. Froude and Mozley. Newman was then in Anglican orders; he had the charge of a parish – first S. Clement's, then S. Mary's; he spent much time upon the preparation of those weighty sermons by which he first became famous, and which were the foundation of his influence with young men. When he studied, it was church history – the Fathers of the fourth century; Athanasius was his hero; he was inspired by the triumph of the church organisation over the wisdom and philosophy of the Hellenic world; that triumph which, to the Humanist, is the saddest moment in history – the ruin of the painfully constructed fabric of civilisation to the profit of the church. Religion was evidently to Newman, in 1830, not only the first but the sole object of all teachings. There was no thought then of ἐν κύκλῳ παιδεία,[8] a genealogical chart of all the sciences; there was not even the lesser conception of education by the classics, as containing the essential elements of humanism. These teachers of the classics had sided with the enemies of humanism. Greek was useful as enabling you to read the Greek Testament and the Fathers. All knowledge was to be subservient to the interests of religion, for which vague idea was afterwards substituted the definite and concrete idea of the Visible Church. Of the world of wisdom and sentiment – of poetry and philosophy, of social and political experience, contained in the Latin and Greek classics, and of the true relation of the degenerate and semi-barbarous Christian writers of the fourth century to that world – Oxford, in 1830, had never dreamt. It is too much to require that the three Oriel tutors should have understood what no one about them understood. But their greater seriousness of purpose – their disinterested devotion to the cause of religion as they understood it – made them more dangerous than the *pococurante*[9] plausibilities who displaced them. In the hands of the three tutors, all of them priests, narrow and desperate devotees of the clerical interest, the college must have become a seminary in which the pupils should be trained for church ends, and broken in, like the students of a Jesuit college, to regard the dictates of the confessor and the interests of the clergy as the supreme law of life. Religion is a good servant but a bad master. In the same volume in which Newman, in 1852, expounds the idea of an all-embracing university organisation, with a breadth and boldness which is not to be found elsewhere, I find the following notion on History, which he speaks of as a science: – 'Revealed religion furnishes facts to other sciences, which those sciences, left to themselves, would never reach. . . . Thus, in the science of history, the preservation of our race in Noah's ark is an historical fact, which history never would arrive at without revelation' (p. 105).

By 1830 Newman had enlarged his views upon the college beyond the circle of his pupils. He now aimed at a moulding of the college of fellows – there were at this date eighteen fellowships – on a mediæval system; at reviving the college of Adam de Brome and Laud, and mounting it as a reactionary machine to resist the formidable progress of 'Liberalism' and the modern spirit. The elections were to be so manipulated that a body of like-minded fellows should be obtained, who should all reside and study the Fathers, not necessarily occupying themselves with tuition. They would form a nucleus of learned controversialists, destined to fight against the vicious tendencies of an unbelieving age. The elections to fellowships for the ten years, from about 1830, were struggles between Newman endeavouring to fill the college with men likely to carry out his ideas, and the Provost endeavouring, upon no principle, merely to resist Newman's lead. Newman did not lose sight of the old Oriel principle of electing for promise rather than for performance; only, instead of looking for promise of originality, he now looked for promise of congeniality. Anyhow, in these contests, the old character of the Oriel fellowship was obliterated, and many inferior elections were made. It may be that the blame of the worst elections lay with the Provost's party, which was not so homogeneous as the opposing party, and possessed no one with the keen instinct, which Newman alone had, for recognising, through an examination paper, the kind of merit and character which he wanted. The capital blunder which was patent to the whole university, when Burgon was taken over the head of Goldwin Smith, must have been made, I think, after Newman had done with the college.

It has often occurred to me to compare what took place at this period, in the fortunes of a small college, with the course of things in the great movement of the sixteenth century. About 1500 it seemed as if Europe was about to cast off at one effort the slough of feudal barbarism, and to step at once into the fair inheritance of the wisdom and culture of the ancient world. The Church led the van, and smiled on free inquiry and the new learning. About the third decennium of the century the resistance of the *obscurantists* was organised, the Catholic reaction set in, and nascent human-ism was submerged beneath the rising tide of theological passion and the fatal and fruitless controversies of Lutheran, Calvinist, and Catholic, to the rival cries of the Bible and the Church. The '*sacrificio d'intelletto*' of Loyola took the place of the free and rationalising spirit with which Erasmus had looked out upon the world of men. It was soon after 1830 that the 'Tracts' desolated Oxford life, and suspended, for an indefinite period, all science, humane letters, and the first strivings of intellectual freedom which had moved in the bosom of Oriel.

CHAPTER 3

THIS IS what I see, looking back after fifty years, to have been the state of Oriel when I entered it in 1832. It must not be supposed that I, the freshman, had the least glimmering of all this which I have now been expounding in these last pages. There was no one to tell me these things, nor should I have understood them if I had been told. I had not so much as made clear to myself what a college or what a university was, nor did I do this for many years after 1832. I suppose I had the same hazy notion of a college – as a school for young men who had outgrown school – which the public still entertains. I have often since wondered at the satisfied ignorance, on all points touching the government and constitution of the University, in which most students pass their time here. They are members of a college three of four years; they take two degrees; they keep their names on its books, and never ask themselves the question – How came there to be colleges, and what is the University as distinct from the aggregate of the colleges?

Certainly in 1832 I had never thought of asking any such question. The 'college' to me was, as it was to my scout, the building at the end of the lane. We were all, I believe, proud of our college. I remember a friend of mine at that time, R. G. Young,[1] confessing to me that he always felt a secret complacency, when he stepped out of the gate into the street, in the thought that he would be recognised as an Oriel man. This was doubtless chiefly the flunkey's estimate – respectability measured by income and position – but I think it contained also an element of hero-worship. We all thought a Fellow of Oriel a person of miraculous intellect only because he *was* one; though I cannot tell how we arranged such exceptional phenomena as W. J. Copleston, J. F. Christie, and another, whom we could not help seeing to be below Oriel par, not only as tutors but as men. Still less could any suspicion enter my mind that I had been wrongly placed at Oriel if the deficiencies in my education were to be made good. Yet when the end of term came I was vaguely conscious of disillusion in two directions. I had built much upon lectures. I had thought now, at last, I shall be put in the right track, having had no guidance so far. But I was not guided; I was not put in any track; I was not shown the method of learning. I had made, as far as books went, no progress.

I don't suppose I was much concerned about this. Time seems infinite to a freshman in his first term. The neglect of a term could be repaired next time. Besides I had had so much else to learn, not derived from books, which boys from a public school bring with them to college, but which I had to pick up *at* college. I had been brought up much like Caspar Hauser in the Bavarian wilds,[2] and had, at eighteen, made my first essay of companions of my own age. Here was my second disillusion. This first contact with my species, though it had brought along with it much necessary to be known, had been disappointment. I had launched out into comradeship with eagerness, because I had been debarred from it, but I had found no sympathy for the better and aspiring part of my nature. I had supposed I was coming into an honourable company of rivalry in the pursuit of knowledge. I wanted not merely to get up my classics, but to penetrate to the secrets and mysteries which I vaguely understood to be somehow wrapt up in books, though they had not, as yet, been revealed to me. I was disconcerted to find that none of my new acquaintance had any share of this yearning curiosity. But though I felt a certain blank, I don't suppose the disappointment was very grievous to me, being overborne and lost in the amusements and novelties which surrounded me during these two months of May and June.†

Commemoration was very late in 1832, and at that time you could not keep your term if you left before noon on commemora-

---

† Compare Lord Lytton's (Mr Bulwer's) experience of Trinity, Cambridge. 'The first term I spent at Cambridge was melancholy enough. My brothers had given me introductions to men of their own standing, older than myself, but not reading men. Quiet and gentlemanlike they were, but we had no attraction for each other. I found amongst them no companion. I made no companion for myself. Surrounded by so many hundred youths of my own years, I was alone' (*Autobiography*, i. 228). Also Edgar Quinet, already quoted. See above, note on p. 39.

tion day.[3] You might suppose I should be desirous of witnessing the prize recitations and other pageantry of my first commemoration. Not so. My frantic impulse was to get back to Hauxwell at the earliest possible moment, and to pour the story of my adventures and experiences into thirsty ears. The new world I had been exploring had been very captivating, but the charm of the old parsonage, under the beeches, exerted at this moment a stronger attraction. On Wednesday morning, 4th July, having paid every shilling I owed in Oxford, I turned my back on the Sheldonian and took the road for Birmingham. On the Friday, at mid-day, I found my father waiting for me, with our carriage, at 'The Salutation' in Leeming Lane.

It may convey some idea of the spell which the home and the family circle was able to exercise over me, if I give here some extracts from my father's letters to me during my first term. I have all his letters from the first. * * * *

HAUXWELL, 8th May 1832

MY VERY, VERY DEAR BOY – Your account has gladdened our hearts; after many and various perusals I cannot perceive one thing omitted that we should have desired to know. This minute and satisfactory despatch has been submitted to the same process, only with elder agents, that a letter from London once experienced in the hands of your sisters – we have nearly learned it by heart. Most cordially do I congratulate you on the commencement of your academical career, the whole of which, I trust, will be honourable and comfortable to yourself, satisfactory to your friends, and subservient to the glory of God. What assistance a parent can render, with these objects in view, you may freely command. I have been consoled for the loss of your society, and my wonted occupation at this table, solely by the reflection that I have done everything in my power to secure your present enviable position. The little rub about the rooms only enhances the pleasure; for, having succeeded so well in mastering all your other difficulties, as they appeared by this fireside, you may well make your account for that. You will no doubt read this in your own rooms. And though, I dare to say, when you opened it you anticipated something of the admonitory complexion, let me relieve you from that apprehension by the assurance that I consider that duty to have been already discharged in this room. Your way is now open before you. My earnest prayers on your behalf are, that our God will direct and prosper you in it. That you like Oxford already I have not the least doubt – you do not belong to me if you do not; and ere this you have surveyed it well; gentlemen 'what's fresh' generally do. Among your visits 'Parker's' has been foremost.[4] Let your Euripides be of the valuable sort, such as, in future years, may call forth from a future freshman the admiration you have bestowed on Mr Christie's library. You call him a scholar. So he must be in the true sense of that word, for my *Vade mecum* (the Oxford Calendar) enrolls him among the fellows. The library of a Fellow of Oriel should be the best in the universe. Even a commoner of that distinguished society should be surrounded by no mean materials for study; and when your rooms are ready, and you wish for a supply, the Stockton steamer shall be put in requisition. Those that now surround me cannot be more usefully and honourably employed than in enriching and storing a mind, the cultivation of which has been the nearest object of my heart for eighteen years. I have procured Tate's *Horace* for you.... We have no tidings that are new for you; no change of any kind except, like the Vicar of Wakefield's, 'from the blue to the brown.' I have removed my shaving apparatus into your room in order to keep up the remembrance of my friend in Oriel. May Heaven's best blessings rest upon him! Write to us frequently at first, and communicate with me freely in any little difficulties that present themselves in your path.

Always, I trust, your affectionate Governor,

M. J. Pattison

This, my first Long Vacation, was spent wholly at Hauxwell. It was very enjoyable, but, as far as mental improvement was concerned, quite unprofitable. I began to read review articles, which I had never done before. I revived my natural history studies, and turned over many books on ornithology. I read, but with little profit, six books of Tacitus' *Annals*. What was really of most use to me this vacation was the free air of the fields and moors, and the long solitary rambles during whole days, in which Nature insensibly penetrated the recesses of the soul, without my having yet become, as I afterwards became, passionate for the poetry of Wordsworth and of country life. At Hauxwell we saw no one except the Squire's family at the Hall, uneducated and uncongenial; we visited with no one, so that there was for four months no break in the bucolic 'secura quies et nescia fallere vita'.[5] As far as manners or conduct among equals went, I must, at the end of this period, have lapsed again pretty much into the fashion of the ploughboy, out of which, for two months, I had been struggling to emerge.

I had, during this 'Long', my first misunderstanding with my father. This was partly about money matters, partly about my reading. In both instances it was I who was to blame, as I easily saw afterwards. He was liberal to me to the extent of his means; wished me to have all the books I wanted, and in the best editions; encouraged me in an occasional ride, and in subscribing to Hall's Boat-Club. In this respect I had nothing to complain of, and I met his liberality by a prudence and economy, the habit of which I established in this my first term, and from which, in fifty years, I have never deviated. I see, in looking at the old account-book, that my total expenses for the term were £78. This included my first establishment in furniture, crockery, etc., £2:10s. subscription to the boats, and, alas! £2 they extracted from me for some memorial – I know not what – to the Duke of Wellington. This was weakness; but how was a freshman to say no when a B.A., a first class much looked up to in college, brought the paper round, and pointed out the names of all the other men in his list?

After I had been at home some time my father expressed a wish to have my bills put into his hands to look over. I ought to have been not only willing but glad to have the opportunity of showing how honest my little expenditure had been. I had not left a sixpence unpaid in Oxford, and what I had laid out, together with the journeys up and down, balanced exactly his remittances. There was not in the bills a single item of which I need have been ashamed. But I had set my heart upon having a fixed allowance, and withheld the bills in the hope that my father's curiosity to see them would drive him into acquiescence upon this point. This was my first fault. The other fault related to a college essay, which I had brought home and exhibited with pride because it had been selected for reading out in Hall! It was the custom then, in all the colleges, to set, each week, a theme or essay; that which was adjudged the best was read before the assembled college on the following Saturday. My father took a great deal of pains over this essay; corrected and even re-wrote parts of it. Mine was no doubt poor stuff, and his was easily so much better that, instead of being thankful to him for his pains, I showed humour at the pitiful figure my scrubby performance cut by the side of his. Besides this instance of bad taste and bad temper I was restive over the Tacitus readings. My father expected me at a fixed hour every morning to read the *Annals* with him. It was true he could not be of any use to me, as he knew little of the language and nothing at all of the history. But it was the only thing he required of me, and I ought to have complied with a good grace, instead of coming unwillingly and finding excuses for shirking altogether.

I returned to Oxford in October with a large stock of good resolutions, both about my reading and about the company I would keep. I was aware now that I should have to look to myself for guidance, as there was none to be had from my official instructors. My desire of improving myself in all directions was not at all abated. I worked blindly and helplessly at some Latin and Greek books without finding the satisfaction I was struggling for – of gaining ground either with language or with literary purpose. But I launched out in other directions besides classics. I engaged a German master at 5s. an hour out of my pocket-money, and thus first entered on the despairing task of contending with the German declensions. I think I had twelve lessons, or £3 worth, and there my German rested for more than ten years, when I had about as many more from another and very inefficient teacher. That was all the instruction in German I ever had. By persevering reading of books, however, on the subjects on which I was interested from time to time, I came to read the literary style without great difficulty. But colloquial German did not become familiar to me till I went to reside in Berlin in 1858.

I also entered my name as an attendant at the evening lectures of the Professor of Chemistry, Dr Daubeny.[6] These lectures were so elementary, so devoted to popular experiments, which generally miscarried, and so rambling, that I did not learn much from them. I had brought up with me a fair knowledge of the chemistry of that day, and had worked over one of the current manuals – Griffin's – as far as a very humble apparatus of blow-pipe and crucible, in a corner of my mother's store-room, permitted. I had also read in but not mastered, the two thick volumes of Henry's *Chemistry*, in which the subject was presented in a more scientific form.

Lastly, in this term I began first to wake up to the attractions of poetry. I picked up at an auction an imperfect copy of Byron's *Works*, in four volumes. This had the charm of forbidden fruit, for Byron had been in the Hauxwell 'index'; and at a later date, when I introduced a copy of Murray's complete edition, in one volume, I did so as one who smuggles cigars for his 'own consumption'. I was amused when my father hastened to borrow it for his 'private reading'. This was later. In 1832 I learned by heart much of the lighter pieces – *Siege of Corinth, Bride of Abydos*, etc. My mind was still so childish that I could not, at first, rise to *Childe Harold*. I also had Pope much in my hand, and was specially delighted with his pictures of the society of his time, and his epigrams on the '*femmes galantes*'. This may seem a paradox; that a rude clown, who had hardly seen the inside of a drawing-room, and was guilelessly ignorant of women, should be fascinated by the most artificial interiors ever painted. Here broke out the native instinct which has led me, in later years, to spend so much time upon the Pope–Addison–Swift circle.

I returned to Hauxwell to spend the Christmas vacation. This was a repetition of the Long Vacation – with its lazy acquiescence in the home circle – to which all intelligent interests were unknown, only that skating on the New-found England pond† took the place of rambles over the woods and fields.

I can score nothing to my credit for Lent term 1833. I was not exactly idle; to this day I never could be; I was always reading something; but at this time I was certainly not making progress. That I returned to Hauxwell to spend the short Easter vacation,

† New-found England was the name of a farm reclaimed from the moor, which had near it a pond on which he used to skate. – ED.

instead of staying in college as I might have done, shows that the cosy and patriarchal life we led at the Rectory, where I never saw any one but my father and sisters, was more pleasant to me than the society of my equals.

In the summer term of 1833 I moved into better and more expensive rooms; the furniture I found there was valued at £60, which my father paid without a remark. These rooms were on the same staircase as, and directly opposite to, Newman's. I had no idea at the time what the neighbourhood was to bring with it in the future. Newman had not, in May, returned from abroad, and he had asserted his statutable right to shut up his rooms and keep them empty, against the Provost and the tutors, who wanted to quarter an undergraduate in them. So that my neighbour was a vacant room, and I barely knew that one of the fellows, by name Newman, was expected soon to occupy it. In this term I had a visit from our old family friend, David Horndon, now of Pencrebar, Callington, who came and spent a week with me. These visits of friends were then, as they are now, fatal to study. Those who know what the summer term is to an undergraduate in Oxford, know that to study to any purpose during it requires one of three things – trained habit, determined will, or absorbing interest in the study itself, of none of which I was possessed at this time. I cannot trace any advance or acquisition to the summer of 1833, though I remember that I luxuriated in the spaciousness and comfort of my new rooms. I completed, however, the first stage of the University curriculum, by passing 'Responsions' at the end of June, the earliest date at which I could then go up for them.[7] I was examined in two plays of Sophocles, Juvenal, Euclid I and II, and Latin writing. The examination was one I could as well have passed the first day I set foot in Oxford. The college had thus spent a year and two months upon me in preparing me to do what I was ready to do before I entered it. Yet, in the face of a system like this, Dr Burgon can assert that 'so long as the trustees of property are faithfully discharging the provisions of a beneficial trust, the State has no right whatever, legal or moral, to interfere' (*Quart. Rev.*, Oct. 1883).

Having thus got rid of Responsions I felt that I had turned a corner, and that I must seriously think of my degree examination. Here again, for want of guidance, I was wholly at sea. The

University prescribed eight books, and you might, by favour of an examiner, get hold of some old papers – those of 1832 were printed, but none had been published since – but no other help was to be had in Oriel. What I had no power of conceiving was, how the books were to be studied so as to acquire the power of answering the questions upon them. As soon as I found myself settled at Hauxwell, with a box of books, I laid out for myself a plan of reading. I have this scheme before me now, for in July 1833 I began a student's diary on the same plan as I have kept up, with intervals, to the present date (December 1883). This diary only exceptionally mentions what I do, or see, or hear, it deals with what I read or write. It is strictly the student's journal, being, in this respect, the counterpart of Casaubon's *Ephemerides*, of which I had not then heard.[8]

My plan of study, allowing for a tone of pedantry which cannot be avoided when such things are written down, is not in itself a bad one. But looking at it as the road to Oxford honours, it has the fatal defect of requiring too much time. It is a scheme of self-education, rather than of the hand-to-mouth requirements of an examination. My scheme required years for its realisation; I may say that I have been all my life occupied in carrying out and developing the ideal that I conceived in July 1833, more than fifty years ago. I may place, in this Long Vacation of 1833, the first stirrings of anything like intellectual life within me. Hitherto I had had no mind, properly so called, merely a boy's intelligence, receptive of anything I read or heard. I now awoke to the new idea of finding the reason of things; I began to suspect I might have much to unlearn as well as to learn, and that I must clear my mind of much current opinion which had lodged there. Not that I saw this with the clearness, or thought of carrying it out with the thoroughness, of a Descartes; but the principle of rationalism was born in me, and once born it was sure to grow, and to become the master-idea of the whole process of self-education, on which I was from this time forward embarked.

* * * had preceded me to Hauxwell and spent the summer with us.[9] As he was so completely one of the family, and confined within the same narrow circle of ideas as the rest of us, his presence made no difference in our way of life. In one respect he caused me serious inconvenience. I used to retire every morning

to my own little bedroom, where I had established my books, and which was the only corner of the house I could use as a study. Solitude was necessary to me; I had not – I have never had – the power of commanding my attention properly in the presence of another human being, and at this date the power of the will over the attention was remarkably feeble. * * * , sociable even in his reading hours, would come in occasionally with his book, and at last established himself there to keep me company. Good-natured creature as he was, and some years older than me, I did not know how to tell him that he put me out. Being then totally destitute of tact, I tried to effect my end by being morose and disagreeable. I succeeded at last, and he retired to his own room, which, as the stranger's bedroom, was a much better one than mine. I had gained my point, but, as so often since, with the uncomfortable consciousness of having done so in a wrong way. I mention this trifling incident because it is typical of my way of doing things all my life.

A walking tour round the Lakes, in company with * * *, this summer, was of great use to me in several ways. It enlarged my knowledge of the country, which had hitherto been confined pretty well within the radius of the two packs of hounds by which our district was hunted. This circle I had traversed in every direction, and knew minutely, but of all beyond I was girlishly ignorant. The tour also first awoke in me a passion for scenery and landscape. It was impossible to have lived in Wensleydale without some sense of this, but so far it had been a latent sentiment. Once awoke, this sensitiveness to the aspects of Nature became soon a powerful element of the poetic enthusiasm by which I was by and by to be possessed. On this occasion, too, were sown the seeds of that passion for rambling and exploring which has since carried me over so many hundred miles on foot, and to which I owe some of the happiest times of early manhood.

The total of reading performed in these three months makes a poor show, as it is summed up in the Diary. The blame of this lay not in the Lake excursion – which was almost the only absence from work that I allowed myself, and only took a fortnight – but in the slowness of my method of working. Neither then nor at any time since have I been able to read in an hour the same number of pages that other men can. But at the time my power of attention was almost none. I fretted much over this defect, as it seemed serious enough to incapacitate me from study. The greater the effort I made to attend, the more my brain seemed to recoil from what I was offering it. Also the new principle I was enforcing on myself – that of never allowing myself to be the passive recipient of any one's thoughts or opinions, but to think out for myself every statement, and to stop upon it until I had found if it ranged with what I had already accepted, necessarily cost me much time.

The Diary in July had opened with the following entry: –

The principal objects which I propose to myself to effect during this vacation are: 1. To read over a few of my heavier books, such as Livy, Herodotus, Pindar, for the final examination. 2. To prepare myself by reading history, and by practising composition, for standing for a scholarship at Balliol in November. 3. To write a Latin dialogue between Cicero, Pompey, and Cato, 'de statu reipublicæ' for a prize of books proposed by the college. 4. To improve and enlarge my mind by every means.

I had discovered one of the many things about Oxford which was hidden from my father, in spite of the close attention he gave to the subject, viz. That if you wanted to get honours you must first get a scholar's gown, and preferably at Balliol. In 1808, it seems, the position of a scholar had been quite different from what it had become in 1833. In my father's time the 'scholars' were not regarded as gentlemen. They did not associate with the commoners, but lived among themselves, or with the bible-clerks. They were nicknamed 'charity boys'. In twenty-five years this had quite changed. The scholar's gown, from being the badge of an inferior order, had become a coveted distinction. It became my ambition to get a scholarship anywhere, where I should have a chance of some help from the tutors. Unfortunately I was getting over age. In October this year I was twenty, which alone excluded me at Balliol. But, had this not been the case, I had as much chance of getting a Balliol scholarship against the public school-men as of a commission in the household brigade. I could only stand at by-places. I went in for the 'Lusby' at Magdalen Hall, then a new foundation, with the tempting prize of £50.† But I withdrew before the examination was closed, in deference to my father's prejudices, who could not understand my migrating from Oriël to a Hall even for £50 a year. The scholarship was obtained by J. E. Giles, against whom I should not have had any chance.[10] On two subsequent occasions I was a candidate at Worcester, where there were scholarships limited to the sons of clergymen. I suppose I did very badly, producing little in three hours; on the second occasion the scholarships were carried off by a nimble Irishman, J. D. Collis,[11] who afterwards became headmaster of Bromsgrove School, and by a schoolboy of the name of Landon, not in any way distinguished.[12] These attempts and failures were at a later date. I return to the Long Vacation of 1833, which the Diary thus speaks of in retrospect: –

That time, which in prospect appeared infinite, is now past, "Thrown down the gulf of time; as far from thee As it had ne'er been thine" (Young's *Night Thoughts*, p. 91, ed. 1853), and how miserably ill have I used it; yet it was better employed than any time before. I might have done three times as much with ease. Such uninterrupted quiet, and regular habits as we had at home, are advantages which I have not got here (in Oxford). And when I look forward and see how fast I am getting on towards my examination, and how little I have done to prepare for it, I cannot help despairing of myself.

I had read the first decade of Livy, Horace's *Satires*, two books of Herodotus, Pindar's *Olympics*, and two plays of Aristophanes. My chief effort had been directed upon Cicero, whom I had worked backwards and forwards solely for style, learning passages by heart, translating and re-translating, primarily with a view to composing a dialogue for a prize of books offered by the college, but also with a view to the general improvement of my Latin style, a point held of much more importance in those days than it now is. I took great pains with this dialogue, writing and

† The MS. gives £100, but this appears to be an error of the writer's memory. The Lusby scholarships, three in number, were and are of the value of £50 each, and tenable for three years. – ED.

73

re-writing it, and thus laid the foundation of a Latin style, which in time attained no little ease and elegance. This accomplishment is certainly in itself of little use, but it adds greatly to the charm of reading classical Latin, which has ever been one of my greatest delights to be got from books.

Being now in the Michaelmas term of 1833 I felt that it was urgent that I should take up seriously the philosophical part of the work for the schools. I was now twenty, and I cannot carry back the dawn of intellect in me beyond this Long Vacation. I do not think my curiosity to know what philosophy was about was sufficiently strong to have carried me through much hard reading at that time; the urgency of the examination was here of great use in setting me and keeping me at work. I began at the beginning, and read Hinds' *Logic*, Whately's *Logic*, Reid's *Enquiry into the Human Mind on the Principles of Common Sense*. But the book which was of most use to me on these subjects was Stewart's *Elements*. I found an odd volume of this in my father's study at Hauxwell. It attracted me; I read and re-read it with increasing satisfaction. To Dugald Stewart, an author now obsolete, I owe the first infusion of a taste for philosophical inquiry.[13] He also grounded me in the principle of strictly applying the Baconian induction in psychology, a principle which has saved me from being led away by the gratuitous hypotheses and *a priori* constructions of Kant and the other German schools.

Another book read this term seized upon my interest in an exceptional way, this was Gibbon's *Autobiography*.[14] The minute history of a self-education, conducted on so superb a scale, was just what I wanted. I had long before got hold of a few extracts from this, which had found their way into Lord Sheffield's Memoir of the author, prefixed to an edition of the *Decline and Fall* which we had at home. Those extracts had fixed themselves in my memory. I now procured the whole work and devoured it, reading it again and again till I could repeat whole paragraphs. Gibbon, in fact, supplied the place of a college tutor; he not only found me advice, but secretly inspired me with the enthusiasm to follow it.

The Diary of studies is continued through this term, and so little now did college lectures count for, in the scheme of my day, that the Diary makes no mention of them. I think it was in this term I was first put into Aristotle's *Rhetoric*; but such a lecture! – the tutor incapable of explaining any difficulty, and barely able to translate the Greek, even with the aid of a crib. As the previous Michaelmas had been my first introduction to Pope, so this Michaelmas I find myself dwelling upon Milton's *Comus* and minor poems with evident gusto. Many years before, my father had read aloud – he read magnificently – the whole of *Paradise Lost*, book by book, in the winter evenings. It failed in affecting me, so that I must infer, as I have already noted, that at fifteen I was less advanced than Miss Martineau at seven, at which age she accidentally got hold of *Paradise Lost*, and 'my mental destiny was fixed for the next seven years' (Mart. *Autob*., i. 42). I must not omit to mention that the prize for the Ciceronian dialogue was awarded to me. So my college had for once been of use to me in stimulating me to take pains about Latin composition, and this at a very cheap rate, as the prize was only £5 in books. They were, however, ashamed themselves of the meanness of the prize, and allowed me to get books at Parker's in excess of that value. What I thought myself of my performance the Diary thus records: – 'Its faults are a vapid declamatory style, without solidity or originality in the matter; it might have been compressed into much less room without loss to the argument. There is not enough of the history of the times introduced; it is confined to general observations.'

The Christmas vacation 1833–34, spent again at Hauxwell, is noted in the Diary as very unsatisfactory, passed either in hunting or in idleness. However, I made an elaborate analysis of Whately's *Rhetoric*, another obsolete book, which was of real assistance to me. I was conscious of great difficulty in composing in English, and I laboured hard to surmount it. James Mill's article 'Education', in the *Encyclopædia Britannica*, fell in my way during this vacation, and was read by me with profound interest. I may mention also Lardner's 'Hydrostatics', a science which exercised, I know not why, a specific attraction over me at all times. I was also incessantly reading Cicero's *Orations* to keep up my Latin style. There were other things, but I mention only those books which I consider to have been factors in my education.

The next Lent term is briefly entered in the Diary as being the idlest term I had yet spent in Oxford. I was unable, amid all the social distractions to which a youth lodged in college rooms is liable, to keep myself steady to work. Perhaps I was weaker than others, but the chief cause was that my mind was not really engaged in what I was trying to learn. Norris† says, 'However strong and universal is the desire of knowledge, men are generally more in love with the fame and reputation of it than with the thing itself.' I had strongly the desire of knowledge, but not at all the desire of that particular knowledge which the examination test prescribes. I read much, but did not concentrate myself upon the legal curriculum, flitting about among any books that took my fancy, e.g. I was captivated by the Greek of Lysias and Taylor's masterly notes upon him, reading many of his speeches, and some of those of Demosthenes – things which didn't pay for the examination, as they were not among the books which I was to take up. I was this term put into a lecture with Denison on Aristotle's *Politics*. As the first step in reading the *Politics* is to be able to translate the Greek, and Denison could do this tolerably, this was the first college lecture I had been in which was of some slight use to me.

The Easter vacation of 1834 I remained in college, only going down to Cheltenham for a week's visit to my uncle Seward. Outside the coach were Philpotts and Crawley;[15] we sat next each other, but, not being in the same set, never spoke a word to each other the whole way. Philpotts had a lighted cigar in his mouth when he got upon the coach, and kept one there till we got off it at the 'Plough' – about five hours – lighting a fresh one from the stump of the one he had finished.

The summer term of 1834 was frittered away over an increasing variety of objects. We set up a book-club among ourselves, and I felt so painfully my want of general information that I gave much time to new books – Bulwer's *England and the English*, Inglis' *Spain*, Silvio Pellico, and others. All this only aggravated the infirmity of mental dissipation against which I was desirous of contending. In this term I also read for the first time Butler's *Analogy*. This book had been recently placed upon the list of books to be taken up for the examination, on the suggestion of Dr Hampden, it was said. This was then considered a great improve-

---

† Norris (John), *Reflections upon the Conduct of Human Life*, etc., p. 9, 2d ed. London, 1691. – ED.

ment, as breaking in upon the monopoly possessed by Aristotle. I worked at this book closely and minutely, but had not yet intellect enough to apprehend its general bearing, or to appreciate the solid structure of logical argument in which it surpasses any other book that I know in the English language. But it is not a book adapted for an educational instrument, as it diverts the mind from the great outlines of scientific and philosophical thought, and fastens it upon petty considerations, being, in this respect, the converse of Bacon's *Novum Organum*. Twenty years later a liberal board of examiners, myself among them, succeeded in removing Butler from the list of books to be taken up. To the time I myself devoted to the book in 1834 I may trace the interest I afterwards took in eighteenth century speculation, witness my contribution to *Essays and Reviews*[16] and my edition of Pope's *Essay on Man*.

CHAPTER 4

THE 23D JUNE I went down to Hauxwell again for the Long Vacation. Much the same account may be given of this vacation as of that of 1833. There was more industry, more work done, but as mistakenly laid out. I gave much time to mental philosophy, read Dugald Stewart and Lant Carpenter over again. Of my classical texts only small portions of Herodotus, Thucydides, and Livy, some Pindar and the Georgics. I wasted time over outlying classics, which did not form part of the degree list. I read with perseverance and regularity – going up to my room for certain portions of each day – but slowly and languidly; my mind did not seem to be awake. It was becoming clearer to me that I could not hope to get my necessary books ready within the time, at the pace I was then getting over the ground. Especially damaging to my prospects was the neglect of Aristotle and of logic. I find no mention in the Diary of the *Ethics*, which, being at that time the principal stock in trade of the examiners, I ought to have had in hand every day. I knew the rational logic of Whately and Hinds, but I had never touched the catch questions in figure logic, familiarity with which was then indispensable. As far as general improvement went the Diary becoming richer and fuller is evidence that this vacation had been more profitable than either of the two former, and this notwithstanding some serious interruptions and calls upon my time. * * * *

Oxford, 19th October. The conclusion of a Long Vacation * * * is, and must always be with me, a very melancholy time. The reflection upon the leisure, tranquillity, and comfort, which I have enjoyed for at least three months out of the four of which the vacation has consisted, and the circumstances that these are advantages I may never have again, lead me sorrowfully to consider how they have been used. It is nothing to say that I have not profited by them in their utmost extent; but how much better

78

might I not easily have used them! I do not wish to conceal from myself any improvement I may have made; I think I may say I feel it more sensibly than after any former period of equal length, but I might, with the same trouble have made much more.

I have no record of the Michaelmas term 1834. * * * I went down to York in the Christmas vacation, and it was settled that I should spend my vacation in York.[1] * * * I can find no diary for either Lent or Easter term 1835. Nor can I remember in what term I first put on a coach. The other reading men in college, whom I have named, did so, and it was necessary at that time for any one who aspired to high honours. In this step I made two mistakes. First, I took a coach, because I had no other help, and because my father urged it, but before I was ready for one. Before you went to a coach you ought to have gone over thoroughly the elementary ground in philosophy – especially to have mastered the text of the *Ethics* – and rhetoric. I acted here in the stupidity of ignorance, as I mostly did, and when I came to my coach found that I could not translate the *Ethics*. A coach is a finisher and not an elementary teacher; I ought to have been ready to take him my difficulties, well prepared for his solutions.

The other error I committed was in the choice of my coach. I went to C. P. Eden, as Fellow of my own college, and of high reputation for ability and for knowledge of his books.[2] What I really wanted was one of those routine professionals, who just supply your memory with the received solutions of the patent difficulties of philosophy, as current in the schools at the time, and who would rapidly catechise you backwards and forwards in the facts you professed to know. Such were, at that time, Richard Michell,[3] Hayward Cox,[4] and Henry Wall.[5] Instead of that, I found in Eden a man who wanted to reconstruct my education fundamentally, from the bottom upwards; who was always ready to discuss with me any theological or philosophical problem and sought to convert me to his own speculative views. These were not very profound in him, but they were really handled, and interested me much. We had heavy controversies over Butler's doctrine of conscience, which my Dugald Stewart training would by no means allow me to accept. Thus we beat about the bush hour after hour; I went to him six days in the week for a fee of £17:

10s., nearly as much as the college tuition fee, £21, which I was also paying and getting nothing in return. All this might have been very profitable towards my general education; perhaps was so. But as the terms went on, I stuck to Eden for, I think, three terms, it was a frightful waste of time, when I expected to be going up for examination in November 1835. I think, too, anything Eden might have contributed to my general building up was counterbalanced by his method, which confirmed me in my slow and dawdling mental habits. I refused to make a single step upon trust; I must think every point out for myself, and required an alarming amount of time in order to do this. The habit that it would have been of most use to me to form at this time, is that exquisitely described by Rousseau in the following passage: –

> Je m'aperçus bientôt que tous ces auteurs etaient entre eux en contradiction presque perpétuelle, et je formai le chimérique projet de les accorder, qui me fatigua beaucoup, et me fit perdre bien du temps. Je me brouillais la tête, et je n'avançais point. Enfin, renonçant encore à cette méthode, j'en pris une infinement meilleure, et à laquelle j'attribue tout le progrès que je puis avoir fait, malgré mon défaut de capacité: car il est certain, que j'en eus toujours fort peu pour l'étude. En lisant chaque auteur, je me fis une loi d'adopter et suivre toutes ses idées sans y mêler les miennes, ni celles d'un autre, et sans jamais disputer avec lui. Je me dis: Commençons par me faire un magasin d'idées, vraies ou fausses mais nettes, en attendant que ma tête en soit assez fournie pour pouvoir les comparer et choisir.... Au bout de quelques années passées à ne penser exactement que d'après autrui, ... je me suis trouvé un assez grands fonds d'acquis pour me suffire à moi même
>
> (*Confessions*, liv. vi. p. 350).[6]

In the summer term I changed from Eden to Hyman of Wadham – from a science coach to a scholarship coach;[7] this was partly with a view to my standing at Worcester. Hyman did me real good, though I only went to him alternate days – £10 worth – reading Aristophanes with me, correcting Latin prose and verse, but above all, offering me in his talk a type of high scholarship which I had never been in contact with before. It was Hyman who gave me a taste for the works and commentaries of the generation of scholars from Bentley down to Porson, which I have retained to the present day.

I may now turn back a little, as this was my last term in college rooms, to say something of the associates with whom I had come to live. The acquaintances I made in my freshman's term – acquaintances due to accident, not choice – early disappeared from the scene. I never can forget my first wine-party. A freshman was not expected to give parties; he was entertained. But when I returned to college after the Long of 1832 I had to make a beginning. I was well supplied by my father with £20 worth of Smurthwaite's port and sherry – other wines were not in fashion – and I am sure that my port and sherry were as good as any in the college, though I should not have known it if they had not been. I had not been brought up upon wine; and my father had great difficulty in coaxing me downstairs to help him and a neighbour with a bottle of port. However, it belonged to the dignity of a commoner of Oriel to invite his friends to drink wine with him. I accordingly asked some of those who had asked me in the summer. I made as good a selection as I could, with a view to the suitability of the guests to each other. A handsome dessert was ordered from Sadler's; the port and sherry decanted. The guests were formally received by me in a cold sweat, so nervous that the few ideas I had fled, and left my brain a blank. I was at all times deficient in that mental activity and quickness of social sympathy to which James Burn, the beggar-boy, in his curious *Autobiography*,[8] ascribes his success in life, in spite of grave defects in regard of the solid parts of character. Oh, the icy coldness, the dreary Egyptian blankness of that 'wine'; the guests slipped away one by one under pretext of engagements, and I was left alone with an almost untouched dessert, to be carried off as perquisite by the college scout. It was long before I summoned courage to give a repetition of the entertainment. I thought I was ostracised, black-balled, expelled from society; I reflected hopelessly on the causes of the breakdown, ascribing it to every cause except the simple one – clownishness and want of the *usage du monde*.

As my first set of acquaintances faded away they had to be replaced by new ones, I did not want, in course of time, for number; one made this way, another that. Standing had probably more to do with making friends than choice. But in 1835 I certainly knew all the men best worth knowing in college. It would be useless to enumerate a string of names unknown to fame. The list would have comprised the names of all who were reading for honours – I think four, besides myself, out of more than sixty. This fact alone speaks volumes as to the state of Oriel. Of the four men reading for honours we looked up to Edward Woollcombe as *facile princeps*.[9] But, as fellow and tutor of Balliol afterwards, he turned out a total failure, giving another disproof of undergraduate estimate. J. S. Utterton[10] obtained a first class, and became afterwards suffragan bishop of Guildford; a wholly prosaic and practical mind, fettered by a narrow type of evangelicalism. Hatsell, though weak in character, had more good stuff in him.[11] He obtained a second class, and immediately after died by his own hand. Among these, my most intimate friends were William Lonsdale,[12] since a chancery-barrister, and James Mozley, afterwards Regius Professor of Divinity.[13] Several out-college men mixed with us on intimate terms, such as Arthur Kensington, who had gone from Oriel to a scholarship at Trinity.[14] All these were men above the average in ability. Woollcombe, Utterton, Kensington, obtained the highest honours, yet our interests were incredibly narrow; we knew nothing of what was going on in the world of science, literature, and art. Arthur Kensington who gained two first classes, a Latin poem, and the Eldon scholarship, seemed to have retained the mind of a boy of fifteen. Lonsdale, I think, was the best informed of us all, spending his time in the Union reading reviews, but he got the best mathematical first of his year. I remember his rushing to my room in the dusk of a December afternoon, when the mathematical class list had just been put out, and throwing his cap on the table, with the words, 'myself and Highton'† – there were only two in the first class that time. I remember the thrill of pleasure I felt – pure pleasure, derived wholly from a friend's success. How fleeting are college friendships! I think in forty-five years I have

† This is an error, for in Michaelmas term 1837 there were only two mathematical firsts; these were 'Childe, George F., Ch. Ch.,' and 'Lonsdale, William, Oriel.' 'Highton, Henry, Queen's' appears in the second class. – ED.

82

seen Lonsdale three times since he left Oxford, yet he has been in London all that time.

Yet with all these, and with many more I cannot now specify, I felt something wanting. I had not yet met with a single man who realised the idea I had formed of a university student. My secret aspirations went for an intellectual sympathy, for a cultivated literary circle, and I could not find my way to either. I wanted a set into the bosom of which I could pour my crude notions about poetry, about morals, about all that was working in one's own inner consciousness, and I had found not only no set, but not even a responsive individual. Were there no sets in all Oxford at that day such as Leonard Montefiore[15] relates his falling into at his very first luncheon party?

> I think of the first luncheon party to which I was asked in Oxford. H. who gave it was himself a freshman, and all of us who were there were freshmen. He had ingenuously told every one much of the rest, and every one was determined to talk his best. And talk we did, with terrible earnestness. How had the ancients described landscape? were Shakespeare's sonnets personal or imaginary? what should children be taught earliest? should women be allowed to vote? and twenty other subjects, till my head ached, and lo! we had sat from one till five talking always
>
> (*Remains of L. A. M.*, p. 308).

I remember one coach drive from Sheffield to Birmingham; I was outside in the front seat, where there were two men, one a Queen's undergraduate, the other a Birmingham (I think) solicitor. They conversed the whole way over the things which I was yearning to learn and to know; things which are now common property, through the *Athenæum*, the *Academy*, and a hundred channels, but which then could only be picked up in a well-informed London circle. I tried once or twice to put in my oar, but it was a failure; I was too far below their level of knowledge; I relapsed into enchanted listening. I thought to myself, 'there exists then such a world, but I am shut out of it, not by the accidents of college but by my own unfitness to enter.'

CHAPTER 5

THE DIARY of studies recommences in July 1835, and from that date to April 1836 I know what I was reading every day. As I began the Long in the belief that I was going in for my degree in November, I can only look with amazement at the fatuity of my arrangements and the snail-like progress with which I seemed to be satisfied. In those days we were expected to know something of the contents of the Old Testament, and I spent an hour every day in reading through the Prophets, great and small, with the notes in Mant's Bible.[1] Of course a cheap manual of divinity would have given me all I wanted in a nutshell, but I was incapable of getting up from manuals – I could not remember them. Then, instead of vigorously attacking the *Rhetoric*, *Ethics*, and *Politics*, and taking up into the memory of a general *résumé* of what I knew already of these books, I dribbled away at bits of them, trying to reconcile them with my Scotch philosophy, and so advancing at the rate of some half-dozen pages of Aristotle per day. It was soon evident that at this pace I could never get through the three science books, and I threw the *Rhetoric* overboard. This was the first, and in those days very serious, damage to the value of the ship's cargo. The *Politics* are, in themselves, of as great or greater weight than the *Rhetoric*; but in those days the examiners knew the *Rhetoric* and did not know the *Politics*. Consequently the questions set on the *Politics* were less well-chosen, and less weight attached to your answer. I again frittered away time over outlying books – Lysias, Cicero *de Legibus*, Terence, and other feather-weights, which counted for nothing in the schools, but with which I had the whim to load my list.

Then there was the early history of Rome. I was taking up two decades of Livy, and set to work to read over the text of both. This, within a few months of the examination, was, Eden said, like trying to gallop over a ploughed field in a wet season. Then the text of Livy alone did not quite fit one out for answering their questions on the early history of Rome. One was expected at that time to know something of Niebuhr's views;[2] I set out to discover these for myself, not in an epitome, as I ought to have done – there were such things – but by reading for myself the two volumes of Thirlwall's translation. A ploughed field was nothing to this. It was a quagmire, a Serbonic gulf, in which I was swallowed up.

When I got into Thucydides for the final review, I find that I did not progress at a quicker rate than some twenty or thirty chapters a day. There must have been idleness to boot, but it is difficult to draw the line between idleness and dawdling over work. I dawdled from a mixture of mental infirmity, bad habit, and the necessity of thoroughness if I was to understand and not merely remember. Whereas the whole of this vacation ought to have been devoted to rapid surveys of what I already knew, here I was, trying to acquire new knowledge in as leisurely a way as I had done when I was three years off my degree.

By September 1835 it became too evident that I could not, with any hope, go in for honours in November. I was under no compulsion to do so; November was the earliest time at which I could offer myself, and few went in as early as they could. I easily got leave from college to postpone till Easter 1836; my father agreeing on condition that I remained over the Michaelmas term at Hauxwell, where I could live free of expense.

I don't think I did much good towards my degree in the Michaelmas term and the Christmas vacation which followed it. I repeated and perpetuated all the faults of the summer; re-read Sophocles, but at the lazy rate of 150 lines a day, instead of going over the difficult places only, which might have been done in a week. I had a handsome black mare on which I rode out most days, and occasionally went hunting. The unbroken leisure and solitude, and the healthy life, formed together the period most favourable to study that I have ever enjoyed. Yet I don't seem to have made anything of it. At the end of the Diary the list of books read amounts to five Greek plays and some fifty-six books, but many of these are very slight things. Among the books of recreation I see Johnson's *Lives of the Poets*. This I took in slowly, page by page, as if by an instinct that here was a congenial subject to which, when free, I would return, and where I would set up my habitation.

I returned to Oxford in February 1836. I had still four months before the ordeal, which now began to press seriously. I do not know if these four months would have sufficed to retrieve the lost ground, even if I had had conduct enough to lay them out judiciously – if, e.g., I had gone at once to Wall and told him that he must get me a first class in June. But I did not lay them out judiciously; I went on on the old plan, pottering over Aristotle in the light of my own ideas, and sauntering through Sophocles at the same snail's pace. I am sure it was not indifference as to what class I got; there were urgent motives enough – such as vanity, and the desire to please my father – but none was so urgent as my desire to settle in Oxford, and my sense that without a first my chances of a fellowship were small. Though I had studied the examination papers I had still but a vague idea how far the stock I was taking into the schools would meet their requirements. When it came within a fortnight of the day I was seized with a panic, lost all idea of a first, and began to fear I should not save my second. I rushed off to Wall and besought him to cram me for the fortnight; he was quite full, and told me it was wasting money; when I persisted he agreed, if I would come to him at eight o'clock in the morning, to give me twelve doses of cram. The first thing he did was to examine me over the *Ethics*, and to shake his head at the result; the next, to give me six questions of moral philosophy to answer on paper. After looking at the answers he said, 'Yours is simply a case of neglect; had you come to me six months ago you might have made your first certain; could you not put off to November?' I could easily have done so; but just about this time I received a disagreeable epistle from my father, which seemed to impute it to me as a serious fault that I had not taken my degree at the earliest time I could. I rushed into the schools and just saved my second – only just, I believe, for on the logic day, which, I think, was the first day, my head refused to work, and I must have sent in an almost blank paper. I supposed I was saved by my translations and Latin composition. When the class list came out I was thankful that matters were no worse, though I saw I must give up my darling dream of getting a fellowship and living a life of study in a college. The same reckless despair drove me to engage myself to a Long Vacation tutorship – the first that offered – of which the conditions were very inferior, but which I thought good enough for me, now that I was disgraced by a second.

I was to go down to my friends for a fortnight, before entering on Mr Snow's tutorship, in Dorsetshire. Passing through London on my way I saw advertised, 'Steam to Hull for 5s.,' and immediately went on board; 5s. were as much as a wretched second class ought to pay for his fare to Yorkshire. There were more than one hundred people on board a crazy Humber boat; berths were out of the question, or even room to lie; you had to sit upon deck. Off the coast of Lincolnshire there came on a terrific storm; every creature sick * * * what could a steward and his boy do among over a hundred passengers? One poor girl went off her head in the midst of all. They got a mattress on deck, and the men took it in turns to hold her down. Her yells and screams audible between the claps of thunder, the scene illuminated by the forked lightning, which we seemed to be entering, made the situation a more frightful one than I can ever remember to have been in. When I got to Hauxwell I was entirely disordered by the strain against sickness, following upon the hard work of the past two months. My father took the generous line of consoling me for my class, with which, he said, he was quite content; tried to persuade me it was not so bad after all, and that it did not make my attaining a fellowship impossible. He pointed out that Oriel, in particular, was noted for correcting the inequalities of the class list, and enumerated the second and third classes who were or had been Fellows there. He gradually soothed my irritation, persuaded me to repudiate the engagement with Snow, and to spend the summer at Hauxwell in reading for a fellowship. In April 1838, a long way off, there were to be two vacancies at Oriel, but there might be chances in other colleges earlier. I was nothing loth; repudiated Snow on the score of ill-health. Hauxwell was very dear to me then with its freedoms and its solitude; the retirement was especially welcome after the rush and anxiety of the summer term. I was also very fond of my sisters, and one of them – the second, Eleanor, – now Mrs Mann – gave promise of soon being able to share my thoughts or studies.[3]

I had always intended, had I got a first, to become a candidate at Oriel; I had flattered myself that, from the turn of my mind towards moral speculation, my chances would be better in the fellowship than they would be in the schools. Oriel did not exact verse composition, or ask questions of philology, in both which I was weak; they employed only the two simple tests of scholarship – translation into Latin and translation from Latin and Greek. Their style of philosophical question and essay was a peculiar one, and I had made a special study of it already. Instead of the eclectic, incoherent ten questions, ranging over the surface of philosophy, and papers by which knowledge rather than original power is tested, their paper had a uniform colour, as if the work of a single examiner. It proposed the simple but everlasting problems of morals and logic in such a way that a candidate, who had thought more than he had read, was inevitably impelled to pour out his very self upon it. Nothing could have been more in harmony with my habits of thought than the Oriel question paper, nor any line of study more congenial to me than that peculiar form of moral and logical science which was encouraged by the college. So I sat down deliberately at Hauxwell to read for a fellowship, and in particular for the Oriel. Not that much reading was demanded; a very few books, well-selected and meditated upon, were, I knew, the best preparation. There was a story current that H. H. Vaughan,[4] elected in 1835 (a very good election), had read nothing all the Long before he stood except Bacon's *Advancement of Learning*, while Shepheard,[5] elected in 1836 (a very bad election), told me that he had been greatly indebted to the writings of Isaac Taylor. These books I looked at with some curiosity, but I relied much more upon the method which I had invented for myself.

At the end of the Long I went back to Oxford to take my B.A.; as the pursuit of fellowships was but a precarious one it was necessary to choose a profession. My father rather seemed to want me to go to the bar, for which I had myself a great aversion; I acquiesced, however, on the understanding that I was to remain for a year in Oxford and try to get on the foundation of some college. In December there were two fellowships at University; one of them confined to Yorkshire. But it was quite understood that W. F. Donkin[6] was to have one of them; it would have been a scandal if he had not, for no one more fitted by science and accomplishments to be a fellow of a college existed at that time in the University. So there was really only one fellowship to be competed for. For this I went in; F. W. Faber, one of those who followed Newman to Rome and became a Father of the Oratory, was elected.[7] I don't suppose that my performances in the examination influenced the election in any way. Faber belonged to the college, in which he was a great favourite, was a dashing talker, though like myself only a second class. There could have been no reason why they should have passed over their own man in order to take me. In April 1837 I had a fall occasioning a severe sprain, which confined me to the sofa for many weeks, and had well-nigh cost me my leg, from the mismanagement of an ignorant apothecary. Fortunately my health remained good, and I got through a considerable amount of reading, especially on the history of the Oriental nations. I began Gibbon, but only got to the end of the first volume. As soon as fit to travel by coach I went down to Hauxwell, where I laid out for myself one of those ambitious schemes of reading which many people have formed, and hardly any one, except Gibbon, carried out. I now first found out Dugald Stewart's *Preliminary Dissertation*, and was enchanted with it, read, re-read, and abstracted it. The Diary has now put on a new tone. Instead of the old complaints of inattention, mental sluggishness, and sauntering over books without reading them, I am now thoroughly interested in what I am doing. I conceived this summer's study to have been one of the most useful periods of my youth. In November 1837 I returned to Oxford. I no longer occupied the elegant and comfortable apartment in the old house opposite Merton College in which Blanco White had lived, but very tiny rooms at the back of Oriel at fourteen shillings a week. This, I thought, was enough for a man to pay who had only got a second; besides that I wished to save my father, who was maintaining me in Oxford while I was 'doing nothing', as they say.

This winter I worked pretty hard. I wrote for the Latin essay, which was got by William Dickinson, scholar of Trinity, but my chief efforts were directed towards preparation for the supreme ordeal of the Oriel Fellowship which came on in April 1838. The conduct of their examination was unusual. Instead of two papers a day, three hours morning, and three afternoon, you went in at ten, and you might stay till dusk, but no lights were allowed. Lunch was supplied at one o'clock, and when the second paper was brought you, the first was not taken away, so that you might have seven hours to elaborate your English essay in. This was much in favour of my slow and hesitating method of writing. The examination was very simple. English essay; Latin essay; Latin composition; philosophical questions; translation from Greek and Latin. What minimised my chances was that there were two Oriel men in besides myself, both of them first-class men; and I thought it hardly possible but that one of the two would be taken. But it was not so. The successful candidates were Church of Wadham, now Dean of St Paul's, and James Cowles Prichard of Trinity, son of Dr Prichard of Bristol.[8] I presume that Church was Newman's candidate, though so accomplished a scholar as the Dean need not have required any party push. I have always looked upon Church as the type of the Oriel fellow; Richard Michell said, at the time of the election: 'There was such a moral beauty about Church, that they could not help taking him.'

I conjecture that the anti-Newman party had endeavoured to elect one of the two Oriel first classes, most probably Woollcombe, and that Newman reasonably enough resisting Woollcombe, parties had compromised upon Prichard, a very clever scholar of the superficial sort. I cannot say that I was disappointed myself, as the odds had lain so heavy against me. Yet I felt sure, from what I knew of some of the others, that my philosophical work was of a style and weight which must have produced an impression. But I was scarcely prepared to receive the message which Newman sent me on the day of the election that there were some who thought 'that I had done the best'.

It will appear strange that I could have satisfied Newman on the questions of morals and logic when I have spoken of myself as having been reared on the strict lines of the inductive philosophy, and being a disciple of Bacon, Locke, and Dugald Stewart. But before this, I had either been seduced from my principles, or from want of clear-headedness, had endeavoured to accommodate them to ideas with which they really could not amalgamate. Early in 1837 I had fallen under the influence of Coleridge.[9] I got all of his books that I could; they had not then been reprinted, and were difficult to procure. The *Aids to Reflection* especially dominated me. The vague mysticism in which he loves to veil himself had a peculiar charm for me. Led on by Coleridge I had read Augustus Schlegel,[10] and I certainly had fallen away from Baconian principles, and passed under the first influences of a realistic philosophy. It so happened that I could not have handled the Oriel philosophy paper in a way to meet the views of the examiners, but for this strong infusion of Coleridgian metaphysics.

I have elsewhere (*Mind*, vol. i.) sketched the fortunes of philosophy in the present century in Oxford. In the present contribution to University history I may draw attention to a fact which did not fall within the lines of my former survey. Ever since 1830, at least, there has been among us an ebb and flow; one while of nominalistic, another while of *a priori* logic. Logic appears to a superficial observer to be merely used in the Oxford schools as material upon which questions may be framed. In spite of this appearance there is always a prevailing or accepted logic asserting itself as true over the opposite system, which it denounces as false. But what is the curious part of the history is, that these oscillations coincide with the strength for the time being of the clerical party. In the '30's, when the revolutionary enthusiasm rose to a height, which for a few years enabled the Government to defy the Church, to suppress her bishoprics, and plunder the cathedrals – in these years Whately's Logic, or some form of nominalism, predominated in the schools. When Tractarianism had made the clergy aware of their own strength, and high sacerdotal doctrines were openly proclaimed, we fell off from Whately, and vague, indefinite, realistic views under the influence of Coleridge and Sir William Hamilton[11] slowly occupied the schools. They established themselves there in a more explicit form when Mansel,[12] a Tory leader and arch-jobber, became the logical legislator of the school, and first introduced Kant into Oxford. But the High Church party received in Newman's secession a blow which for the moment seemed fatal to their cause. Coincident with this was the appearance of Mill's great work, and Oxford repudiated at once sacerdotal principles and Kantian logic.[13] There was, in the language of the clerical platform, an outbreak of infidelity. For more than a quarter of this century Mill and nominalistic views reigned in the schools. But gradually the clerical party rallied their forces, and since the Franco-German war have been advancing upon us with rapid strides. This fresh invasion of sacerdotalism has been accompanied by a renewed attempt to accredit an *a priori* logic, though in less cumbrous form than the Kantian, bristling as that does with postulates and assumptions – ideas of the reason, ideas of the understanding, the two *Anschauungsformen*,[14] and all the other *Begriffsdichtungen*[15] with which the Kantian loves to decorate his imaginative chamber. What is curious is that this new *a priori* metaphysic, whoever gave it shape in Germany, was imported into Oxford by a staunch Liberal, the late Professor Green.[16] This anomaly can only be accounted for by a certain puzzle-headedness on the part of the Professor, who was removed from the scene before he had time to see how eagerly the Tories began to carry off his honey to their hive.

CHAPTER 6

IT MAY be thought that Newman had tried to carry me as a man fit for his ecclesiastical purposes. This was not at all so; and I think I have now come to the point where I ought to relate how and when my connection with Newman grew up, and became the influencing fact of several years of my life.

I have said that my third set of rooms was exactly opposite Newman's. He returned from the continent in the summer of 1833; but this contiguity had no consequences. Newman, however, became dean about 1834, and the business of the dean was to look over the weekly themes. Whereas former deans had contented themselves with writing their initials in lead-pencil at the bottom of your (unread) essay, with the words good, bad, or indifferent, Newman took this office *au sérieux*, sent for you, made you aware where you had gone off the point into sophistry, or where you had left out the main feature of your case. Once my English was selected by him as the best of the week for being read out in hall. But before it could be read, it had to undergo various alterations, which he pointed out. I patched at it as well as I could, but it is not easy to run a theme in another man's groove without rewriting. I was probably too lazy to rewrite, and took and read it before the assembled college with such botches as I could make of it. Denison certainly would not have heard, and I counted upon Newman's not hearing or not attending. Nothing of the sort. Newman was in high indignation at having put his *imprimatur* upon matter which he disapproved, and which he characterised by some strong epithets. I retired crestfallen, and had learnt to fear both the watchfulness and the sternness of the new dean. This was in 1834, and our acquaintance made no further progress till I became a B.A. at the end of 1836. As a B.A. residing for purposes of study, Newman sent me occasional invitations through the year 1837 to his common-room evenings. He was very hospitable to all the college, and invited any one he thought would like to come. But previous to 1838, when we stood for the fellowship, he had not only no reason for considering me a proselyte, but some reason to set me down as most unlikely to become so. He must have known, for he had his eyes everywhere, that I openly and ostentatiously took the side of Hampden in the matter of the Regius Professor of Divinity. The fact was, I was delighted with the Bampton lectures. Their tone of omniscience imposed upon me, and as I had not yet abandoned my nominalist foundations, the dissolving power of nominalist logic applied to the Christian dogmas was wholly to my mind. On a later occasion, I well remember a personal incident on one of those evenings which must have wounded my vanity deeply. The conversation turned on some point of philosophy, no matter what, and I, who must always be pushing myself forward when something I did not understand was going on, offered some flippant remark, such as young B.A.'s are apt even now to deal in. Newman turned round and deposited upon me one of those ponderous and icy 'very likelies'; after which you were expected to sit down in a corner, and think over amending your conduct. I am sure that up to April, 1838, the only sentiment Newman can have entertained towards me was one of antipathy.

Under the influence of solitary study and much meditation on philosophical themes I was relapsing into that habit of self-consciousness out of which I had struggled in my first years. The world was fast becoming a sphere which moved round myself as a centre. Such a rebuke as that of Newman's was exactly what I wanted to warn me against the dangers of conceit and egotism. But I do not mention it for its own sake, but only as evidence that Newman, in praising my examination, could not have been influenced by party favouritism.

Now as to the steps by which I was finally drawn into the whirlpool of Tractarianism I am enabled to trace them minutely by the aid of a very full student's diary for 1838. This diary shows that I did not begin by catching the infection of the party spirit which was lying about on all sides like contagious matter in cholera time. I began from within; I had been brought up as a boy in sentiments of profound, I may say abject, piety. Undergraduate life had rubbed this off the surface, and I find my father remonstrating with me because when at Hauxwell I was slack in attending church, and seldom put in an appearance at the morning exercise, having been out in the fields probably since six o'clock. But this was all on the surface. The *fonds de piétisme* lay too deep to have been so quickly lost. The Diary of 1838 is evidence that this *piétisme* was slowly recovering its ascendency over me. I was an instance of the phenomenon which is recorded by William Palmer in his dreary *Narrative*. He says:

> The complete organisation of the party, and the amount of truth which underlay their system, produced great and permanent results in society. One of its benefits was the interest which it excited in the young in all religious practices and exercises, ... it ... promoted religious exercises and seriousness of character, and a keen interest on many religious questions which had been matters of indifference (p. 60).[1]

This was the side I was first taken by. I am astonished to see what hours I wasted over religious books at a time when I ought to have been devoting every moment to preparation for the Oriel examination. Nearly all these books were of an evangelical colour; indeed, while I was at Hauxwell, no others were accessible to me. Scott's *Force of Truth*,[2] his *Refutation of Tomline*, Gregory's *Letters*, *Mammon*, and a quantity of second-rate stuff of a similar kind, are carefully read and digested. It is true I combined with these books a passion for studying the Fathers; a passion which was more caught from Gibbon than from Tractarianism, and was an integral part of my plan for a life of study in college rooms. I also find of the same date an elaborate statement of the Anglican *via media*, so correctly drawn that the driest Anglican, William Palmer himself, must have been well satisfied with it.

In spite, however, of occasional depressing fits of conscientious superstition, there is a healthy secular tone carried through a great part of the Diary of 1838. But I am gradually being warped round, for I find myself on the 19th of August in that year beginning to suspect Hampden's Bamptons of 'unsoundness'. However, they interested me sufficiently to make me spend six pages on an analysis, not a disapproving one, of some of Hampden's leading views.

After Oriel, I offered myself at two other colleges. First at

University, for Mr Glaister's fellowship, vacated by his accept-
ance of a college living. This was in June 1838. There was at this
time no formidable in-college candidate; the others were seconds
and thirds, and otherwise undistinguished like myself. I had by
practice got such a mastery over examinations that I had now no
difficulty in turning off any number of pages of foolscap in three
hours. I accordingly went into the hall at University with better
hopes of success than ever before. I sat down to the table, and
after reading over the questions, raised my eyes to scan the
candidates. What was my amazement to see among them the
well-known figure of A. P. Stanley.[3] It was impossible – Stanley
was not eligible by the statutes. The fellowship was confined by
the founder to the 'parts nearest Durham'. As Durham was
always interpreted of the bishopric, not of the city, and as
Hornby, my birthplace, was within six miles of the bishopric,
my county claim was a close one. Of course Stanley, not being
statutably eligible, could not have come in unless he had been
invited to do so; if invited, he must have received private assurance that he would be elected, as he was at that time the most
brilliant figure in the University. What then was the purpose of
submitting five or six men, backed by a county claim, to a three
days' examination, when the fellowship was already settled? Did
the electors mean to cover their breach of the statute by pro-
nouncing the rest of us unfit in point of letters to hold a fellowship
in a college like University, generally filled with common-place
men? I could put no other interpretation upon the situation in
which I found myself. Of course Stanley was elected. I was
advised to appeal to the Visitor; but the Visitor being the Lord
Chancellor was sure to find some loophole for confirming the
election. I refused to appeal, and to put my father to what might
have been a considerable expense.

It became evident that the conscience of Travers Twiss, who, I
suppose, managed the plot, was not easy at what he had done.[4] It
was obligatory to write a circular Latin letter to the fellows of
University, announcing your candidature. This Latin letter
ought to have been purely formal; but I could not help introducing into mine a quotation from a speech of Livy, which seemed to
me pat for the occasion. It was an *étourderie* to do it such as I was
too often committing; but the quotation in itself was as innocent

as a lamb. Twiss came over to the Provost in a rage, and tried to make this bit of quotation a ground for rejecting me as I had written an impertinent letter. Travers Twiss' subsequent performances before the world have been of a nature which, I think, justified me in thinking that the whole indignation was simulated by that astute lawyer. The Provost, who hated me as a suspected proselyte of Newman's, instead of throwing his fatherly shield over me, and laughing Twiss out of the room, pretended to be duped, sent for me and remonstrated.

Great was the indignation in Durham and the North Riding at what had been done. It got about in the county that I had written ever so furious an indignation letter to the Master of University, and I got highly applauded for my spirit in not putting up quietly with a wrong done to county claims; so that an innocent bit of Latin was turned as a serious pretence against me, while a letter which I had never written, was highly commended by the clergy and other fathers, who might be looking forward to placing their sons at University to take advantage of their birth.

Once more I went in for a fellowship in November 1838, but it was an act of despair, not of hope. There were four fellowships at Balliol, and the unusual number drew the whole University. The general opinion was that one out-college man would be taken, and the other three filled up from the Balliol scholars; each out-college man thought he might be the lucky candidate. Public expectation was fulfilled, they took one out-college man, and three Balliol scholars, two of whom have since amply justified their choice. The out-college man taken was Woollcombe, and as this selection turned out afterwards to be a very great mistake, one can hardly help thinking that the act was done in order to show Oriel what *they* ought to have done in April. In other respects the Balliol examination was vastly inferior to the system pursued at Oriel. Odds and ends of literary lore, collected up and down commentators and handbooks; there was neither unity nor character about the papers. I can hardly think that the election was influenced by the examination, but that Balliol acted on the principle, not a bad one, of selecting those three of their scholars of whom they had otherwise reason to think well. The two colleges did for a long time pursue opposite paths; Oriel was noted for being '*noverca suorum*',[5] while at Balliol their geese are always swans.

With this adventure closed my fellowship campaign, the colleges seemed resolutely to have closed their doors against me, my darling hope of leading a life of study as a Fellow completely blocked. Which way should I turn? I had long given up all thought of the Bar, though my father pretended to carry on the scheme longer. With my increasing religiosity, it was natural that I should think of Orders. Being a clergyman's son I knew well the routine of a country clergyman's life. In my present frame of mind the idea of pastoral duty was agreeable to me; but I was not without a side-glance at the many learned clergymen whom the annals of the Church of England can show as having led a life of study and obscurity in the by-ways of England. My father wrote me one of his disagreeable letters, overflowing with pious resignation and moroseness.

> The hearts of electors are not exempt from the common dispensation, which places them in His hands, who turneth them whithersoever He will. And if He seeth good for you, I sincerely hope you will have it, because I am persuaded your future happiness is involved in it. I have lived long enough to have seen men, after ten or fifteen years' miserable enjoyment of a fellowship, ten thousand times more anxious to get rid of than you can be to procure one. I burnt but the other day an old letter of Mr Page's, in which he says, "Mesech and the tents of Kedar were a mere joke to what I am now enduring;" i.e. while an Emmanuel living was slowly passing down the list of Fellows, and might possibly come down to him.

Accordingly I turned my attention towards Orders in the winter of 1838–39. Meantime I was glad to close as a temporary expedient, with an offer made me by Newman. Pusey had taken an empty house in St Aldate's,[6] with a view of filling it with the young B.A.'s, whom he would employ upon some of his many projects, the Library of the Fathers or other. We were to live in common, rent free, and pay a very small sum a week for our frugal diet. I did some odd jobs for Pusey, collated MS. of Cyprian in the Bodleian: when Newman projected a translation of Thomas Aquinas' *Catena Aurea* on the Gospels, I undertook Matthew and Mark, but afterwards contented myself with Matthew, passing on

Mark to another hand. Even Matthew took me nearly the whole of 1839. The translation is often incorrect, and wants revision; it was extremely useful to me in one way; it brought me acquainted with the whole range of patristic bibliography. Aquinas never gives chapter and verse for his citations; only the name of the Father, sometimes also of the particular work. I hunted up the whereabouts of all the quotations in each case in the best edition of the Fathers; I spent hours and days over the work in the Bodleian, and would not be beat. By the end of 1839 or 1840 I had established quite a Bodleian reputation for finding my way about among the writings of the Fathers, genuine and supposititious. Even Jacobson[7] would come and ask me for a suggestion.

All this while I was rushing into the whirlpool of Tractarianism; was very much noticed by Newman, who thought I translated better than most, – in fact fanaticism was laying its deadly grip around me. In October 1839, being discontented with one or two of the inmates of the 'house', I seceded and took again a private lodging. This was a most fortunate accident, for on 4th November James Mozley and Ashworth of Brasenose came running at 8.30 to my lodgings, to say, didn't I know that there was a Yorkshire Fellowship at Lincoln, for which the names were to be handed in that very day; several candidates, but none thought formidable.[8] Of course I gave in my name. The misfortune was that for more than a year, while I had been occupied upon the *Catena*, I had not touched the Classics, had not written a line of Latin prose, had left philosophy on one side, and of course forgotten all my secular history. I was in the situation of a man suddenly called upon to row in a race after being twelve months out of training. Lincoln was noted at that time for being, with Magdalen and one or two others, a rigid anti-Puseyite college. Of course old fellows did not in those days know much about the character or sentiments of the rising generation. I am sure if Calcott,[9] Thompson,[10] and Kay[11] had really known how deeply I was tarred with the Puseyite brush they would have taken anybody sooner than me. Especially, what was the lucky point was that a few weeks before I had seceded from Pusey's house, and was found at that moment in a private lodging. They did elect me, and oh, the joy of relief! No moment in all my life has ever been so sweet as that Friday morning, 8th November, when Radford's servant came in to announce my election, and to claim his five shillings for doing so.[12] I had seen with the despair of an excluded Peri all the gates of all the colleges shut against me, and here, in the most unlikely quarter of Oxford, I had really got the thing I had so eagerly desired. I was quite off my head for two or three days, and must have exhibited myself as a *jeune étourdi* in the eyes of the Rector and Fellows of Lincoln. The joy at Hauxwell equalled my own. My father penned quite an enthusiastic letter, thought that fellowships were excellent things, and talked of bringing up two of my sisters to pay me a visit in the following summer. I poured out thanksgivings in the pages of my Diary to Almighty God, to whose sole agency I ascribed my election. And really a concurrence of fortunate accidents had to converge on a single moment, or the thing could not have been done.

Done it was, and I began to lay out my life on new lines. There was no study so vast and arduous that I would not attack it, nothing that I did not feel capable of conquering. But there was one temper which was not let loose without restraint, my high church fanaticism. When that came in the way, nothing could stand before it; I became a declared Puseyite, then an ultra-Puseyite; I saw a great deal of men like Jack Morris, whose whole conversation was turning the Church of England into ridicule, and who adopted as their motto, 'Tendimus in Latium'.[13] Jack Morris, however, took me also by my student's side. He passed his whole day up the tower of Exeter College reading the Fathers, and cutting jokes upon our step-mother, the Church of England. My reason seemed entirely in abeyance in the years 1840, 1841, 1842; I moved entirely with the party, was loudly prominent in all their demonstrations, and judged of good or bad, according as any event or person was docile or otherwise in Newman's tactics.

To what extent this fury of zeal would have run I cannot tell. I must have been enveloped in the catastrophe of 1845, as were so many of those with whom I lived, but for one or two saving circumstances. One of these was my devotion to study. It must not be supposed that I passed the whole of my day in these years in haunting *conciliabules*, and reading fiery articles in the *English Churchman*, and *British Critic*; I carried on a tolerably steady line of reading, though chiefly theological. Especially church history fascinated me; but I formed stupendous plans for works I would write on the history of the Middle Ages; the history of monastic establishments with several other things, each of them a task for a life. Of course what I was to write was all to tend to the glorification of the Catholic Church, but still, schemes which require method and long preparation have a sobering effect upon a heated brain. In the winter of 1839 I wrote again for the Latin essay, and unsuccessfully, Stanley carrying it off. In 1841 and 1842 I was twice successful for the Denyer prize. I carried through the press my translation of the *Catena Aurea* on Matthew; I wrote an elaborate article in the *British Critic* on 'Earliest English Poetry', for which I spent months of study, and got to know all that was then known on the subject. I wrote two *Lives of the Saints* in Newman's Series, upon which I spent an amount of research, of which no English historian at that time had set the example.[14]

All these were the acts of a sane man, however wild and warped my public conduct and talk may have been. In 1843 another circumstance occurred, which contributed powerfully to save me. Radford offered me a tutorship of the college. Already in 1839 my classics had got sadly rusty, and as I had never touched them since, it may be supposed I was not in a fit condition to work a tutorship even of pass men. But I was not daunted. I immediately set resolutely to work and made good my lost ground. By confining my first lectures to those books I had known best I gained time, and in two years' time I was at least a fairly efficient pass lecturer. This cost some very hard steady work, and gave me a serious object in life, beyond holding up one of the banners of the Puseyite party. I think it was chiefly owing to this that when the crash came in 1845 I did not follow Newman. Not that my belief in the necessity of finding and joining the Catholic Church was as yet shaken, but I would take time and examine my conscience a little further.

In the Diary which begins 1845 there is a much larger infusion of secular matter. I find myself deep in the literary history of the eighteenth century, reading Gray's *Correspondence*, Prior's *Life of Goldsmith*, Hume's *Life and Correspondence*; and as all this was when Newman was preparing his going over, I must have been looking on with equanimity.

Then I saw that I must soon be called upon to share the Honours lecturing in the college with William Kay, and I was making all the efforts I was capable of to get a mastery of Aristotle, and the principles of logic. These things excluded those gloomy thoughts, which weighed down so many of my contemporaries. There was not room for the question – if I died outside the pale of the Catholic Church, what would become of me? It put itself aside rather than answered itself; for I do not see that I had begun to doubt the efficacy of the only saving Church in 1845. Not only had I not begun to doubt, but I find breaking out in the Diary in these years evidence of abject prostration of mind before some unseen power of which it is not clear whether it is God or the Church.

Indeed I have great difficulty with the Diary in my hand in making intelligible the exact state of my mind and opinions in the whole of the four years from 1843–47. I do not see a single page in the Diary which savours of rationalism, I mean the application of the common reason to religion. I see a great deal of degrading superstition, of fasting and attending endless religious services. I adopted the plan which many others did, of reciting the Hours of the *Roman Breviary*, and seemed to please myself for some time in this time-wasting and mind-drowning occupation. I once, and only once, got so low by fostering a morbid state of conscience as to go to confession to Dr Pusey.[15] Years afterwards it came to my knowledge that Pusey had told a fact about myself, which he got from me on that occasion, to a friend of his, who employed it to annoy me.

Perhaps the best way of exhibiting my state of mind in this period is to give some extracts from the Diary, kept during a stay of a fortnight with Newman in his Littlemore retreat.[16] Newman had bought some land at Littlemore, and turned a row of single-roomed cottages into cells connected by a sort of cloister; had built a library for his very considerable collection of patristic literature, and got some of his young disciples to join him in a kind of semi-monastic life. The place came to be called popularly in Oxford 'The Monastery.' The warden of Wadham of those days, B. P. Symons,[17] a flourishing Evangelical, who poked his nose into everything, one day knocked at the door. Instead of a servant, the door was opened by Newman himself. Symons asked if he might see the monastery. 'We have no monasteries here,' was the answer, and the door was slammed in his face. On Saturday,

30th September 1835, I went by invitation on a short visit. The Diary is as follows: –

Newman kinder, but not perfectly so. Vespers at eight. Compline at nine. How low, mean, selfish, my mind has been to-day; all my good seeds vanished; grovelling, sensual, animalish; I am not indeed worthy to come under this roof.

Sunday, October 1. – St John called me at 5.30, and at 6 went to Matins, which with Lauds and Prime take about an hour and a half; afterwards returned to my room and prayed, with some effect, I think. Tierce at 9, and at 11 to church – communion. More attentive and devout than I have been for some time; hope I am coming into a better frame; 37 communicants. Returned and had * * * breakfast. Had some discomfort at waiting for food so long, which I have not done since I have been unwell this summer, but struggled against it, and in some degree threw it off. Walked up and down with St John[18] in the garden; Newman afterwards joined us. Newman stated to Rivington the possibility that an outcry might be made against things in the *Lives of the Saints*, which might oblige Rivington to drop it; this, therefore, provided for in the agreement by which the title goes to Newman, not to Rivington. Newman thinks Rivington very well disposed; took up the Oxford Tracts just about the time that the P. C. K. Society was taken from him. Edward Churton[19] mentioned for (editor of) the *British Critic*,[20] but Newman has no idea who it will be. Odd enough that W. Palmer should have been thought of, who is, at this very time, engaged in writing a pamphlet against the *British Critic*. At 3 to church; then Nones; walked in the garden till dinner – interesting talk; sat till 7.30. Some unknown benefactor sent a goose. Newman had not heard till to-day of Litton's marriage, that is to be, to a relation of H. Shepheard. When ill abroad Newman had choice of being bled in his arm or his foot; chose the latter as safest; only took two ounces of blood from him with a round lancet with three heads. Pseudo-Dionysius, certainly in Newman's judgment a late writer; monophysite and much neoplatonism in him. The sermons of St Methodius also given up. When Dionysius is quoted by the Council of Trent, or by a pope, this only sanctions the piece quoted = St Paul quoting Menander. Talk of some Rosminian nuns coming to England; though an order, and under the three vows, they do not renounce possessions in the world; yet they live together. They evade the Mortmain Act by vesting property legally in the name of a member, while really it is at the disposal of the general. They aim to embrace the whole Church. The Pope is their head. The Jesuits always and everywhere opposed and despised; St Ignatius prayed for this. Wiseman opposed the Jesuits at Rome, and does so here: proof of his sincerity.[21] 'Father' is usually applied to a regular, but not so in Ireland. Father Matthew provincial of the Capuchins. Vespers at 8, Compline at 9: the clocks here very backward. Very sleepy and went to bed at 10.

Monday, 3d October. – I shall not note any more the regular proceedings of each day. Unwell and very sleepy; could not read or pray as I wished. Silence not literally observed, gives way to necessity. Began Moehler *On Unity*, French translation. Read Wharton's Preface to *Anglia Sacra*, vol. ii. St Remigius transferred to-day.[22] Mrs Seager lodging here in Newman's old lodging. Newman rents some college land, and has planted a belt round the church. Walked alone in the fields, towards Garsington, between afternoon prayers and dinner. Lockhart's mother much distressed.[23] Probably at the separation more than at the conversion, which she must have expected some time.... His friends say that Sibthorpe will not stay where he is, but change again before long.[24] I asked Newman how to take religious language when used by the poor. The dilemma is, if you don't check it, they think they can impose upon you by it; for nine times out of ten they use it hypocritically; if you do check it, you seem to banish religion out of conversation, almost out of all your intercourse with them. N said England was almost in the condition of a heathen country, and he supposed the Early Christians did not use Christians' language when they went among the heathen; quoted our Lord's replies to the man who said, 'Good Master,' etc.... The air of Littlemore quite different from Oxford air, so that invalids are sent out of Oxford to Littlemore, which is upon sand.

4th October. – Very poorly this morning, but more calm and more composed in my mind.... N mentioned to me having just received the account of a lady who, having in conversation declared that she thought the Church of Rome the true Church, had been refused the communion by her minister, he thus telling her in so many words to go to Rome.

5th October. – Awoke poorly this morning, but got gradually better, yet did not make a thoroughly good use of my time. Coffin[25] came to-day to stay; says the college at Chichester in great want of discipline. The principal does not live with them, and Lowe has not much authority. Men to be found in the billiard-rooms, and set up a tandem; many come only to cram for the Bishop's Examination. . . . How uncomfortable have I made myself all this evening by a childish fancy that once got into my head – I could not get out of it – a weak jealousy of N's good opinion. Oh, my God! take from me this petty pride; set me free from this idle slavery to opinion; fix my affections on things eternal. . . . Coffin more subdued and less thoughtless than usual.

6th October. – Much better this morning, but not thankful to God for it; my mind still disturbed by the bad feelings of yesterday. Bloxam[26] walked up to church yesterday afternoon, and brought confirmed account of Sibthorpe's apostasy. He has received the communion in our church at St Helen's I. O. W., but to what communion he will attach himself is not so clear. Says Rome is Babylon, etc., and the strange thing is all that he alleges as the ground of his change are the trite objections about idolatry, etc., which he must have heard and got over often enough before his conversion. . . . When the Bishop of London visited B. Smith[27] he went over the church, and made no remarks; the rowing came in a letter next day. As he was leaving the house, Smith asked him for his blessing, and was about to kneel down for the purpose; the Bishop abruptly turned away with 'Good morning; I'll write to you to-morrow.'

6th October. – St Faith in Salisbury breviary.[28] More comfortable in mind to-day. Walk with N and Coffin to Sandford. Much talk about the English saints. The Carthusians have no miracles.[29] The Bollandists talk of legends of St David as 'Fabulosæ.'[30] A well in one of Wilberforce's parishes called St John's Well, was from St John, Beverley.[31] The Paduan edition of St Athanasius has many additions to the Benedictine. N thinks the fourth oration a patchwork of different pieces. He had overlooked Mansi's chronology, and given the received chron., but thinks now that Mansi's is the right.[32] The MS. of Athanasius in Bodl. is of the fifteenth cent. Mr Goode's quotations about παράδοσις taken unacknowledged from Suicer.[33] Dr Bull's nickname, when a young man, Jemmy Jessamy;[34] his houses both at Oxford and Exeter in most trim order now.... Bowles pressed me so to preach, in his quiet gentle way, that I thought it would be unkind to refuse any longer, and I consented, though I do not know what to do for a sermon.

7th October. – Newman showed me a specimen of the *Lives of the Saints* come down to-day. Compared number of words with Lardner's *Cyclopædia*. The *Lives* has one line more in the page and one word more in the line, that is about forty-five words more in the page than the *Cyclopædia*; but something to be deducted on the score of Herschell's long words. Talk at dinner about St Bernard. The Cistercians objected to decorations in churches.[35] Not all the papal bulls are in the *Bullarium magnum* – not, e.g., those relating to particular orders. Mr Valentine, brought up by a Catholic priest, said to M. Lammaire, a French apostate to our church, that he hoped he might live to repent of what he had done. M. L gave French lessons in Chichester; now gone back to France, and a professor in a Protestant seminary. After dinner we went with N into the library; he went round showing us the books, giving us their history, etc. A book of prints, *Shores of the Mediterranean*, led him to speak of his illness in Sicily.[36] Caught a fever by sleeping in some out-of-the-way place, and laid up in consequence three weeks at Castro Juan (Giovanni), the ancient Enna; had a Neapolitan servant with him, who since came to England, and is servant to Lord Carrington. Priest came once to see him, but he not in a state to have any conversation; people dying all around and bells going continually for them; people of the house thought the heretic couldn't bear the bells; was given over for a week. First place he went to, on getting better, the cathedral – old Norman; might have fancied himself in England. Left CG so weak he could not walk; when he got to Palermo people considered him dying; sea-air restored him. Used to walk up and down at Palermo till the vessel could sail; was a fortnight

on the voyage from Palermo to Marseilles, a whole week becalmed. Then at Lyons fell ill again; legs and ankles swollen;
thought to be erysipelas. All this time his friends in England
heard nothing of him. Six weeks in anxiety. Sicilian almost unin-
telligible. N could speak a little Italian, but it went from him
while he was ill. Corresponded afterwards with his landlord in
Latin. Suspected the priest wrote the letter. . . . The two things I
have to guard against most at present are, I think, acting to be
seen of others and going through religious duties, services, etc.,
in a formal legal way. Oh that I may go to communion to-morrow
with more devout and abstract meditation, more true thankful-
ness of heart for this great benefit!

8th October. – Communion at 7, breakfast at 8. N detailed the
history of his taking the *British Critic*. Campbell, late secretary of
the S. P. G., was once editor, under Boone; while C was editor,
Whately had the *Review* turned out of Oriel C. R. for an article on
Croly's book on the Revelations. Whately had a correspondence
with C on the subject, and against one passage in the Oriel copy,
to the purport that 'Balaam's ass was a type of Mr Croly,' is
written in Whately's handwriting, 'Mr C assures me that this was
written by a gentleman and a Christian.' It was on the point of
being given up under Boone when Mr Watson persuaded Rivington to have another number. Then N stepped in, and agreed to
furnish four sheets a number gratis in order to keep it afloat.
When B gave it up Maitland[37] took it; very unfit, as not knowing
anything of men or parties; wrapt up in his books. N continued to
contribute, M getting shyer and shyer, but not liking, or not able,
to do without him. Then M appointed archbishop's chaplain, at
which time Pusey wrote his review of the Eccles. Com., which
blew them out of the water. N, wishing to bring things to a crisis,
and not any longer to be a thorn in M's side, offered Pusey's art. as
the contribution for the quarter, almost expecting that it would
be refused and they sent adrift. It was inserted, but Maitland
resigned, and N took it, never intending to keep it long. Boone,
by the way was turned off by Rivington for his laxity, particularly
for some things he said in favour of Bp. Stanley. . . . Connection
between the University and the Vicar of St Mary's formerly much
closer; e.g. if a preacher did not come for his turn it would have

been usual to ask the vicar to take it. The parish sermon has not been customary for more than twenty years. The Bishop began it. Morning daily prayers began the day after St Peter's Day, 1834. The image of the Virgin in the spire a famous one. The Pope asked some Oxford men who were presented to him what had become of St Mary of Oxford. . . . We sat till Vespers, and had a long and interesting conversation about the state of the Univ. I stated my impression of the restless emulation which the classes and open scholarships produce among the undergrads., and of the ambition and preferment-hunting among the M.A.'s. N took a more cheerful view; defended the class system as having done so much to rouse the Univ. He thought that the tutor who aimed at leading and forming his pupil's mind, even supposing him to have at the time less weight than the successful cram-coach, might succeed in making an impression which would gradually gain upon the pupil as he got older, took his degree, got out of the influence of the schools, and began to see things in a truer light. Talking of Lord Ashley's memorial,[38] N said it did not answer for Heads to turn out their tutors in a body; they put themselves entirely in the power of the succeeding tutors, it being a measure they could never repeat. Instance at Oriel, when Hawkins turned out three of his tutors, – if Wilberforce had gone down to his brothers one Sunday during term there was a regular sitting upon it as a grave offence. Well, Denison came in in his place, and took a curacy, to which he went out every Saturday, and oftener, and the Provost could no nothing. About 1770 the worst time in the Univ.; a head of Oriel then, who was continually obliged to be assisted to bed by his butler. Gaudies a scene of wild license. The object of men at that time seems to have been to get over time. At Ch. Ch. they dined at 3, and sat regularly till chapel at 9. Same divisions and party spirit going on in N's younger days, only on different subjects. Jealousy between Oriel and Ch. Ch., Whately and Lloyd.[39] Lloyd said that W had σαφήνεια,[40] and nothing more. Copleston always in a state of irritation at something; thought he ought to have been promoted before. His plans for extending Oriel; asked [J.] Dean to give him up St Mary Hall, and complained of his unreasonableness in refusing, 'though he offered him the best lodgings in High St.,' on which [Cotton] headed one of his chapters – Orielensibus ingenio exundantibus barbare denegatur aula B. V. M.[41] Lord Ripon, Copleston's patron [Sir] D. K. Sandford, stood at Oriel and rejected; wrote furious arts. in the *Ed. Rev.*

9th October. – The Oriel Bible clerk used to wait to dine after the high table, so that he said grace twice before he began to dine. Tyler, when Dean, sent away four men for coming to high table too late. . . . Another interesting talk with N alone, on the present prospects of the Ch. in England; he thought persons in lay communion, and thus not bound by the arts. and p. book, remaining in the Eng. Ch. and advocating Catholic views, would be irresistible. Has as little hope as possible himself, but thinks it wrong to be without hope; H. Wilberforce[42] most sanguine; said persons were being drawn in daily; the non-jurors not a parallel case;[43] they made a schism; bad bishops quarrelled among themselves on trifling points, and yet made no difficulty at being severed from the Catholic Church. But Laud's influence has been permanent,[44] e.g. the sacramental doctrine rescued by him, and, so to say, restored to the E. Ch. What persons in authority want is to get quickly rid of the Tractarians; he is afraid men may be impatient, and yield to the force of opinion and to temptation, and go to Rome. How to understand the fact that the recent converts have been mostly weak persons, e.g. Mr Spencer? Thought me too gloomy about influence in Oxford; when a man can be set down as a Puseyite he loses influence with one class of persons, but not with others, and those the most worthy. But even with the opposite party, however they may talk, there are times when they are, in spite of themselves, obliged to pay deference to conscientious men – they mistrust their own principles.

10th October. – Thirty years old to-day; ripe and mature in age, but only beginning, if, indeed, I am beginning, Christian life. A child in knowledge and judgment. When I ought to be able to teach, guide, and influence others I am still only a learner. Spent nearly two hours this morning in devotion and self-examination; with some fervency and, by God's grace, I trust, profit, at least I have felt more peace and calm through the day than I have known for some time past. . . . Ogilvie read Herbert's *Country Parson* with his class, and as the practical comment on it, asked them to dinner on Friday. Copleston, when Provost, used to torment probationers; his saying to Newman, 'We don't help sweetbread with a spoon; butler, bring a blunt knife'; and reproving him for not taking wine with the company; very much irritated at the Ch. Ch. hunters being exercised outside his windows; his horror of going to bed.... Talk at dinner about ancient meal-times and wonderful abstinences; the Jesuit rule wisely adapted to our enfeebled condition. The Cistercians never had their minds in vigour; could hardly ever be said to be thoroughly awake. St Macarius turned out of an Egyptian monastery from envy of the monks of his superior powers of endurance. Stood upright in his cell for a week without eating anything, but chewed a palm-leaf out of humility. St Goderick stood all night in the river up to his neck, and frozen.

On a review of the whole time I am thankful for much, much happiness. I felt lifted more into the world of spirit than ever before; thought I had more faith, but how much evil was mixed up with this in my heart; thought so much of little mortifications, yet talked as if they were familiar to me; felt so anxious for N's good opinion, and suffered my mind to wander miserably in prayers.

This fairly exhibits the state of my mind in 1834. I see no trace of change of feeling in the Diary for several years from this time; but I do observe that the fanatical instincts did not gain ground, as I presume they usually do when indulged; mine remained at a dead level. My thoughts were much occupied during term time with my college work, which I saw would necessarily grow indefinitely as I threw myself into it. And in vacation I had abundance of literary work, besides the *Lives of the Saints* mentioned above. I was a good deal employed by the editor of the *Christian Remembrancer*, which had succeeded the *British Critic* as the organ of the High Church party, but much more moderate in tone. These articles were literary, not theological, and it was a novel delight to me to find that I could turn out a literary article of a superior finish, without a trace of the church bigot about it.

This seems like literary vanity; there was, no doubt, much of that, but that was by no means all. The truth was that I was now turned of thirty; my brain had consolidated itself, and the forces of the reason were slowly beginning to assert themselves against the masses of imported superstition or native tendency to pietism, which had hitherto had it all their own way. This power of reason did not come into direct conflict with the blind beliefs to which I was so devoted. I never questioned for a long time any of the things I had hitherto believed and taught; there was no internal debate. But as I had been drawn into Tractarianism, not by the contagion of a sequacious zeal, but by the inner force of an inherited pietism of an evangelical type; so I was gradually drawn out of it, not by any arguments or controversy against Puseyism, but by the slow process of innutrition of the religious brain and development of the rational faculties.

I may appear in the above extract from my Diary to have been closer to Newman than I really was; I always felt there was some secret barrier between him and myself which did not exist between him and the other young neophytes of my own standing. These also I will not say kept aloof from me – we were most friendly – but they certainly suspected me of being in some point not like themselves. Was it possible that Newman's insight into character was keen enough to detect already a rationalising element, of which I can myself see no trace in anything I wrote for a long time after? H. O. Coxe[45] told me many years afterwards that Newman should have said of me, 'Ce garçon ira loin', or some equivalent phrase in English. Now I, on my part, had a great and growing dissatisfaction with the greater part of the men into whose society I was thrown by my opinions. I have mentioned that I left the Pusey house because I was discontented with some of its inmates, and I could not but feel that the young apostles I was amongst in these years (1843–45) were not intellectually equal companions. Indeed it was a general wonder how Newman himself could be content with a society of men like Bowles, Coffin, Dalgairns, St John, Lockhart, and others. I venerated Newman himself as having been so much to me in so many ways; and I had too little knowledge to see how limited his philosophical acquirements were. The force of his dialectic, and the beauty of his rhetorical exposition were such that one's eye and ear were charmed, and one never thought of inquiring on how narrow a basis of philosophical culture his great gifts were expended. A. P. Stanley once said to me, 'How different the fortunes of the

Church of England might have been if Newman had been able to read German.' That puts the matter in a nut-shell; Newman assumed and adorned the narrow basis on which Laud had stood 200 years before. All the grand development of human reason, from Aristotle down to Hegel, was a sealed book to him. There lay a unity, a unity of all thought, which far transcended the mere mechanical association of the unthinking members of the Catholic Church; a great spiritual unity, by the side of which all sects and denominations shrink into vanity.

I had gone abroad for the first time in the summer of 1843.[46] I took Catholic introductions, as I had a notion that foreign Catholics, not being converts, might be of a better mental stamp than these neo-Catholics that I had to do with at home. In a very few weeks I was undeceived. I saw Kenelm Digby, the author of *Mores Catholici* – fine monument of learning and industry.[47] But I found there was no mind underneath; it was all accumulation in support of Catholic dogma. I found also rife in Parisian Catholic circles a spirit of credulity so vulgar that it could not have existed had it ever been brought into the light of day. The religious people lived among themselves; they believed every miraculous story which was brought in, and simply because it was miraculous; their mental habit had become so inexact that the idea of truth seemed to have perished from among them. The question was, Does this alleged fact redound to the glory of the Church? If it does it is not to be questioned; if it is against the Church it is a fiction of the Voltairians.

Something of the same kind I observed during my visits to Littlemore; there was a lurking fondness for stories of miracles. One I find recorded in the Diary –

> C mentioned case of a fellow in Leicestershire who was blaspheming in a public-house, and using the common oath, Strike me blind! *was* struck blind by a flash of lightning on the instant. C added that he had become a Cistercian, and that on his first reception of the sacrament had recovered his sight.

On the 9th October 1845 it was known that Newman had resigned his fellowship. On 10th October, Church showed me a note from Newman to him, announcing his approaching reconciliation to the Catholic Church by Father Dominic. It is impossible to describe the enormous effect produced in the academical and clerical world, I may say throughout England, by one man's changing his religion. But it was not consternation; it was a lull – a sense that the past agitation of twelve years was extinguished by this simple act; and perhaps a lull of expectation to see how many he would draw with him. Instead of a ferocious howl, Newman's proceeding was received in respectful silence, no one blaming. But as there must be always an *advocatus diaboli*, this part was sustained on this occasion by the Vicar of St Thomas(!) who went about inveighing against Newman's honesty in putting out the theory contained in his last sermon; 'He didn't believe it when he wrote it.'

Of course the neophytes were also scattered like chaff. Ward[48] and Oakeley[49] had gone before, but there still remained a small band of us more stable, to keep each other in countenance and meet at Manuel Johnson's[50] for our Sunday dinner – Church, Marriott,[51] Copeland,[52] myself, and others. M Johnson jocularly proposed to write the history of Absquatulation.[53] He called upon Marriott to provide a theory to cover us. Marriott, who could not see a joke, answered seriously, 'We are in a state of appeal – appeal to a general council.' When this was repeated to Lewis, who was strong in canon law, he said, 'Didn't Marriott know that an appeal must be lodged within thirty days?'

The tone of the Diary for the years 1846–47 seems to me distinctly more trivial than that for the two preceding years. In the first place, the principal figure round whom so much interest was gathered has disappeared from the scene; the sense of suspense, which had quite a dramatic effect in giving unity to the day-by-day entries, is lost. Secondly, I myself am evidently in a very depressed state, both of body and mind. Friends used to think that this depression was due to the painful severance which had taken place from Newman and others. Others, again, would ascribe it to an intellectual conflict going on within me similar to that of which so harrowing a detail is given in the life of Blanco White. Both of these were wrong. I was neither so close to Newman personally as to miss him as a friend, nor had his perversion, so long looked for, and therefore mentally discounted, at all fallen upon me like a blow. Up to nearly the end of

1847 I see no trace in the Diary of anything like internal struggle. On 14th October 1847 I find this entry which negatives the idea of anything like what they call scepticism having consciously arisen within me: –

> Went up to Froude, who engaged in writing a novel to expound his views; had long talk with him, with something of confidence on both sides, though no satisfactory result – a sincere desire on my part to sympathise with his scepticism for the purpose of helping him through it.[54]

J. A. Froude had made much shorter work with it than I could possibly do, not having had in early youth that profound pietistic impression which lay like lead upon my understanding for so many years of my life. I remember, too, though it would hardly be gathered from the Diary, that in these years, 1846–47, I was making very strenuous efforts to make my share of the college tuition real and influential. I may take this opportunity of explaining what my position in college as tutor was at this time. At that time there was no subdivision of labour such as is now established in the form of combined lectures. The tutors of each college taught everything that was taught in the college to all its students. Under this monstrous abuse, of which I have written the history several times in other places, a zealous tutor was entirely baffled as to what course to take; if he wanted to make a good lecture on any one classical book, say Herodotus, he must devote an amount of time to his preparation for it which was quite inconsistent with his also doing well the other lectures he had to give – looking over Latin writing, teaching English composition, seeing that men know their divinity, and the vague but heavy duties of personal inspection and advice. I never could let routine be routine, or do anything with any comfort to myself, unless I tried to do it as well as I could. It so happened that among other lectures Herodotus fell to me. I took vast pains with this; read up everything I could, and after some terms' apprenticeship and much bungling, became able to give what was for those times a really good lecture. But then to do this it was impossible to keep up equally well with Livy and Sophocles and the Greek Testament, and perhaps another book or two. I had the mortification of sitting there and hearing men translate Sophocles to me unprofitably, as knowing I could not teach them the niceties of Greek erratic [Attic] idiom. Here I was but struggling with the fetters of an impossible system, though it was not till years after that I came to conceive where it was that the fault lay. I was honestly labouring to make the best I could of my Sparta. But I had other college difficulties to contend with in my colleagues.

Lincoln had been let drop very low in the rank of colleges during the tutorship of Rose[55] and Radford.[56] Rose was gone long since; Radford had become Head in 1834. Richard Michell had come in as tutor and had immediately raised, by force of character and a singular knack of teaching, the tone of the tuition. Every Lincoln man felt this. We were all proud of Michell, who, by his genial, jovial sociability, represented Lincoln before the world. The other fellows were a bad lot, the tradition of 1750 surviving into the nineteenth century. Queen's and Magdalen, Jesus and St John's, were bad enough, but none of them could show such fossil specimens of the genus Fellow as our Kay *senior*, Thompson, Calcott, Meredith.[57] The juniors, Green,[58] Kay *junior*,[59] Perry, and myself, formed an opposition contending for discipline, decency, order, and religion (outward). We were always honourably supported by Michell, though he cared for none of these things. But we were always outvoted by the seniors, with the Rector and his casting-vote. They besides could fetch up from no great distance – Northampton – another wretched *crétin* of the name of Gibbs, who was always glad to come and booze at the college port a week or two when his vote was wanted in support of old abuses.[60] In spite of a majority, we had managed to turn the corner, and get a moral reform initiated. At the end of 1847 I could not but look with some complacency at the great change which had been effected in the discipline and tone of the college in seven years. Not that this was all my doing, far from it. Michell, as I have said, was loyal to us with his vote, but having a low type of intellect and *moral*, was not helpful in some of the main points.

My other colleague, William Kay *junior*, on the other hand, was a man of most vigorous intellect and sternly disciplined *moral*. In religion of strong evangelical sentiments and passionately anti-Puseyite * * * he had distinguished himself at the local Grammar School (Knaresborough), and been sent to college by the assistance of friends, who justly judged that such a genius would make his way if he got the chance. He justified their prevision, getting a first class in classics and a second in mathematics at the same time, and was immediately elected Fellow of Lincoln about a year after me. * * * I could not but admit to myself the superior intellectual force of this young Hercules. I was still only a shy abstract student, unready and unequal to a dialectical conflict. I resisted, but was always over-crowed. If I had been less unequal to the contest, the fight – for it was a constant warfare – might have given me nerve; as it was, it only contributed in these years to the other causes of depression already enumerated. In the end I am sure I received great benefit from what was at the time most fatiguing. I had never before been at such close quarters with so robust and aggressive an intellect. Not that William Kay was of a speculative or sceptical turn of mind: quite the reverse. He remained for a long time the narrow Puritan he had been brought up. Though emerging afterwards into orthodox Anglicanism, he had no philosophical interest to carry him on, and remains, I suppose, to this day intellectually where he was when he was thirty. What so vigorous an understanding has been able to satisfy itself with I know not. He went out to India as Principal of the College at Calcutta. * * * *

The Diary in these years is a good deal taken up with these college squabbles – the joint resistance of us juniors to the voting majority of the Rector and seniors, and my personal altercations with Kay to be allowed to do anything that I wished. Kay, with his superabundant energy, was extremely useful in the college, made as good a bursar as I had made a bad one, knocked the men about with his horns of iron, waking them up and rebuking their vices. Vice there was enough among the students, even after all our reforms – drinking, gambling, the old tradition of the college, were by no means extirpated. In dealing with the students I soon became aware that I was the possessor of a magnetic influence, which soon, not perhaps at this early date, gave me a moral ascendency in the college, to which at last everybody, the Rector even, the students, the very servants, even at last Kay himself, succumbed. In this fact, which was very slowly making itself felt in the years of which I am now writing, lies the true secret of my not having followed Newman. Not that I should by any means have gone when he did in 1845; I was not ready; I was always more deliberate; but I think in 1847 I might have dropped off in some moment of mental and physical depression, or under the pressure of some arguing convert – for the converts never left you any peace; they were always at you like Christian's conscience in the *Pilgrim's Progress*, urging you to flee from the wrath to come. The question, What would become of me if I died outside the pale of the Church? long had its terrors for me. I give as a specimen a letter written to me from St Chad's, Birmingham, in the year 1846, from my old crony, Jack Morris: –

MY DEAR PATTISON – I hope you will excuse my earnestly pressing upon you the duty of facing your grounds for remaining a Protestant, and of going by the greater probability as to which is the Church. You seemed to me to be getting quite towards scepticism last time I had a talk with you, and that is one reason why I urge you not to delay. Depend upon it that you cannot expect more than probability out of the Catholic Church, and that you really ought to act on that, whether you feel inclined to do so or not.

People say that converts are 'cocky,' but that impression arises in part from the fact that they who have it have no more than doubtful evidence for what Catholics have certain proof. This is not a conviction arising from my own case, but from all I see and hear around me. It would be 'cocky' in me to say so, but I don't care what it is, so as I may urge you not to be slow about the 'unum necessarium' of caring for your own soul.

I hope Faber's pamphlet will come out, and push on you that stay in darkness, which I am sure you hate as much as I do. I was too long by a good deal. – Ever yours truly,

J. B. MORRIS

I have hitherto abstained from mentioning one of the most important factors in my general education from a very early date, which then grew into an influence driving me into my frantic Puseyism, and which, at the date I am now at, was a powerful weight in the scale of going over to Rome.

I had a female cousin, three years older than myself, living with her mother, a widow, in great seclusion in the country not many miles from Hauxwell.[61] This girl early developed a masculine understanding. It was as dominant and urgent an element in her constitution as I have described William Kay's. But she possessed what was wanting in Kay – a speculative activity which urged her, would she or would she not, through all the abysses of philosophic thought. Her perseverance in learning equalled her powers; after the governess age, in which she learnt French, the globes, etc., she began to educate herself. She taught herself Latin, Greek (which seems incredible), Italian, German, mathematics – not, I suppose, very far. She had a command over the range of history, ancient and modern, that I have never known in any one since; and her memory was such that if you called upon her suddenly for aid about some out-of-the-way person, lived he under Charlemagne or was he a member of the Johnsonian circle, it was strange if she could not tell you something. I have known some of the wittiest, the ablest, and the best read men of my time, but I do not exaggerate when I say that this woman at about thirty-five was a match in power and extent of knowledge for any of them. Of course one great field of learning, i.e. the classical lore which an Oxford scholar possesses, she did not possess; but this only because she did not choose to follow it up and become a Madame Dacier.[62] She was wisely content with using Latin and Greek as instruments for making her acquainted with the body, soul, and spirit of ancient literature. This she knew as literature – I can vouch for it – in the year 1847, more extensively than I did.

I may as well say at once that there never was between us any sentiment of a more tender kind than that of companionship, or any approach thereto, though inobservant relations, who could not explain our fondness for each other's company otherwise, may have fancied that there was. We corresponded upon books, upon everything we thought or read, from as early a period as I remember, she taking the lead and I following. As long as I lived at Hauxwell I was constantly riding over to Enderby to pass two or three days. During my undergraduate time at Oriel I dropt fearfully behind her, so that the interval between us had become very wide indeed. After 1836, and during the two or three profitable years which followed it, I, with greater advantages of books and external stimulus, made up some leeway, and we were beginning to resume our philosophical speculations together when the rising tide of Puseyism carried us both off – me first, and her through me; for up to 1836 we had both been Liberal. And as whatever she was she was it passionately, she was, I think, before taking up with Tractarianism, an extreme Liberal * * * When her Tractarianism grew to white heat it took the shape, not of a devotion to the tenets promulgated in the Tracts, but of exaggerated antipathy to everything that savoured of Anglicanism. Her mother, a good and sensible woman, became alarmed, and thought to stop the mischief by removing from Yorkshire to some place where Anglican privileges could be enjoyed in their plenitude. No place could surely surpass Hursley in this respect; and to Hursley they went. But it was too late. The daughter had got the Roman fever in her veins; everything about the services at Hursley was contemptible, disgusting, odious, and Keble himself, so far from being a saint, was discovered to be an addleheaded old hypocrite. Of course there was nothing for it after this; my cousin was received into the Church of Rome, and compelled her mother, who lived but for her daughter, to go in with her. I think, but am not sure, that their perversion preceded that of Newman some time in 1845. I think they settled first at Bath, but they soon removed to Paris, where the ministrations of the Church could be had more completely.

I suppose I had persuaded myself so far, out of antagonism, as to profess to believe that our Church was no branch of the Catholic Church, but I had never gone the length of exasperation against everything belonging to it which my cousin ran. Still there is no doubt that the parting with one with whom I had been for so many years in close friendship gave me an additional shake, and was something to be got over. Not that our friendship was at all interrupted. As long as they continued to live in Paris I went over to visit them twice a year, or oftener, and was always most affectionately received by my aunt. But all intellectual intercourse between myself and cousin was at an end. Her conversation had come to be a passionate invective in monologue against Protestantism, Anglicanism, and everything except what was Roman. They lived about a great deal in Italy, etc., afterwards, and had every opportunity of seeing the seamy side of practical Catholicism; but my cousin saw it not * * * Can such a wreck of a noble intellect by religious fanaticism be paralleled?

CHAPTER 7

THE YEAR 1847 was the zero of my moral and physical depression, partly from injudicious fasting, partly from the moral causes above enumerated.[1] I began to be troubled with palpitation of the heart and sleepless nights. I was in Paris in June with my aunt and cousin, and after my return I tried in September the air of Wales, but I had to come back to London to take the advice of Dr Williams, or Dr Latham, I forget which; he sent me to Brighton for a month. I had just a month before term began, and was obliged to go back to college to take up my work in an extremely languid state. All through Michaelmas term 1847 I dragged on in feeble and complaining discomfort. For the proctorial year 1847 I had acted as pro-proctor to Green, the other pro being Kay; and in the spring of 1848 Green did me the essential service of nominating me examiner in the School of Lit. Hum. It was wonderful that he ventured to do so; a public examiner in those days was a much more important person than he now is, there being then only four of them, whereas now there are ten or twelve times as many. A proctor was quite free to nominate any friend of his own, as far as the statute went. But he was really subject to a very stringent public opinion – to select only a person who had sufficient scholastic distinction to command the respect of the tutors and their pupils. I certainly at that time could show no such claims. Entangled as I had been by my church connections, and still hardly cool from the Tractarian frenzy, I was only known, so far as I was known at all in the University, as a violent partisan and controversialist. And at that time, if you were able to describe a man as a Puseyite, he became, *ipso facto*, unfit for any public appointment. The little that could be set on the other side were my articles in the *Christian Remembrancer*, read but by few. Those articles, too, were literary, and no proof of classical acquirements, and my industry as tutor within my own college was hardly as yet distinguishable from what was done by the other tutors. As for my wretched second class, and that more than ten years before, it must have reckoned, if anything, against me, when there were so many first class men about, all longing for the appointment. In spite of everything, Green ventured to put me in. Of course whatever was said was kept from me; but from various indications I gathered that there was a good deal of disapprobation felt among the tutors of the best colleges. I did not mix in the strictly tutorial circles, from which examiners had to be taken, but I looked up with humble reverence to all first class men as necessarily my superiors. My first essay was in May 1848, when I found myself the colleague of three first class men – Muckleston,[2] tutor of Worcester; Bode, former censor of Christ Church;[3] and Landon, who had formerly carried a scholarship at Worcester against me, and was now Fellow of Magdalen. Oh, my terrors and qualms and timidities! I felt I was on my trial; the other three were taken for granted, but I was the weak place in the board. This was my first chance of showing if I had any good stuff in me, i.e. for what they call university work, and I knew if I failed it would be my last; nobody would ever give me another appointment. I dreaded also the discredit I might bring upon my good patron, Green.

I must say I was amazed myself at the discovery I made with what a slender outfit of knowledge all the other three men set about, light-heartedly and easily, going through their routine duty. Muckleston was a fair Latin scholar, and knew his books, as the slang went, *memoriter*, that is the six or seven books in which he gave lectures in college, but knew nothing of any classics outside this cycle. Bode was also a good general Latin scholar, according to the measure of those days, and knew one book – namely, Horace's *Odes*. Landon, who, I think, came up from a parish in the country, had neglected his books, and, I ventured to think, was hardly at par in what we then called Greek scholarship. Before the examination was over the tables were certainly turned completely round; my Greek scholarship was, I should say, distinctly feeble, but it was quite as good or better than that of any of the other three. Of Latin I had made a special study and was become by this time a good judge of Latin composition. My 'books' I knew as well as Muckleston, with this difference, that what he knew mechanically and memorially I understood in its formation and its relations. And as far as the strictly philosophical portion of the work went (there was then no division of labour) I soon found that I had it all my own way. The others – I don't know if any of them are living now – were very generous, and admitted me at once on a comfortable footing with them. My triumph was complete, and all adverse tongues were silenced for good by the handsome report which my colleagues made of me. The real discovery which I had made was not so much that my classical acquirements were worth something. If I did not know it then, I soon came to know how childish and elementary they were; what I had discovered was how slender was the outfit of those men whose names carried scholastic weight in the University.

My ambition was fairly roused by this incident of the examinership. I began to see that I might aspire to something in the University as well as others, but I did not relax my industry. My commonplace book of this year (1848) astonishes myself by the vast range and variety of general information its pages exhibit. How I found time, with the work of the college and the schools, to look into so many books, and select so much solid matter from them, I cannot tell. For I remember what the commonplace book takes no notice of, that I was making strenuous efforts to acquire a profound and philosophic hold upon Aristotle, having become aware that my knowledge hitherto was unreal and merely textual.

A partial explanation of the work I got through is that I was in much better health in 1848 and 1849 than I had been for several years past; this was in some degree attributable to my having taken to riding. I bought a horse by an agent in Yorkshire, and had him brought up by an old Yorkshire groom of ours. The fellow was highly delighted to find himself in Oxford, of which he had heard so much, and in half an hour after his arrival he was dead drunk, and remained in that condition till his departure early next morning. All this winter I rode regularly, and often went to look at the hounds.

I have spoken of the sudden lull which fell upon Oxford, and, indeed, upon all clerical circles throughout England, the moment the secessions to Rome were announced. The sensation to us was as of a sudden end of all things, and without a new beginning. We felt that old things had passed away, but by no means that all things had become new. Common conversation seemed to have collapsed, to have died out for want of topic. The railway mania of 1847 and King Hudson was the first material that rushed in to fill up the vacuum.[4] G. V. Cox says, 'Instead of High, Low, and Broad Church, they talked of high embankments, the broad gauge, and low dividends. Brunel and Stephenson were in men's mouths instead of Dr Pusey or Mr Golightly;[5] and speculative theology gave way to speculation in railway shares' (*Recollections*, p. 238). Then came the railway crash, a new and still greater interest, as many fellows of colleges lost their savings in it. Finally, in 1848, the universal outburst of revolution in every part of the continent. It seemed incredible, in the presence of such an upheaval, that we had been spending years in debating any matter so flimsy as whether England was in a state of schism or no.

This was the view which Newman's conversion presented at the time to a man who saw all things only from their outside. The truth is that this moment, which swept the leader of the Tractarians, with most of his followers, out of the place, was an epoch in the history of the University. It was a deliverance from the nightmare which had oppressed Oxford for fifteen years. For so long we had been given over to discussions unprofitable in themselves, and which had entirely diverted our thoughts from the true business of the place. Probably there was no period of our history during which, I do not say science and learning, but the ordinary study of the classics was so profitless or at so low an ebb as during the period of the Tractarian controversy. By the secessions of 1845 this was extinguished in a moment, and from that moment dates the regeneration of the University. Our thoughts reverted to their proper channel, that of the work we had to do. As soon as we set about doing it in earnest we became aware how incompetent we were for it, and how narrow and inadequate was the character of the instruction with which we had been hitherto satisfied. We were startled when we came to reflect that the vast domain of physical science had been hitherto wholly excluded from our programme. The great discoveries of the last half century in chemistry, physiology, etc., were not even known by report to any of us. Science was placed under a ban by the theologians, who instinctively felt that it was fatal to their speculations. Newman had laid it down that revealed truth was absolute, while all other truth was relative – a proposition which will not stand analysis, but which sufficiently conveys the feeling of the theologians towards science. More than this, the abject deference fostered by theological discussion for authority, whether of the Fathers, or the Church, or the Primitive Ages, was incompatible with the free play of intellect which enlarges knowledge, creates science, and makes progress possible. In a word, the period of Tractarianism had been a period of obscurantism, which had cut us off from the general movement; an eclipse which had shut out the light of the sun in heaven. Whereas other reactions accomplished themselves by imperceptible degrees, in 1845 the darkness was dissipated, and the light was let in in an instant, as by the opening of the shutters in the chamber of a sick man who has slept till mid-day. Hence the flood of reform, which broke over Oxford in the next few years following 1845, which did not spend itself till it had produced two Government commissions,[6] until we had ourselves enlarged and remodelled all our institutions. In these years every Oxford man was a Liberal, even those whom nature had palpably destined for obstructives. There still survive many of this generation, who, having been caught up by the spirit of their day, and having then committed themselves to the Liberal colours too definitely to withdraw, are uncomfortable in their position, and present the laughable spectacle of remaining Liberal in spite of nature and constitution.

In any case a Liberal reaction must have come. But had it come by the ordinary slow steps it would not have done its work so thoroughly as it did. The clerical virus would have lingered in the system, and interfered with the complete recovery of the patient. Purged off and got rid of as it was, all at once the new generation had a clear field, entered, as it were, upon a new phase of life. It were no wonder if, in the first rush of intellectual freedom, we were carried beyond all bounds, sought to change everything, questioned everything, and were impatient to throw the whole cargo of tradition overboard. It is not to be denied that the reforming movement was pushed into extravagance in more than one direction. In the much needed reform of our studies the love of examination has been carried to a mischievous extreme, from which we are now suffering. The sudden withdrawal of all reverence for the past has generated a type of intellect which is not only offensive to taste but is unsound as training. The young Oxford, which our present system tends to turn out, is a mental form which cannot be regarded with complacency by any one who judges an education, not by its programme, but by its *élèves*. Our young men are not trained; they are only filled with propositions, of which they have never learned the inductive basis. From showy lectures, from manuals, from attractive periodicals, the youth is put in possession of ready-made opinions on every conceivable subject; a crude mass of matter, which he is taught to regard as real knowledge. Swollen with this puffy and unwholesome diet, he goes forth into the world regarding himself, like the infant in the nursery, as the centre of all things, the measure of the universe. He thinks he can evince his superiority by freely distributing sneers and scoffs upon all that does not agree with the set of opinions which he happens to have adopted from imitation, from fashion, or from chance. Having no root in itself, such a type of character is liable to become an easy prey to any popular charlatanism or current fanaticism.[7]

There is a letter of Kant, written in 1790, in which he answers a correspondent who had consulted him as to the means of checking the *Schwärmerei*,[8] which seemed to be over-running Germany like an infectious complaint. 'This mental disease,' replies Kant, 'arises from the growth in the nation of a class which has not thorough science, and yet is not totally ignorant. It has caught up notions on current literature, which make it think itself on the same level of knowledge with those who have laboriously studied the sciences. I see,' he says, 'no other means of checking the mischief than that the schools should reform their method, and restore thorough teaching instead of that teaching of many things which has usurped its place. I would not have the desire of reading extinguished, but directed to a purpose' (Kant, *Werke*, v. vi. p. 72, ed. 1867).

Our *élève* resembles that gamin of Paris of whom Renan says, 'Écarté par une plaisanterie des croyances dont la raison d'un Pascal ne réussit pas à se dégager',[9] and which it took Renan himself six years of laborious study to work his way out of.

It is therefore quite in the order of nature that after thirty years of freedom we are now (1884) threatened with a clerical reaction in the domain of fact, and with a philosophical reaction in the region of thought. The feeble fabric of opinion in young Oxford, run up without labour and held without conviction, must give way before the steady pressure of the vast ecclesiastical organisation, which, after having spread itself over the face of England, is now laying siege to our University as the stronghold of freedom of thought and disengagement from the fetters of traditional dogma. The assault from without is aided by the reappearance within of an *a priori* philosophy, which, under various disguises, aims at exempting Man from the order of nature, and erecting him into a unique being whose organism is not to be subject to the uniform laws which govern all other Being that is known to us.

A reactionary wave, such as now seems imminent, may not improbably have a salutary effect upon our University. As a chastisement for the egoism and the ignorant adoption of fashionable freethinking, which now characterises young Oxford, it may do good service if it merely restore to us the lost virtues of humility, reverence, and recognition of a power beyond ourselves. The galvanised Kantism, which seems to be coming into esteem, will lead to a re-examination of the old problem of thought, and thus a reasoned conviction may arise to take the place of a lazy and thoughtless acquiescence in the opinions of the fashionable periodicals. Whenever such an examination takes place the history of philosophy from A.D. 1400 shows us unmistakably what the result must be. Science, periodically baffled and checked by Catholic reaction or the interferences of Government, has ever reasserted itself.

If any Oxford man had gone to sleep in 1846 and had woke up again in 1850 he would have found himself in a totally new world. In 1846 we were in Old Tory Oxford; not somnolent because it was as fiercely debating, as in the days of Henry IV, its eternal Church question. There were Tory majorities in all the colleges; there was the unquestioning satisfaction in the tutorial system, i.e. one man teaching everybody everything; the same belief that all knowledge was shut up between the covers of four Greek and four Latin books; the same humdrum questions asked in the examination; and the same arts of evasive reply. In 1850 all this was suddenly changed as if by the wand of a magician. The dead majorities of head and seniors, which had sat like lead upon the energies of young tutors, had melted away. Theology was totally banished from Common Room, and even from private conversation. Very free opinions on all subjects were rife; there was a prevailing dissatisfaction with our boasted tutorial system. A restless fever of change had spread through the colleges – the wonder-working phrase, University reform, had been uttered, and that in the House of Commons. The sounds seemed to breathe new life into us. We against reform! Why, it was the very thing we had been so long sighing for; we were ready to reform a great deal – everything – only show us how to set about it and give us the necessary powers.

Among the shipwrecks of this yeasty time one of the most memorable was that of Professor Conington. I pause upon this because the dexterous friendship of his biographer has, without misrepresenting the facts, contrived to conceal from his readers the true history. John Conington was at this date not only the most distinguished scholar whom the University had turned out, but was, much more than a scholar, a man whose words and opinions came with weight as from a full and powerful mind. Perhaps verbal memory at all times existed in him in disproportion to other mental faculties, and he never shared that tendency to the exercise of the speculative intellect which was at that time so pronounced in Oxford. He had, however, very decided opinions upon the questions then agitated, and, up to the year 1854, belonged to the small section of advanced Liberals. So prominent a place did he fill in this left wing of the reforming party, that I remember Arthur Haddan,[10] who was one of the best representatives of the enlightened Tory and Anglican section, saying to me 'If we were only rid of Halford Vaughan, Goldwin Smith, and Conington, the University would go on very well.' Conington's partisanship was more political than theological, and more academical than either. His antipathies were most strong in regard to the reigning authorities and the occupants of the higher posts in the University. He would declaim with great bitterness against the Professor of Greek, as not doing what he considered professorial work. One of his earliest appearances in print, was a review of William Sewell's translation of Vergil's *Georgics*, in the *Ed. Rev.*, the bitterness of which was out of all proportion to the demerits of the book. Sewell's version had obvious faults, but it was evident on the face of the review, that there was a motive of antipathy behind. Conington seized an opportunity of venting his spleen against one who was at the time (1846) one of the men of highest worth in the University, and also belonged to the opposite camp. The Nemesis which awaited this transgression was that in after years Conington himself translated Vergil, and with far less success than his victim. The editors of Conington's *Remains* prudently omitted this review when they collected Conington's papers in two volumes in 1872. His temper was naturally very irritable, and his eagerness for University reform was mixed with much personal animosity from this cause. Of his irritability on small occasions I myself became aware accidentally. It was at a very early period of his career, and before our acquaintance began, at a time when he did not even know me by sight. It was in the year 1847 at the Encaenia[11] when I as pro-proctor had to keep one of the doors of the theatre. Conington had the Latin prize poem for the year, and came up with his prompter to make his way to the rostrum or pulpit from which it was to be recited. His chaperon asked me for the Latin rostrum; I was perhaps not very *au fait* at my new duties, and may have hesitated as to pointing out the right entrance, on which Conington turned to me, and with a face distorted by passion, and a voice trembling with rage, thundered out 'the Latin Rostrum'. This irritability grew upon him and constituted a large part of his reforming *animus*. Combined with a large share of vanity, growing out of his sense of his high accomplishments as a scholar, it became in time a personal discontent at not getting a professor's chair. His sarcasms against the Greek professor, and his complaints that Latin scholarship was not represented at all in the University, too obviously meant that he himself was wronged in not being appointed to a Latin or Greek chair. He thought himself equally qualified for either.

In 1854 the Corpus Latin professorship was founded, and to the great joy of Conington's friends he was chosen by the electors to fill it. Latin was being neglected among us, and we anticipated great things from the general vigour and high reputation of the new professor. His principal performance, so far, had been in Greek – an edition of the *Agamemnon* full of originality and promise for the future. I might have remembered the instances, not many but still some, e.g. Ruhnken, who were equally eminent in the two languages, and never doubted that the power Conington possessed could be given in new directions.

When we came back after the Long Vacation of 1854 we became aware that something had happened. It gradually oozed out that Conington had been 'converted', and not by the seduction of piety, but by the terrors of hell. He attended chapel assiduously, refused to read anything but religious books on Sunday, or to dine out or visit on that day. He took an opportunity of giving publicity to his revulsion of sentiment by going to vote against opening the Union on Sunday, while all other M.A.'s thought it wiser to leave the point to be settled by the public opinion of the undergraduates. But it soon appeared that the change in Conington extended farther than to theological view. He began to broach Conservative sentiments, as well in politics as in University affairs, and very soon ranged himself with the followers of Dr Pusey, who at that period commanded a majority in congregation. During this period such was the tyranny of the High Church party that church views were made the test of eligibility to all office or place. Every one was excluded who did not belong to the party; they would not allow me even to be a curator of the Bodleian. Conington championed their acts, and spoke for them in congregation. Everything in him was changed but his temper. He was more irritable than ever. He could not endure the smallest opposition to his new opinions, and could not control the expression of his irritation even in public debate. This provoked irritation on the other and weaker side. I never remember any single academic of my time against whom there existed such a bitter feeling, as was felt towards Conington by the Liberals at that date. From this time forward Professor Conington never roused himself to any intellectual exertion worthy of him. He revised undergraduates' Latin verses; he wrote one or two articles in reviews on liturgical subjects, and perhaps a short paper or two in his own proper person in the *Journal of Philology*.† Otherwise he abandoned himself to the laziest of all occupation with the classics that, namely, of translating them into English; he translated Horace, I daresay no worse and no better than the scores who have translated it before him; he translated Vergil, I think, more than once through, and it is remarkable that he who, as a young critic, found no expressions sufficiently

---

† He also edited, with notes, *Vergil* and *Persius*. – ED.

depreciatory for William Sewell's *Georgics*, produced, on the whole, a translation of much less merit. Yet all this while Latin philology on the continent was rapidly growing to those vast dimensions which we see it to have now attained; a growth with which our Latin Professor made no attempt to keep pace. But, though Conington had sunk from the high promise of his youth into an ordinary theological partisan when, on our return from the Long Vacation of 1869 it was announced that he was dying, not one of us but felt a shock, and what a luminary of the University was suddenly extinguished! – An insignificant ailment, a pimple on the lip, was fatal to him.

Ὄσσιχόν ἐστι τὸ τύμμα καὶ ἁλίκον ἄνδρα δαμάσδει.[12]

THEOCR. iv. 55

One MS. Professor Conington left behind him which would have been of surpassing interest even beyond the circle of those who had known him. This was a daily journal to which he committed without restraint the whole current of his thoughts and feelings; the executors in the discharge of their duty considered themselves called upon to destroy it. The loss of this document to University history, and as a genuine psychological study of a remarkable mind, can hardly be overrated.

In my own college the transformation worked in 1850 was probably more thorough than in any other. Two of the old Fellows, Thompson and Meredith, had gone off on college livings, Michell was removed to the Vice-Principalship of Magdalen Hall, William Kay *junior* had gone out to Bishop's College, Calcutta. I was therefore senior tutor, with two juniors assisting me, both docile and amenable men. The old Rector retired into his study or lived out at Coombe,[13] and left the college entirely to me. For about three years I was much more absolute master in Lincoln than I ever was after I became Head. In 1850 Lincoln could have been cited, and was so, as one of the best managed colleges in the University. It must not be supposed because I was a Tractarian that I was ever a Tory at any time. I used to *afficher* Tory principles as a part of the lot. But I never could bring myself to sympathise with Charles the Martyr, or do other than wish success to William III. I have said that I sympathised with Hampden in 1836; in 1846, when Paterson carried round for signature an address to the Bishops deploring the nomination of Hampden to the see of Hereford, I obstinately refused to sign; my example was followed by the rest, and I triumphed in knowing that Lincoln had been drawn blank. Whether or no I might at times have hoisted Tory colours, in vote or conversation, there never was any one to whom it was more impossible not to be a Liberal than it was to me. I had from youth up a restless desire to be always improving myself, other people, all things, all received ways of doing anything. This was a mental instinct which lay far below any adopted opinions in politics, and has been a cause of no little trouble to me. It is impossible for me to see anything done without an immediate suggestion of how it might be better done. I cannot travel by railway without working out in my mind a better time-table than that in use. On the other hand, this restlessness of the critical faculty has done me good service when turned upon myself. I have never enjoyed any self-satisfaction in anything I have ever done, for I have inevitably made a mental comparison with how it might have been better done. The motto of one of my diaries, 'Quicquid hic operis fiat pœnitet',[14] may be said to be the motto of my life. The same is true of anything I may have written. I write, rewrite, revise, and then with difficulty let it go to press, seeing how much better another review would make it.

So in 1850–51 the University was alive with projects of reform. In August 1850 the promised Commission was actually issued; it was a Royal Commission of Enquiry. Jeune[15] and Liddell and Tait[16] were on it; A. P. Stanley was its secretary. It was embraced with enthusiasm by the younger section of us, and received with sulky terror and bitter mortification by the Tories, who banded together for one last desperate stand. At Trinity, e.g., there still remained a body of seniors, who, having outlived many generations of juniors, had still been able to keep the then set of juniors at bay. The Heads of Houses, who knew their authority threatened, took the trouble to take counsel's opinion as to the legality of the Commission, and of course got the decision they wished. They got by it a *quasi* sanction for withholding documents, and for other mutinous conduct, which was only vexatious, as the Commission had no difficulty in obtaining in other ways all the information they required.

We, on our part, were roused into a new activity, of which there had hitherto been, in my experience, no example in Oxford. Every tutor had his scheme; we went about comparing them; discussing them point by point; endeavouring to mature our views, which were, for the most part, crude enough. Jeune, one of the Commissioners, confessed to Lake[17] that his mind was still quite a chaos on the subject.

For my part, I was familiar with Sir William Hamilton's articles on Oxford;[18] but they had not opened my eyes, as they might naturally have done, to the true function of a university. I still wore the college blinkers. I was so proud of the success which had attended my own exertions as tutor that I could not as yet see beyond that narrow point of view. My imagination was wholly preoccupied with the beneficial relation which the college system establishes between tutor and pupil. We had this, and I could not bring myself to contemplate its being broken up. As usual with me at that time of my life, I could only see one side of a question, but saw that in intense vision. I spent much pains and time in drawing up my evidence. I made very many radical proposals; among other things I urged the abolition of residence within college walls as a condition of keeping term. This was an innovation which was at that time pronounced by the most competent authorities to be subversive of morality, but which has since become a part of the University system without evil consequences of any kind. I could not help turning aside to twit the Hebdomadal Council with their unwisdom in keeping the G. W. R. out at Didcot,[19] an arrangement which added ten miles to our distance from London, without being the smallest hindrance to what they professed to have feared – viz. undergraduates running up to London for the day.

But the weight of my evidence centred in an elaborate vindication of the tutorial as opposed to the professorial system. I charged in this direction with all the force of which I was capable. The case I made for the college system is as good a case as I have ever seen in print, and a much better one than Pusey's long rambling invective against professors printed in another volume (*Report and Evidence on the Recommendations of the Oxford Univ. Comm.*). Now as the superiority of the professorial to the tutorial system was a prime article of the Liberal creed, and as every other young reformer, whose evidence was included in the volume, had something to say in favour of professors, my evidence acquired a peculiar importance and notoriety, as being the solitary defence of the *status quo* coming from the Liberal side.

In after years I became one of the most strenuous advocates for the endowment of professors. It was easy to suppose that I had simply changed my mind and gone round to the other side, because it was the popular Liberal creed. Like other things in which change has been imputed to me, this was not an instance of shifting of opinion, but of development. I have never ceased to prize as highly as I did at that time the personal influence of mind upon mind, – the mind of the fully instructed upon the young mind it seeks to form. But I gradually came to see that it was impossible to base a whole academical system upon this single means of influence. Teachers, it was plain, must know something of what they profess to teach; and my own limited experience had shown me that a tutor could thoroughly master only a single branch of classical learning even; and then there was the whole field of knowledge outside classics to be furnished with teachers who could only be professors of the University. It was only very slowly, and after long study of universities, both in theory and in history, that I gradually rose to the full conception which I drew out in my *Academical Organisation* in 1868.[20] It required many experiences both at home and abroad, and years of reading and reflection, before I arrived at the results exhibited in that book. When that volume was published its recommendations seemed so startling and paradoxical that very few dared to declare themselves in their favour. Within less than twenty years the colleges and the University have been arranged by a Commission in conformity with the spirit, if not the letter, of my proposals.

I have spoken of the pride with which I was able to look on the internal condition, tone, and discipline of the college. This was so at those times when I could take a general retrospect; but the Diary of these years (1850–51) shows by what efforts, through what vexations and defeats, this general result was attained. The Diary at this time has entirely ceased to be a diary of studies – there was no study but desultory reading – and has become one of college management, showing how my thoughts were engrossed by administration. Entries of the following kind occur constantly: –

25th January 1851. – Never felt more heavy and reluctant to work; no satisfaction in contemplating the term or the Lecture list; all my zest for any mental exertion gone.

12th May 1851. – Sadly heavy work last week setting the engine in motion; seemed as if I had forgotten everything.

14th June 1851. – Very great dissatisfaction with lectures and college work altogether.

But these fits of depression only marked the ups and downs of the struggle; they are indeed often only indications of physical and mental exhaustion. I was attempting much more than I had strength for. One term I had four successive hours' lecturing every day; one of these classes was in the *Ethics*. In this class I was not living on my old provision, but was reducing Aristotle's doctrines, which used to be delivered to us as mere formulae, into the substance of real truths, which could be assimilated with such ideas on morals and psychology as the student could be supposed to possess. I believe that my mode of teaching the *Ethics* was at that time quite unknown in Oxford. This lecture, simple as it became to me in later time, cost me vast efforts to inaugurate in these years in which I was inventing it.

I had also established a custom of addressing the students assembled in chapel twice in each term. I say *addressing*, because I tried to make what I had to say as unlike a sermon as possible. I had no text or formalities, but stood up after prayers in my place and went straight to the two or three pieces of advice I wished to give. But these addresses were not extempore, and the preparing them, both as to style and thought, cost me as much labour as anything I ever did. One of the students being accidentally drowned,[21] I endeavoured to enforce the solemn reflections which such an event in a college gives rise to, and I remember I had to sit up the whole night to be ready with it.

Nor did I spare myself in vacation. I adopted a plan of taking four favourite pupils, one year to Bowness, and another set the next year to Inverary, for a month each time. I thought the living together might enable me to make more impression upon them than mere college relations allowed of. I did not coach them in their books, but tried to get them interested in poetry and litera-

ture, having found that even our best were very narrow and
schoolboy-like in their reading. In this respect the plan did not
answer my expectation; but I can never regret an experiment
which left me as its residuum two of the most valued friendships I
have enjoyed since – that of R. C. Christie and William
Stebbing.[22]

All this exhausting effort carried with it one consequence
which was soon to tell with disastrous effect on my rising fortunes. It was impossible to do what I was trying to do and yet live
the life of easy sociability to which tutors of colleges were then
accustomed, and which had been traditional in Lincoln. The
college dinner hour was five, and at eight I began work again, and
inspected men singly from eight to ten. This withdrawal from the
common-room, notwithstanding that its reason was well known,
gave offence.[23] It was not so difficult when we were alone, but
when, as usually happened, there were guests dining you had the
appearance of breaking up the party, and were obliged peremp-
torily to decline a hand at whist. It also made it impossible to
accept invitations to dinner out of college, as you could not leave a
C. R., where you were being entertained, at eight. I have no
doubt, too, that the lassitude and depletion of spirits, occasioned
by overwork and absorption in my occupation, made me a less
congenial companion than I might have been. I incurred much
unpopularity in consequence, and was gradually set down as
unsociable, ungenial, and morose. I had little notion how dear my
devotion to the work of tuition was soon to cost me.

This not having time to mix with other men in the practical life
of the place carried with it other disadvantages. I have said that
when I was younger I was always blundering into some
étourderie[24] from want of the average amount of usage du monde. I
was now thirty-eight, and much as I had advanced in knowledge,
I had not equally advanced in knowing how to deal with men –
men my equals, I mean, for the treatment of young men was then
my speciality. But I was deficient in the ordinary tact which every
man of the world has acquired long before he arrives at thirty-
eight. I was conscious of this defect, and conscious also that in the
life I was leading it was impossible for me to get over it. On one
occasion I gave a signal instance of this want of discretion and
ready wit. There had grown up a kind of standing feud between

Michell and myself. The Fellowship which Michell vacated by marriage was confined by the statute to the diocese of Wells. When it had to be filled up, his brother, Rowland Michell, presented himself as a candidate. Rowland was a wooden dunce, a reproduction of all his brother's Tory prejudices without his abilities. I supported another candidate, viz., G. G. Perry,[25] against Rowland Michell, and Perry was elected. This Michell never forgave.

But there were other causes of Michell's strongly pronounced antipathy to me. When he gave up the tutorship, on being promoted to Magdalen Hall, he naturally expected that the college of which he had been so long the mainstay would collapse. So far from this being the case, he had to see it every year rising both in reputation and numbers in the hands of junior men, whose politics and principles were the antipodes of his own. Michell was now in the mortifying position which is sometimes called a disappointed man, i.e. he had lingered on till late in life without attaining any preferment to which his academical reputation might have justly entitled him. He had tried for many things and not got them; and found himself shelved as Vice-Principal of Magdalen Hall, and could not but see that the sun of his reputation was gradually sinking. All this was certainly very hard to be borne – would have been so in any walk of life; but when it is considered what a University is – how rife with personal jealousies and emulations – and what hotbeds of party cabal common-rooms are, it will be understood how intense the feelings of envy, hatred, malice, and all uncharitableness can become. Nor could he conceal his animosity; he never lost an opportunity, private or public, of running me down. It was, I think, at the Gaudy[26] of 1850 that in an after-dinner speech – Michell excelled in after-dinner oratory – he thought proper to insult me so grossly that it was impossible for me to let pass what was said in the face of the assembled college. In what he said he had laid himself so open to retort that a dexterous nimble-witted man would have laid him on his back with ease, and carried the company with him. I was not such a man; and being naturally in a state of boiling indignation, I went at the enemy in a blind fury, hardly knowing what I was saying, and of course placed all the company on the side of the assailant. Five minutes afterwards I was bitterly repenting the folly of my tongue; but I little thought at the time what use was to be afterwards made of it against me.

There were other minor slips of conduct, all of which were carefully hoarded by Michell against the time that he might want them. But, as if I was determined to be my own worst enemy, I committed about this time another blunder which had very serious consequences for me. The old statutes of Rotherham, by which we were then governed, enacted that every Fellow, when he should have completed eight years from the conclusion of his necessary regency,[27] should proceed to the degree of B.D.; and further, that after six years from the B.D. he should take the D.D. The penalty for neglect of this regulation was the *ipso facto* forfeiture of the Fellowship. A majority of the society had the power, if they saw fit, of dispensing the Fellow from proceeding to the higher degree, but the same power of dispensation was not allowed in the case of the B.D. Being quite ignorant what was meant by 'completing his necessary regency', I had applied to Dr Bliss for an explanation.[28] Dr Bliss, the Registrar, was 'so exact and methodical in the arrangement of his papers, so full of information, as well as so ready to give it, that other persons had become careless of acquiring a knowledge of University matters, being quite sure of getting from him full and prompt information. Ask Dr Bliss, was the answer to all inquiries; he knows' (Cox's *Recollections*, p. 344). All this was strictly true; yet oddly enough, on two occasions where I was personally concerned, Dr Bliss made mistakes. The first of these was one of the two years in which I wrote for the Latin essay. I sent in my composition conformably to the regulations, placing my name in a sealed envelope, on which my motto was inscribed, and inscribing the same motto on the cover which contained the essay. The Registrar, when he came to sort the compositions, tore off my cover and threw it away without looking at it, and then noted on the outside of the essay, 'This essay was sent in without motto or sealed envelope.' That was mistake No. 1, but I don't suppose I should have got the essay had it not occurred.

The second occasion on which he misled me was more serious. In answer to my question, 'When did I complete my necessary regency?' he furnished me with a memorandum of the date in his own handwriting on one of his well-known slips of paper. I put the memorandum carefully up in my pocket-book and relied upon it in blind confidence. He had dated the completion of the regency, and consequently the time at which I was due for my B.D. degree, a whole year too late. I well remember the time and manner in which the awful discovery burst upon me that I had *ipso facto* ceased to be Fellow of Lincoln. The old Rector, who, as a rule, never came near me, came in a white rage to my rooms, and informed me bluntly that I was no more Fellow of the college than the porter. One would have thought that he would have had compassion upon my condition, slaving away as I was day and night for the college and never thinking of myself, and would have tried to find some method of helping me out of the scrape. Far from this, he treated me as a malefactor, who had broken the fundamental laws of the college, and so placed myself outside the pale of humanity. It was now in the power of the Fellows to have turned me out of college, by which each of my juniors would have gained a step. Such harshness occurred to none of them. They did the best they could for me; a college meeting was held, at which *pro forma* my Fellowship was declared to be *ipso facto* vacant; at the same time a unanimous petition, the Rector joining, was sent in to the Visitor, explaining to him that I had acted, not in contempt or fraud, but in error, and humbly praying him to exercise his visitatorial power and restore me to my place. He did so on condition that I should proceed at once to take the degree of B.D. This I did, and the incident was considered by all in college as closed.

But there was a watchful enemy outside, who made a note of the fact, and let it be known that he intended to use it against me if ever an important election should be determined by my vote. For he denied that the Visitor had the power of dispensation in the case of the B.D. degree, or the power of restoring to his Fellowship a Fellow who had forfeited it under an express statute.

I cannot remember that I did anything more just then than calculate the damage to myself; therefore fortune took it in hand, and began to declare against me. On the 16th July 1851 the junior fellow, Richard J. Ogle, died suddenly, or after a very short illness. He had been a pupil of mine, and was the first Lincoln man I had had the satisfaction of placing in a first class. He was a staunch friend, and could be counted on as a true and sure supporter. I felt in his death that I had somehow received a fatal wound.

I have said that ambition, a motive quite unknown to me before, was first roused in 1848. This was so only in a quite vague and general way. In these years 1848–51 my absorption in the college was total, and excluded all other thoughts. When, therefore, in the spring of 1851, Symonds began to say that the Rector (Radford) could not possibly live more than three months I had no other feeling than that of alarm, lest under some new Head I should lose the almost absolute authority I was then wielding, the possession of which I knew was necessary to work the college machine as it was being worked. When, then, one of the junior Fellows, G. G. Perry, first hinted to me that in case of a vacancy the juniors wanted to have me for the Head, I was struck with surprise and amazement. The Heads in those days, as they alone constituted the governing body of the University, were placed on an elevation, from which they have since had to descend. I could hardly believe that such a sudden exaltation could be within my reach. With a manner which I believe suggested conceit, I had really a very low estimate of myself as compared with others. I could echo what Bishop Stanley writes of himself in his journal: 'My greatest obstacle to success in life has been a want of confidence in myself, under a doubt whether I really was possessed of talents on a par with those around me. This painful doubt has of late certainly increased,' – this in his sixty-first year. (Stanley's *Life of Stanley*, p. 89).

Radford's funeral took place on the 29th October. All the Fellows who were in England were present at it. William Kay *junior* and Bousfield were abroad. The 13th of November was fixed for the election, at which there would be nine electors, therefore five votes would be required to elect. The three junior Fellows, Perry, Andrew,[29] Espin,[30] voluntarily and heartily supported me, so with my own I had already four votes. My three supporters were all regular residents, and it was our four votes which had succeeded, in spite of the resistance of the old *régime*, in introducing all the reforms and improvements which had been established in the college and in totally changing its tone. The other five votes were Calcott and Gibbs, the rump of the old Lincoln of the days of degradation; Metcalfe, whom we had taken without knowing enough about him from Cambridge, and who had gradually gravitated towards the old set;[31] finally, Washbourne West, who, though only recently elected, was old in age and attached to the traditions of the bad time.[32] I had strenuously opposed West's election, and had urged his being declared *non habilis* upon the examination. He had therefore, not unnaturally, a grudge against me and an injury to revenge. I may observe here how very little one can judge at the time of electing how a Fellow will turn out. I was keen to get Metcalfe elected * * * I was equally keen to keep out West, the Fellow to whose financial genius the college owes more than to any one since Dr Hutchins.[33]

These four would therefore certainly go against me; and it followed that the determination of the Headship lay entirely in the hands of the ninth Fellow, J. L. R. Kettle.[34] On the evening of the funeral we all dined in C. R. After dinner Kettle called me out, and held in my own room a long and friendly conversation with me. The substance of it was that he, being resolved that none of the 'old set' should come in, being determined not to vote for Kay *senior* or Thompson, saw that William Kay *junior*, Principal of Bishop's College, and myself were the only persons, in his opinion, qualified. He concluded, with a heartiness and frankness not natural to him, and which might have roused my suspicions had I not been so absurdly ignorant of the world, by promising me his vote. Espin happening to come up at the time, he repeated the pledge in his presence. I said, 'Well, Kettle, you know I have four votes already, so you understand that yours gives me the Rectorship.' Upon that we shook hands and parted. From that time my friends in college considered the question settled, but I never told out of college, even to my own family, that I was in actual possession of a majority. Something unforeseen might happen, e.g. Bousfield, with whose views I was unacquainted, might return from abroad within the time. And though I knew I could rely on the other three, I did not somehow feel the same towards Kettle, in whose manner there was something sinister which I could not interpret. My thought, however, did not amount to suspicion. It did not go beyond contemplating the possibility of failures. My caution in not speaking of the promises I had received was owing to doubts as to my own adequacy for the office – doubts which forced themselves the more strongly on me in proportion as I found myself brought near the position, and saw the great opportunity of usefulness it opened.

Kettle's promise was given to me on the 29th October, and from that time till the 7th November I did not suspect that anything was wrong. But I learnt afterwards that immediately after the funeral Michell had gone up to London and had taken Bethell's (Lord Westbury)[35] opinion as to whether he could not be elected himself. As Wells Fellow he was expressly excluded from the Headship by the Statutes, and he knew that he must be displaced on appeal. But he wished to be elected, though with the certainty of being removed, because it 'would do him good in the University.' In order to induce Thompson's friends to vote for Michell it was represented to them that the time consumed in the appeal would allow for Bousfield's return from the continent, who, they assumed, would support Thompson. This scheme was dropped on Bethell's pointing out that if a disqualified person were to be elected by a majority and set aside by appeal, the consequence would be, not a fresh election, but that the person who had the next largest number of votes would be declared Rector by the Visitor. Thus, unable to do anything for himself, the only line remaining to Michell was to keep me out. It might have seemed a hopeless game, with Kettle's promise already passed to me, but Michell's adroit diplomacy was equal to the occasion. He began with attempts to shake Kettle's vote by undermining his opinion of me. Kettle, though opposed to Michell in general politics, being a professed Liberal, yet had always viewed all college matters with Michell's eyes. He not only sapped Kettle directly by suggesting everything he could to my disadvantage, but caused statements to my prejudice to be conveyed to him by other indirect channels. Kettle (letter to me of 9th November) informed me afterwards that the representations were 'many,' and that they were made for the purpose of showing that my election as Rector would not be desirable on my own account or on that of the college. That it would not have been desirable in the interests of the college was so notoriously untrue that that allegation was afterwards withdrawn; and in the final wording of the ground of objection it is laid upon 'the personal feeling which exists' ('I am sure you would have been elected but for the personal feeling which exists' – Kettle, printed Letter, p.

22). I may say on this that there was but one of the Fellows of whom it could be said with any truth that there was a personal feeling against me. This was Metcalfe. With Calcott, Gibbs, and West I was on perfectly good, though not intimate, terms personally. They wished to have a Rector out of the old set, naturally enough, but bore me no ill-will, except so far as West might resent my opposition to his election.

When Kettle intimated that he had been attacked by statements to my disadvantage, and my friends began to fear that Kettle was shaken, they endeavoured to meet them by counter-representations on the points of professed attack. I myself was at first quite unsuspicious, and believed what Kettle wrote, viz. that he was sincerely concerned at what he heard against me. I wrote privately to A. P. Stanley, and asked him to speak to Kettle on my behalf. He replied that he had seen Kettle, but he feared with little effect; his knowledge of the points attacked was so slight that he felt himself 'both unauthorised and incompetent to defend them.' He concluded by saying, 'I have, however, done what I could – I hope not too much.' It would be idle now to repeat or to refute allegations against me of so old a date – allegations which were not made in sincerity or even believed by those who brought them. Kettle, after the election, raked together all he could get of this kind and printed it in a pamphlet designed to cover or excuse his desertion of his friends. I daresay copies of the pamphlet can be consulted by the curious in college libraries. It may be placed by the side of the odious picture of me which * * * once drew in a sermon from the University pulpit;[36] or with * * *'s caricature of me * * * .[37]

At what period Kettle was gained over I am unable to say. He not only relinquished me and my friends, but went over to the support of the old set, for whom he had repeatedly declared he never would vote. They now distinctly put forward as their candidate William Kay *senior*, who dated from very far back times, and had for many years retired upon a Yorkshire living. When Kettle had, on the grounds alleged, changed his opinion of my eligibility, I conceived the least he could have done should have been to have stated to me his objections, to have given me a hearing, and if I was unable to satisfy him, to have then called on me to release him from his pledge, which I must have immediately done. This would have been straightforward conduct. Instead of this the line he took was to keep us in the dark as to his desertion of his party, and alternately to amuse and alarm us by writing (to Perry) letters hinting doubts as to me, but always ending by leaving us to conclude that he intended after all to vote for me. The impression made on my mind by these missives was that they were only intended to enhance his own importance as the holder of the fifth vote, between four on either side, but that he must end by voting for me. A letter I received from him, on the very morning of the day preceding the election, reasserted his intention of voting for me, but with the following saving clause, 'unless a person of equal claims could be brought forward and supported.' As W. Kay *senior* was the only person at this time thought of, we read this letter as decisive of Kettle's intentions in my favour. For it never occurred to us that after Kettle's often declared opinion of the old set, and of Kay in particular, he could thus turn round and say that he thought him as eligible as myself. It was not till late in the evening before the election that I had a definite notice from Kettle that he had gone over to the old set and to Kay. This was on the evening of November the 12th.

It was not till afterwards that I learnt that as early as the 7th of November Kettle came down from London, collected the opponents of college reform at the Mitre, and endeavoured to bring them to unite on Kay. On the 10th of November Michell went up to town, and there finally pledged Kettle to support Kay. It was necessary for him to keep his treachery to his party secret till the last moment, as otherwise it would have been defeated. We should have looked out for a third man in whose favour we could have detached one of the old set. Kettle's attempt against me could only succeed by being carried on under false colours and in my own camp.

The great difficulty under which the enemy's party laboured was to unite the five votes upon Kay; to unite Kettle, pledged to university and college reform, with Calcott and Gibbs upon Kay, a thorough Conservative and anti-reformer. So desperate, indeed, did the enterprise seem that Michell, hopeless of obtaining five, said to them, 'Give me only four votes for Kay against five for Pattison, and I undertake to work it.' N.B. – He intended to make use of my having been too late in taking my B.D. degree. I suppose this was thought too risky, as I had a Visitatorial order restoring me, which order *might* be confirmed by a higher court if appealed against. What had to be done, then, was to combine Calcott, Gibbs, and West, generally opposed to all reforms and novelties, in the same boat with Kettle, an eager Liberal, who now felt the indecorum of abandoning, in the election of a Rector, the principles he had hitherto upheld in the election of Fellows. The chief practical point of repulsion was probably the local restrictions on fellowships which Kettle, in common with myself, was desirous of abolishing, but which Calcott, Gibbs, and West as sternly maintained. The expedient which was had recourse to in this dilemma was one worthy of Michell's astute diplomacy. He had by this time acquired such an ascendency over Kettle that he could play with him as a child. He succeeded in making Kettle believe that in the retirement of his Yorkshire parsonage Kay senior had become a convert to university reform; that he now regretted the part he had consistently taken while resident, and was now prepared to enter on a new career with new principles. Kay wrote, at Michell's direction, a letter to Kettle which was to satisfy him on this point. This change in Kay's politics had to be kept a close secret from his supporters, Calcott, Gibbs, and West, who thought that in voting for him they were erecting an effectual barrier against the innovating tendencies they so much dreaded in myself. To give them full security on this point Kay was directed by his manager to write another letter to Calcott, asserting in firm though general terms his continued adherence to his old principles, and his repudiation of the Liberalism now in fashion in the college. This letter had to be kept a secret from Kettle. On the evening of November the 10th Michell felt so secure of having effected his purpose that, at a party at Richard Greswell's,[38] he boasted publicly 'by three words I can determine the election at Lincoln.' He meant, I presume, that by showing the Tory letter to Kettle, or the Liberal letter to Gibbs and West, he could at once break up the combination.

All these arrangements were unknown till afterwards to myself and friends. We were relying in security on Kettle's still unretracted pledge to me, and on the impossibility, as we conceived it, of his ever being brought round to support a relic of the old times, brought back from the country in which he had vegetated for some years. It was not till the night before the election that Kettle informed Perry that he recalled his promise to me, and had, under cover of it, secured the return of another man. We were quite unable to understand how this result had been brought about. All that we saw was, that at a late hour on the evening of Wednesday, the evening before the election, we were betrayed by one of our own friends. We saw, of course, that as far as I was concerned the game was up, and the only question was, whether anything could be done to save us in our extremity from being delivered over, bound hand and foot, to the old set, from whom it had cost us so much labour to deliver the college. Our first attempt was on Calcott, the senior Fellow; he was a gentleman, and a man of some education – Kay was neither of these – but thirty years of the Lincoln C. R., such as it was, had reduced him to a torpor almost childish. Espin and Perry called him out of bed at midnight and tendered him the Rectorship if he would vote for himself. They argued that a pledge to vote for another man is never held good against yourself, should it turn out that you could be brought in. Calcott afterwards said that Espin's casuistry on this occasion was worthy of any of the greatest canon lawyers. But here we were baffled; Calcott's feelings of honour would not allow him to do what nine men out of ten would have thought permissible to them. During the attempt to negotiate with Calcott I sat in Perry's room smoking, and endeavouring to reconcile myself as well as I could to the thought of having 'old Kay' over me. When Perry came back and announced that Calcott was immovably fixed you would have thought that all was up. Not so Espin and Andrew. West had repeatedly been heard to say that he was for 'Thompson to the last gasp.' Would he consider the pledge he had given to Kay as conditional only on Thompson's having no chance? They knocked him up at 3 A.M. and negotiated this. West thought that his pledge to Kay might be regarded as always subject to a prior and perpetual pledge to Thompson. Espin and Andrew came back to Perry and myself, who were in ignorance of this last move, and hinted at the possibility of Thompson. It had never occurred to me, as Thompson was the very last man I should have wished to see elected. Yet I could not but also see the deliverance which it held out to us from the meshes of the net which had been so industriously woven round us. Thompson had at least this qualification that he blocked out Michell for ever, that he came in as our friend, owed his election to us, and, what we probably felt most of all in our desperation, thwarted a plot, the near success of which had roused in us a transport of indignation.

Kettle published an angry and indiscreet pamphlet in vindication of his conduct.[39] He could make no defence for the violation of his pledge to me and of his secretly working against me while pretending to be one of my supporters. To make a case at all he had to vilify me by every insinuation that he could gather together, for in defence of his own candidate it was impossible for him to say anything. Espin published a defence of Thompson – calm, temperate, and forcibly reasoned; but it was no less impossible to say anything in defence of Thompson, who was a mere ruffian. It was, however, true that this ruffian was the only member of the college at that time who was acquainted with the college estates and with college business. The real defence was that we had been driven by Michell to choose between two totally unfit men, and had preferred that one of the two whom we could bring in ourselves to the other, who was being carried, as it were, in triumph over our dead bodies.

I also wrote a statement in justification of my own conduct and handed it about in MS. among my friends; I never printed it, as the *fiasco* was so terrible that I did not feel it worth while trying to keep up appearances. What the Oxford public thought about the election was of very small consequence by the side of my own sense of the overwhelming nature of the catastrophe. Kettle never understood the extent of the damage he had done, because he had never known what the college had become under my management. The proverb says, 'One fool can destroy in an hour what ten wise men cannot build up in a generation.' To gratify his vanity he had burnt down the Temple of Ephesus. But he never knew the value of the building he had sacrificed.

For myself, what I have called my nascent ambition was dashed to the ground. The greatest prize in the college had been placed by fortune within my grasp only to be snatched from it again, and that under circumstances which seemed to close my academical career. But I can truly say that the personal disappointment was a minor ingredient in the total of mental suffering I had now to go through. My whole heart and pride had in the last few years been invested in the success of the college. It belonged to my narrowness at that time to be only able to care for one thing at a time: this was the thing on which I had set my affections. In a single night the college was extinguished for all the purposes for which I had laboured. My Satan had triumphed, and had turned my little Paradise into a howling wilderness. It was the return to the reign of the satyrs and wild beasts – Thompson was nothing better than a satyr. The stone I had rolled to the top of the hill with so much pains had rolled back upon me in a moment. I had had disappointments before – a great one, e.g. in my class; but I was then twenty-one, with life before me to retrieve the disaster. I was now thirty-eight, and no other path than the one in which I had embarked all my hopes and energies appeared open. My mental forces were paralysed by the shock; a blank, dumb despair filled me; a chronic heartache took possession of me, perceptible even through sleep. As consciousness gradually returned in the morning, it was only to bring with it a livelier sense of the cruelty of the situation into which I had been brought. For many years I had not been in bed as late as 10 A.M. I now lay commonly till that hour, in the hope of prolonging the semi-oblivion of sleep. I could set about no work. If I read, it was without any object beyond self-forgetfulness. Friends were very kind, and did what they could in the way of consolation and sympathy. I can never forget four who especially stood by me to cheer me at this trying moment – J. M. Wilson (afterwards President of C. C. C.); Manuel Johnson of the Radcliffe Observatory; W. C. Lake (now Dean of Durham); R. W. Church (now Dean of St Paul's).

For many days the question what I should do did not occur to me. I was benumbed and stupefied – too stupefied to calculate the future. For the moment, too, it was not necessary to decide, for of course there was an appeal to the Visitor against the election, and that would take time to hear. It might be months before Thompson could be installed and confirmed. I dragged on a weary routine of tuition for the rest of the Michaelmas term and the Lent term of 1852; went through the forms of lecturing, but the life and spirit were gone. I now loathed teaching as much as I had delighted in it. My tutor's back was broken; I knew that, whatever might happen about the appeal, I could never take up again college work with any spirit or hope of success.

Early in 1852 the Visitor pronounced against the appeal and confirmed the election; he had no choice but to do so, as we had proceeded throughout with statutable regularity. Baffled here, my Satan proceeded to wreak his vengeance upon me. He set about the attempt to oust me from my fellowship on the ground that the Visitor, in restoring me, had exceeded visitatorial power. Here was a new abyss opened beneath my feet! I supposed I had fallen as low as I could in being deprived of my dear occupation and my position in college. Now my bare livelihood, for I had nothing except my fellowship to live upon, was threatened; it seemed not unlikely that I should be turned into the streets to starve. Visitatorial law, what it might contain! It loomed before me like an Indian jungle out of which might issue venomous reptiles, man-eating tigers for my destruction. I was told that the limits of the jurisdiction between the Queen's Bench and a Visitor was a moot point of law as to which there were conflicting cases. By the Master of Pembroke's (Jeune) advice I went down to Riseholme and saw the Bishop (Kaye) myself. He was polite, but shook his head and said it was quite true; in restoring me to my fellowship he had done an act which exceeded his powers, and which was therefore now invalid. The truth was, the Bishop was a weak, timid man, as afraid of the lawyers as I was; he had been quite cowed by the mere name of Bethell, out of whom Michell and Kettle had got some sort of an opinion that a *mandamus* from the Queen's Bench might issue, compelling the Visitor to order the college to fill up my fellowship.

I was now fairly at my wits' end, when a deliverer suddenly arose in an unexpected quarter. Roundell Palmer (Lord Selborne)[40] was spending his Christmas at his father's parsonage at Mixbury, some twenty miles from Oxford. He sent me a message to come over to see him, which I did, and put him in possession of the facts. He told me that I need not go through the form of approaching him through an attorney, but that in a day or two he would send me an opinion. It was one of his masterly arguments, searching every corner of the case, and couched in a tone of decision and authority which, it seemed to me, nothing could stand before. The poor Bishop, who had had skirmishes with Roundell Palmer before, was almost more afraid of him than he was of Bethell. Armed with this opinion I went up to town and put it into the hands of the solicitor, William Ford. Ford, after many delays and frights given me as to my precarious position, got together a consultation – Sir Fitzroy Kelly and Phillimore. We drew up a petition: the Humble Petition of Mark Pattison, praying the Visitor to confirm the sentence of restoration which he had formerly issued, and informing him that these three luminaries of the law, Roundell Palmer, Kelly, and Phillimore, were of opinion that it was within his power to do so.[41] I am not certain that this petition was ever presented, nor can I find any document which should have issued from the Visitor on the occasion; the college register is silent. I paid the lawyer's bill; Roundell Palmer took no fee for his opinion, and I heard no more of the matter.

I had now my fellowship to rely upon: £200 a year – a fellowship of Lincoln was not more in those days – which sufficed for my personal expenditure in the economical style in which we lived at that time in college. I was therefore free to consider my plan of life, and I took time to do so. As on a former occasion, I would do nothing precipitately; I would carry on the college tutorship for a term or two, though I now hated the work as much as I had delighted in it; and I would consider whether anything that could be called prospects could be saved from the wreck. If Thompson behaved well to me, perhaps in time I might recover tone and begin tutorial work again as before. If he behaved ill I would throw up the college tutorship and take private pupils for a term or two.

In this gloomy, almost desperate, frame of mind I dragged through the year 1852. The Diary abounds in entries such as the following: – 'Dull, insensible wretchedness.' Again, 23d April: 'Returned to-night to college for the first time for many years that I have done so without any pleasure.'

Again, about the same date: –

The miserable depression of these days is not to be forgotten. From supreme power to have come down to be the least among my Lord's servants is little; but to see everything, small and great, going the wrong way [then I enumerate many small points of discipline] . . . In a fortnight has been undone all the work of my sub-rectorship. May God give me patience in time; but I cannot sit by and with equanimity look on at the retrograde course of things. I try to fix my thoughts on the subjects I am now proposing to myself, but I do not succeed in getting anything like absorption in them.

19th September. – Read prayers at Launton and preached twice, being the first time I have done any duty since my illness; was indifferent and uninterested in preaching; my unhappiness comes between me and everything; good congregation and attentive, but I could not give my mind to what I was saying.

28th September. – Reading Socrates [? Isocrates] all yesterday and to-day; not more happy but less disquieted days; mind more taken up by what I was reading. Read an article in *Westminster Review* on Sir Robert Peel, which did me good, and for half an hour made me resolve to work and redeem my misfortune, but soon went off when I recollect my friendless and helpless condition.

On 1st November 1852, the first Gaudy after the catastrophe, I went up to London to be out of the way: 'to escape the bitter heartache of being in college; did in some measure deaden the bitter pain, but that was all.'

13th November. – Hunc diem satis misere, ut semper, transegi.[42]

4th December. – My unhappiness not abating.

> *Aut ego profecto ingenio egregie ad miseriam*
> *Natus sum; aut illud falsum est quod vulgo audio*
> *Dici diem adimere ægritudinem hominibus.*[43]
>
> TER., *Haut.*, iii. 1–11

18th December. – Began to read Carlyle's *Life of Schiller*. Very weary and wretched both yesterday and to-day; all the savour of life is departed.

26th December. – Very wretched all yesterday and to-day; dull, gloomy, blank. Sleep itself is turned to sorrow.

19th May 1853. – Sympathising visit from Sanderson, who has been among the undergraduates, and reported their wretched and deteriorated condition.

9th August. – A depressing feeling of melancholy came over me in the evening at the thought of the summer tour having now come to an end. I have nothing to which I look forward with any satisfaction; no prospects; my life seems to have come to an end, my strength gone, my energies paralysed, and all my hopes dispersed.

Of course Thompson behaved badly to me – any one with any knowledge of the world would have known that he would; he treated me as Hawkins treated Newman.[44] He wanted to get me out as an unconformable element in the mechanical system of government which was now substituted for the human and personal relations into which I had entered with each undergraduate individually. He offered me such hard terms as to the tutorship that I indignantly threw it up, and, to earn some income for the moment, fell back on private tuition. My credit in the University as a philosophical tutor was now such that I had no difficulty in getting some of the best men who were going to read with me. Jowett sent me men from Balliol;[45] and J. M. Wilson, who seemed to have the power of making everybody do what he wanted, compelled an unfriendly vice-chancellor to nominate me a second time examiner in the honour schools.

All these things, however, did not restore my equilibrium or repair my unstrung nerves. What was in the end more useful to me than any honours and employments were long fishing excursions which I got into the habit of making in the north of England and Scotland. Since my boyish days I had dropped out of fishing – forgotten its charms; and, during the fever of Tractarianism, had not felt the want of its gently soothing properties. Fortunately a year or two back the fly-rod had accidently come into my hands; it was now precisely the resource of which my wounded nature stood in need. I arranged the classes of private pupils for Lent and Michaelmas terms only, keeping the summer term free. About the middle of April, after long and anxious preparation of rods and tackle, with a well-selected box of books and large store of tobacco, I set out for the north. My first stage was Hauxwell, from which I fished the Ure or Swale; then passed on to the Eden; then up the Border, fishing everywhere, where I could get leave – trout only, I would have nothing to do with salmon – all the way to the

Bridge of Tummel in Perthshire. This humble inn, kept by simple and friendly people, became my home for many weeks at a time. I made lengthened excursions from it into the far north, Ross-shire, the Isle of Skye, etc., and returned again to the Bridge. So it was not till July, at the earliest, that I became sufficiently tired of idleness, or satiated with solitude, to begin to think of returning home. My habit in these years was to seek Oxford for a few weeks in the middle of the Long Vacation, to renew acquaintance with my books and review my literary plans, and then, about the middle of September, to go off for a ramble in Germany. In this way I visited on foot large tracts of central and southern Germany, delighting in discovering nooks and corners unknown to guide-books. After I gave up private tuition, as I soon did, I prolonged those German tours into November, settling at some university; e.g. in 1856 I passed some weeks at Heidelberg, attending as a guest the course of Dr Richard Rothe, who was then at the height of his celebrity as pioneer of a new school which was to unite the utmost liberty of philosophical thought with Christian dogma. Then I would return to my rooms in college, and live there among my books till April and the 'March Browns' came round again. I lived these months in the college which I had governed as a stranger, knowing nothing of college affairs, averting my eyes from a misrule of which I would know nothing, and only noticed by the authorities when I was summoned to a college meeting to make a quorum. Two or three seasons of this *régime* went some way towards restoring my mental equilibrium, and giving me back something of my old energy.

The Diary of these years bears traces of mental and moral deterioration; it has quite ceased to be a diary of studies, and records scarce anything but the names of the men I met in the course of the day, and the subjects, but not the detail, of our conversations. These ran at this time largely upon two subjects: 1. The reform of the examination system; 2. University reform. I appear to have taken a great interest and no little share in both changes. The aim of the new modelling of the examination statutes was to take off the strain of the final schools, the requirement of the poets and scholarship, along with philosophy and history, having been found too heavy. When we had created a new examination, moderations, and detached the scholarship portion of the examination, assigning it to the students' second year, we congratulated ourselves on having notably alleviated the burden of preparation. Little did we foresee that we were only giving another turn to the examination screw, which has been turned several times since, till it has become an instrument of mere torture which has made education impossible and crushed the very desire of learning.

The other and greater question of university reform consumed a still larger amount of time and thought. As it invariably happens when you have to frame a scheme, the great outlines disappear under a multitude of details, and these assume at the time an importance in your eyes which, on a retrospect, is ridiculous enough. However, life is made up of details; one cannot be always chewing the cud of great principles; so far the Diary faithfully represents my broken life in those years of defeat and despair. It was probably well for me that I was able to take so deep an interest even in these profitless discussions.

I do not underrate the value of what was done by the Executive Commission of 1854. The abolition of the close fellowships opened the colleges to an amount of talent and energy hitherto unknown in them. They had hitherto been peopled by a class of inferior men – clergymen waiting for college livings, and going through a feeble routine, which was dignified by the name of tuition, to fill up the time till a living dropped in. This was the rotten and indefensible system which the Tories fought for to the last gasp, and which the *Quarterly Review* would gladly see restored. It seems it is necessary, in the interests of the Church, that the college endowments should be reserved for men of capacities and energies below the average. But this sweeping away of local claims was nearly all the good that the Commission of 1854 effected. After all the contention about the professoriate, what the Commission did in this direction was without method – crude, sporadic. Meantime an influence had been growing up among us – an influence which the Commission did but little to help or further – one of which we said little, and that little not approvingly, but which was destined to work a revolution in the scope and functions of Oxford life far greater than has been effected by two successive Commissions. This was the Museum, and through the Museum the introduction of the thin end of physical science.[46] It is to the silent permeative genius of science that the growth of a large and comprehensive view of the function of the University and the desire to discharge it has spread among us. I have said that, immersed in the details of our examination statute and our suggestions to the Commissioners, we spoke little of this pregnant germ of the scientific spirit which was silently diffusing itself among us. I say we, as I do not mean the obstructionists, who were still in a large majority; but the minority of liberal-minded men with whom I now lived paid little attention to this fact, and scarce knew whether they approved of it or no. I remember on one occasion, when a grant of £10,000 for Museum purposes was before Convocation, that our party was divided as to whether we should support it or no. But even more astonishing than our reluctance to give money was the blindness in which we still lived as to the claims of science in the realm of knowledge, and our naive assumption that classical learning was a complete equipment for a great university.

These, then, were the desultory and unsatisfying occupations of these years of famine, during which the mind seemed to be suffering rather than growing, and in which a disproportionate time had to be allotted to that fresh air and solitude which seemed required to repair the moral nature after the humiliation which had paralysed it. All the spring and summer I wandered like Bellerophon about the Aleian fields, shunning the encounter of men my equals.[47] This retired life developed in me a kind of reserve or aloofness from other men, or rather it reopened that cleft which seemed to separate me from my species, under which I complained at my first entrance into college life. I was growing brooding, melancholy, taciturn, and finally pessimist.

But though neither sun nor moon nor stars appeared for many days, the vessel was not entirely without a compass. I have said that my earliest aspiration was to get a fellowship, that I might devote myself to study. This was from very early days my ideal of life. I had the vaguest notions of what I would study. My curiosity was sufficiently awake when a boy in various directions; but it was not the satisfaction of my curiosity that I sought, but a studious life – the βίος θεωρητικὸς – for its own sake. I daresay the special pursuit to be favoured varied from year to year. As early as 1830 my cousin * * *[48] and I used to take in, she the *Literary Gazette*, I the *Athenæum*, and we kept up a lively correspondence in comparing notes over what we read. This desultory reading was interrupted by my trying for classical honours at Oriel. For a short time after my B.A. degree I returned to the old love, and read voraciously whatever came in my way, but all slight and without a purpose. Then the flood of Tractarian infatuation broke over me and gave an object to this plan of a studious existence; I would devote myself to the reading of the Fathers and of Church history from the point of view of the Catholic Church. This phase took some eight years out of my life; and before I had quite cooled down in 1846 I found myself engaged, without choice of my own, in a new and absorbing occupation – that of teaching and forming the young mind. This engrossed all my energies till the catastrophe of November 1851, when this occupation was abruptly withdrawn from me. Slowly the old original ideal of life, which had been thrust aside by the force of circumstance but never obliterated, began to resume its place. Here again there was no act of will or choice on my part. I lived for two or more years in a state of passive wretchedness; as tone and energy returned, the idea of devoting myself to literature strengthened and developed. I never at any precise moment made a formal devotion of myself as Goethe did, who, on entering his thirtieth year, 'resolved to deal with life no longer by halves, but to work it out in its totality and beauty – Vom Halben zu entwöhnen, Und im Ganzen Guten Schönen Resolut zu leben.'[49] (Goethe, *Gesellige Lieder, Generalbeichte*.) With me, on the other hand, there was no intervention of the will; I was moved by a power beyond myself, and by imperceptible steps, to approve and deliberately adopt that course of life which old instinct, like a fate, had chalked out for me. I began to form many ambitious schemes of books to be written, any one of which might have occupied my lifetime. My interests were too diversified, and my mind suffered accordingly. I am astonished, when I look over my C. P. B. of this period, to see how omnivorous was my appetite for both facts and ideas. I was also still, at least as late as 1857, very far from having formed the pure and unselfish conception of the life of the true student, which dawned upon me afterwards, and which Goethe, it seems, already possessed at thirty. My ideal at this time was polluted and disfigured by literary ambition. I had in short essays proved to myself that I could write that which attracted men's attention. I wanted to be doing more of this sort – to be before the world, in fact, as a writer. I shared the vulgar fallacy that a literary life meant a life devoted to the making of books, and that not to be always coming before the public was to be idle. It cost me years more of extrication of thought before I rose to the conception that the highest life is the art to live, and that both men, women, and books are equally essential ingredients of such a life.

This last suggestion belongs to a later period. At the epoch of which I am now writing – about 1856–57 – what was necessary for me? The thing of first necessity for me was a definite direction to reading; so that reading might become serious study, study might become research, and, if it might be, literature might become learning. One subject I seem to have already appropriated as my own, i.e. the history and organisation of universities. This topic was indeed only a subordinate branch of a larger form of investigation which constituted the framework within which my thoughts habitually moved – viz. the laws of the progress of thought in modern Europe. At first I attempted to work this out through the filiation of successive systems of philosophy. I soon found that this was a task beyond me, and besides it had been already attempted with various success by many others. Buckle's *History of Civilisation* appeared and took the reading world by storm.[50] I was carried away by Buckle's vast reading and the appearance of wide induction which his pages bore, a quality which I had now come to require in any book. I gave much time to the study of Buckle; I not only wrote a review of it for the *Westminster* – a review which I have since found from Buckle's *Life* was the only one which he considered to have touched the merits of the book – but I brought all the attention of which I was capable to meditate upon his main thesis – viz. that the actions of mankind, at any point whatever of their history, are determined by their knowledge. I found myself compelled not only to reject this theory, but came to see the impossibility of reducing the theory of progress to *any* single law.

I therefore dropped the pursuit of any such comprehensive idea as progress or civilisation, and tried to confine myself to some one manageable section of the subject. The readiest at hand was the history and function of the universities; and as through the '50's the topic of university reform was a leading topic both at Oxford and Cambridge, in following out the bent of my own studies I had by accident got hold of a popular topic. I returned again and again to it in essays, articles, addresses; and when, in 1867, I thought I had exhausted all I had to say upon the subject in my book on Academical Organisation, there suddenly sprung up a new development in the question of the endowment of research. I would willingly have left this new outgrowth to be looked after by others; but I was compelled, partly by Dr Appleton's importunity, partly by thinking it cowardly to shrink from standing by an unpopular cause, to take a much larger part in that movement than I wished to do.[51]

But the history of universities was but one of many rivals in my intellectual interests. The movement of theological sentiment in modern Europe had long had a peculiar charm for me. It was a subject, too, that had never been touched by any English writer, with the exception of one Unitarian sketch by J. J. Tayler – *Retrospect of the Religious Life of England* – a volume not known beyond Unitarian circles. I saw the impossibility of attempting, as Tayler had done, to survey the whole course of religious thought in England, and I therefore selected a special period which had peculiarly definite limits. It had always struck me as a surprising fact that Deism, which had been the prevailing form of thought among the educated classes in England during the first half of the eighteenth century, should have abruptly disappeared somewhere about 1760, giving place to a revived Puritanism in the form of Methodism and Evangelicalism. I saw clearly that the usual solution offered by the orthodox, viz. that Deism had been triumphantly refuted in argument, did not explain the fact. I attempted an original inquiry, of a kind new in this country, into the philosophic causes of the sudden rise and as sudden extinction of Deism in the last century. I inserted this essay in the volume of *Essays and Reviews*. So wholly extinct is scientific theology in the Church of England that the English public could not recognise such a thing as a neutral and philosophic inquiry into the causes of the form of thought existing at any period. Our clergy knew only of pamphlets which must be either for or against one of the parties in the Church.

The study of the sources and the collection of the materials occupied me for nearly two years. The essay as it stands was hastily written and crudely and awkwardly composed. But the dominant idea which governed the writer was, as I have said, that of a scientific history of the self-development of opinion. This attempt to present the English public with a philosophical monograph on one special phase of religious thought was singularly unsuccessful. To judge from the reviews, it never occurred to any of our public instructors that such a conception was possible. Clerical or anti-clerical, from the *Westminster Review* to the *Guardian*, they were all busily occupied in finding or making contradictions between the writer's words and the thirty-nine articles.

It is possible that the fault was partly chargeable on the essay itself, which, hastily written, may not always have maintained the tone of historical investigation; yet to foreigners it seemed to do so. The Protestant historian – Dorner – going over the same ground a few years afterwards,† accepted the essay for what it was intended to be – a history, and not a party manifesto. Dorner's chapter, 'Der streitende und siegende Deismus', makes much use and ample acknowledgment of my essay. Another exception to the chorus of blatant and ignorant howling, with which my poor venture was received, I will record. Soon after the publication of *Essays and Reviews*, happening to come down from town in the train with Father, since Cardinal, Newman,[52] whom I had not seen for a long time, I was in terror as to how he would regard me in consequence of what I had written. My fears were quickly relieved. He blamed severely the throwing of such speculations broadcast upon the general public. It was, he said, unsettling their faith without offering them anything else to rest upon. But he had no word of censure for the latitude of theological speculation assumed by the essay, provided it had been addressed *ad clerum*, or put out, not as a public appeal, but as a scholastic dissertation addressed to learned theologians. He assured me that this could be done in the Roman communion, and that much greater latitude of speculation on theological topics was allowed in this form in the Catholic Church than in Protestant communities.

Whatever may be the case in the Catholic Church, I do not see

---

† In his *Geschichte der Protestantischen Theologie besonders in Deutschland*, pp. 497 *seq.*, München, 1867. See also English Edition, 1871, v. ii., p. 496. – ED.

how an English writer is to confine theological discussion to a class of professional theologians, even supposing there existed such a class. If he writes in Latin he might as well not write at all – he will remain unread; and if he publishes an English dissertation any one who can buy the book may read it. No topic excites the English world more than a religious topic, yet there is no public in this country for a scientific treatment of theology. This absence of a professional public, and not the restraints of our formularies, seems to me the true reason why a real theology cannot exist in England. Every clerical writer feels himself bound to decide every question of criticism or interpretation in favour of the orthodox view. It is demanded of him by public opinion that he shall be an advocate and not a critic. Science or knowledge cannot exist under such a system; it requires for its growth the air of free discussion and contradiction.

For myself, I refused to attempt any defence or to enter into controversy with my critics. We were at cross purposes, and there was an end. But I resolved to wash my hands of theology and even of Church history, seeing that there existed in England no proper public for either. So, as philosophy was too difficult for me, or its interest was exhausted, I fell back upon another special portion of the great story of progressive civilisation, which had attracted me from a very early time. I have mentioned under the year 1835 the fascination exerted over me by my tutor Hyman's style of annotation on Aristophanes, and the first introduction I got through him to the personality of Bentley, Brunck, Porson, etc. This first suggestion fructified in my mind, and from time to time, among other miscellaneous reading, I dipped into the Latin commentators, Ernesti, Ruhnken, Valckenaer, without going farther back than the eighteenth century. In 1851 the Clarendon Press printed the *Ephemerides* of Isaac Casaubon. This curious book immediately riveted my attention. I saw what a mine of inquiry was opened into the progress of classical learning, from the Renaissance down to Niebuhr. I began also to see how full of biographical interest and local colour were the lives of the great philologians of the sixteenth century. I immediately acted on Dr Priestley's advice to a man who asked him how he might get to know something of a subject he named, 'Oh sit down and write a book upon it.' I sat down and wrote an article on Casaubon, and sent it up to the *Edinburgh Review*.[53] My article was immediately returned by Empson with the message that Casaubon's *Ephemerides* had been placed in the hands of an old contributor. Here was my usual luck; nothing that I attempted was to succeed. However, I tried the *Quarterly*. It so happened that the *Quarterly* was then, for a too brief period, in the hands of a man with the genuine tastes of a scholar. It was inserted in the next number, and the editor was not sparing in praise. I must always feel grateful to Mr Elwin[54] for thus giving me the first encouraging impulse to a path of research, then new and untrodden, which has been my main occupation for the thirty years that have elapsed since that article was written.

My first scheme, now that I had discovered a subject to which I could thoroughly devote myself, was to write the history of learning from the Renaissance downwards. One's ambition is always in the inverse proportion of one's knowledge. I soon discovered how much I had miscalculated my powers. I contracted my views to a history of one only of the schools of philology. It should be the French school, beginning with Budæus, and coming down at least to Huet and the Delphin editions. It was not long before I found that even on this reduced scale, I could not hope to execute a thorough piece of work. There had not been enough preparatory investigation of single points by others. There was an outline, *Geschichte der Philologie*, by Fr. Creuzer very slight, apparently notes for a course of lectures. The chapters on classical learning in Hallam might furnish a skeleton.[55] But Hallam did not pretend to appreciate the scholars as he did the *littérateurs* from his own reading; he only transcribed the judgments of the *ana*, or the vague *éloges* of prefaces and dedications.

Of the ambitious plan I had first conceived I have only executed fragments; one exhaustive monograph on Isaac Casaubon, and some slighter sketches, first draughts, as it were, for the lives of Henri Estienne, Salmasius, Huet, and F. A. Wolf. What was to have been my most elaborate study was that of J. J. Scaliger. To this I devoted myself in a different spirit. In the case of Casaubon I had been animated to my work, less by interest in the personality than by the biographer's gratification of finding in London, Paris, and Geneva, a mass of unpublished material, which I was the first to bring into a connected story.

No literary vanity or ambition mingled itself with the pure enthusiasm which animated me in the study of J. J. Scaliger.[56] As C. Neate writes,

> Posterity owes to those who have effectually worked for its benefit the debt of a grateful curiosity; that debt it is, in matters of learning, our part to pay. It is a debt we can repay at little cost, or rather we shall grow richer by the repayment. . . . In this way only can we keep up that glorious continuity of the human mind which gives, . . . even to the new-born thoughts that are here engendered, the nobility of many generations and the hope of an enduring succession
> (*Legal and other Studies at the University*, p. 10)

I soon came to view in Scaliger something more than the first scholar of the modern age. The hint was given me in a conversation I had with Chevalier Bunsen at Charlottenburg in 1856.[57] Speaking of Bernays' masterly monograph on Scaliger, just published, he pointed out that Bernays' creed had interfered with his seeing in Scaliger the Protestant hero. He showed me that Scaliger was the central figure of his time, and that the whole literary effort of the Catholic reaction for a quarter of a century had been directed to beating down his fame by an organised system of detraction and vilification such as has never been played off against any other man who was not a political leader. He suggested to me not to translate Bernays' volume, but to rewrite the life in connection with the religious history of the time from which Bernays had detached it. I imposed it on myself as a solemn duty to rescue the memory of Scaliger from the load of falsehood and infamy under which the unscrupulous Jesuit faction had contrived to bury it. So elaborately planned had been their campaign that they had even trained a double – a kind of mock sun – or harlequin Scaliger in the person of Dionysius Petavius, whose burlesque was to make the real Scaliger forgotten. The French *literati* of the next generation, indifferent to truth and the slaves of epigram, lazily copied the Scaliger as depicted by the Jesuits. And as one French biographer copies the one before him without examination, the *Scaliger hypobolimæus*[58] has become the permanent Scaliger of their dictionaries and books of reference. I have been nearly thirty years getting together the materials for my *vindiciæ.* In the autumn of 1883 I returned from the Tyrol with the full purpose of devoting the next twelve months to complete the composition of the *Life*, of which many portions were already written out in their definitive form, when I was struck down by the malady which has cut off all hope of my ever being able to execute this or any other literary scheme.

With the year 1860 I close for the present this brief memoir. Of the three-and-twenty years of life which have been granted me since, what little account there is to be given must be reserved for another time, which may never come. The fortunate possessor, by my election to the headship of my college, of unrivalled academic leisure, there is even still less to say about these twenty-three years than there has been about those which preceded them. I do not flatter myself that the outline of my mental development which I have drawn can have interest for many beyond the circle of my own acquaintance. In looking back on the course which self-formation has taken with me, two points seem to me chiefly noteworthy.

1. The minuteness of the germ out of which a wide and full intellectual life has been evolved. A writer in the *Spectator* says, speaking of Anthony Trollope,

> There exists in some men a mental husk or shell out of which they grow, as they grow out of physical weakness or uncouthness. It is not that they conceal their powers or neglect their powers, but that the powers are not there. The germ must exist, but it may for effective purposes be so crushed as to be temporarily dead. Such men's minds do not simply grow, they break through also. What it is that happens in such cases no one can say; but it does happen, and more frequently to women than men; and there is, as is evident from the analogy of sleep, no reason why it should not happen. Why should not the explanation of Anthony Trollope's boyhood be that he, the clear-sighted novelist, able man of business, and successful public servant, actually was, till he was twenty-five, a disagreeable dullard?

This is nearly my mental experience; my first consciousness is that of stupidity. A very feeble germ of intellect was struggling with a crushing mass of facts, ideas which it could not master, and with the tyrannical force of more powerful intelligence in the persons around me. Instead of starting, as I saw other young men do, with a buoyant sense of mental vigour and delight in the masterful exercise of the intellectual weapons, I was wearily nursing a feeble spark of mind, painfully conscious of its inability to cope with its environment. At twenty-one I seemed ten years in the rear of my contemporaries.

Slowly, and not without laborious effort, I began to emerge, to conquer, as it were, in the realm of ideas. It was all growth, development, and I have never ceased to grow, to develop, to discover, up to the very last. While my contemporaries, who started so far ahead of me, fixed their mental horizon before they were thirty-five, mine has been ever enlarging and expanding. I experienced what Marcus Aurelius reckoned among the favours of the gods, μὴ πρὸ ὥρας ἀνδρωθῆναι, ἀλλ ἔτι καὶ ἐπιλαβεῖν τοῦ χρόνου (i. 17),[59] and the growth of anything that could be called mind in me was equally backward. But slow as the steps were, they have been all forward. I seemed to my friends to have changed, to have gone over from High Anglicanism to Latitudinarianism, or Rationalism, or Unbelief, or whatever the term may be. This is not so; what took place with me was simple expansion of knowledge and ideas. To my home Puritan religion, almost narrowed to two points – fear of God's wrath and faith in the doctrine of the atonement – the idea of the Church was a widening of the horizon which stirred up the spirit and filled it with enthusiasm. The notion of the Church soon expanded itself beyond the limits of the Anglican communion and became the wider idea of the Catholic Church. Then Anglicanism fell off from me, like an old garment, as Puritanism had done before.

Now the idea of the Catholic Church is only a mode of conceiving the dealings of divine Providence with the whole race of mankind. Reflection on the history and condition of humanity, taken as a whole, gradually convinced me that this theory of the relation of all living beings to the Supreme Being was too narrow and inadequate. It makes an equal Providence, the Father of all, care only for a mere handful of the species, leaving the rest (such is the theory) to the chances of eternal misery. If God interferes at all to procure the happiness of mankind it must be on a far more comprehensive scale than by providing for them a church of which far the majority of them will never hear. It was on this line of thought, the details of which I need not pursue, that I passed out of the Catholic phase, but slowly, and in many years, to that highest development when all religions appear in their historical light, as efforts of the human spirit to come to an understanding with that Unseen Power whose pressure it feels, but whose motives are a riddle. Thus Catholicism dropped off me as another husk which I had outgrown. There was no conversion or change of view; I could no more have helped what took place within me than I could have helped becoming ten years older.

Das Werk wächst concrescirt allmälig und langsam, wie das Kind im Mutterleibe: ich weiss nicht was zuerst und was zuletzt entstanden ist. Ich werde ein Glied, ein Gefäss, einen Theil nach dem anderen gewahr, d. h. ich schreibe auf, unbekümmert, wie es zum Ganzen passen wird; denn ich weiss, es ist Alles aus einem Grund entsprungen. So entsteht ein organisches Ganzes und nur ein solches kann leben.[60]

The same evolution which thus worked out my conception of the supreme law of the universe prevailed in all the subordinate branches of investigation through which my studies led me. I never began, as I believe many men do, with the highest generalisation, and then gradually narrowed it down as I got to know more facts. An ovum was deposited in the nidus of my mind, blind, formless, with no quality but life. Incubation warmed it; it differentiated itself into logical members, then threw out tentacles, which grasped with avidity all matter which they could assimilate from their environment, till the whole conception presented itself organically complete and articulate. It was thus, e.g., that I arrived at last at the idea of a University. I began with the most rudimentary notion, the personal relation between teacher and taught, and obstinately refused to admit any other consideration into my mind along with it. This indeed historically was the origin of universities; – as when Abelard[61] attracted his five thousand pupils to St Geneviève, it was the personality of the man in which the magnetic influence resided.

In the second place, I cannot help observing the remarkable force with which the Unconscious – *das Unbewusste* – vindicated its power. The weight of this element in human affairs is so unmistakable that whole theologies have been founded upon the observation of the working of this single power, e.g. Calvinism and Mahometanism. By whatever name you call it, the Unconscious is found controlling each man's destiny without, or in defiance of, his will. The unconscious instinct of a studious life, having its origin in the days of early boyhood, reasserted itself again and again against untoward external events, until it had compelled me into the career which alone my reason approved, and to which I have been faithful for the last thirty years. Once or twice only in this period have I for a brief moment deserted literature. In 1858 I went out to Berlin for three months as *Times* correspondent. But in this case the attraction to me resided not in the political reports I had to transmit to my paper, but in the opportunity afforded me of making acquaintance with men and things, of the sort that touched my special interests, in a new sphere. Again, in 1859, I went over North Germany as commissioner, to inquire into German elementary schools.

Besides these two occasions, I was once or twice nearly thrown off my balance by the practical urgencies of a life led in the University. When the new Hebdomadal Council was first instituted in 1854 I fancied, or friends persuaded me, that I should like to be elected into it. I tried to be so on two occasions; fortunately for me I was left in a minority each time, or I might have wasted years in the idle and thankless pursuit which they call doing university business. When the Vice-Chancellorship came to me in 1878 I had the moral courage to refuse it; and I am fairly entitled to say that, since the year 1851, I have lived wholly for study. There can be no vanity in making this confession, for, strange to say, in a university ostensibly endowed for the cultivation of science and letters, such a life is hardly regarded as a creditable one.

Thus the catastrophe of 1851, after all the agony that I suffered in consequence of it, turned out to be a substantial blessing. In writing my *Life of Milton* I could not but be forcibly reminded of my own experience when I had to describe the poet, after the crash of 1660, returning to thoughts of poetry and the composition of *Paradise Lost*, which he had forsaken for more than twenty years for a noisy pamphlet brawl and the unworthy drudgery of Secretary to the Council Board. Surely Milton, who was at one time so carried away by the passion of a party whose aims he idealised that he boasted of having lost his eyesight in bombarding Salmasius with foul epithets, must, amid the inspiration which poured forth *Paradise Lost*, have come round again to the opinion of Goethe that 'a purely poetical subject is as superior to a political one as the pure everlasting truth of Nature is to party spirit.' For myself, I can truly say that daily converse with the poetry and literature of all times, ancient and modern, has been to me its own sufficient reward; the classics have lost for me nothing of their charm; on this very day – New Year's Eve, 1884 – I can read Sophocles with greater delight than I ever did.

> J'ai profité des jours, des années qui m'ont été données pour vivre dans la familiarité des grands esprits de tous les temps.
>
> Ces bons génies qui ont illustré le monde ne m'ont point dédaigné. Sans me demander mes titres, qui j'étais, d'où je venais, ils m'ont admis dans leur compagnie. Ils m'ont ouvert leurs volumes; ils m'ont laissé lire dans leurs pensées, dans leurs secrets; ils m'ont laissé m'abreuver de leur douce science; j'ai oublié dans cette occupation les mauvais jours qui s'étendaient sur moi.
>
> ... J'ai osé moi aussi vivre de leur vie, de cette vie ailée, magnifique, toute puissante par laquelle ils disposent en souverains de la réalité. Comme eux j'ai osé faire profession de penser. J'ai joui de l'intimité des choses. J'ai conversé avec les idées, embrassé le possible; car dans ces moments, je m'oubliais moi même, et en suivant le beau cortège des intelligences qui m'ont précédé, j'ai joui comme elles de l'univers moral dont elles m'avaient ouvert l'entrée.
>
> (Quinet, *Hist. de mes Idées*, p. 95)[62]

There seems to have fulfilled itself for me that adage of Goethe which, when I first came upon it, appeared a mere paradox –

> *Was man in der Jugend wünsche,*
> *Hat man im Alter die Fülle.*
>
> *(Of that which a man desires in youth,*
> *Of that he shall have in age as much as he will.)*[63]

APPENDIX

The Lincoln College Election of 1851

DR JOHN RADFORD, Rector of Lincoln College, Oxford, died on 21 October 1851. The election of his successor rested, as laid down by college statutes, with the fellows of the college, eleven in number. Two of these, William Bousfield, who was chaplain on St Helena, and the younger William Kay, who was Principal of Bishop's College, Calcutta, were abroad and so disqualified from voting; that left nine fellows as the decisive electors. It was obvious that Mark Pattison would be one of the candidates, but, for a time, no one was sure who would be his rivals. Several other fellows were mentioned as possible candidates. Pattison told his sister Eleanor that he had been called on by the senior fellow, John Calcott (fellow 1815–64):

> Johnny called on me this morning, and proceeded to allow himself to be comfortably ensconced in the great chair, after which he read a letter from another former fellow, Clarke Jenkins [fellow 1803–23, rector of Great Leighs, a college living], placing himself at the disposal of the College. He followed this by a similar letter from the elder Kay [William Kay, fellow 1823–40, incumbent of Kirkdale, Yorkshire].

Finally, he 'produced a shabby little envelope wh. in a very nervous way he threw upon the table, requesting me to read it after he was gone'. This revealed that Calcott too was willing to place his hat in the ring.

> I shewed my contempt visibly ... It really begins to make it rise in one's estimation when the eagles flock after it [the headship] so. Really as I stood opposite Calcott at the altar-table on Sunday, I could not help a feeling, very untimely at that place, that I should be supposed to be engaged in a competition with such a snubby, dirty, useless little dog. We are wondering where is Martin [Green, fellow 1837–49]. I fully expect a letter from Winterborne [in Dorset where he was rector] by every post, and really compared to any of the men yet in the field, Atkinson [Miles Atkinson, fellow 1834–9] excepted, Green would be fully justified in offering, and would make a very average head.

Another former fellow, James Thompson [fellow 1823–46], who was rector of the college living of Cublington, near Aylesbury, was also a possible candidate.

It was obvious, however, that in so small a constituency in which Pattison had three strong supporters among the fellows, Andrew, Perry and Espin, that the conservatives would lose if the vote was divided. They decided to place their votes with a former fellow, the senior William Kay. He was promised four votes: those of Calcott, Gibbs, Metcalfe and Washbourne West, the bursar, who admitted that his real preference was for James Thompson. Since Pattison was allowed, and indeed expected, to vote for himself, he too had four votes.

The decisive vote would be that of a non-resident lawyer, the only layman in the company, J. L. R. Kettle. Kettle had wanted to nominate another former fellow, Richard Michell (fellow 1830–42, and now Vice-Principal of Magdalen Hall), but the fellowship which he had held, the Somersetshire Fellowship, disqualified him by statute from being a candidate. Nonetheless, Michell, an Evangelical cleric with a subtle mind, was a powerful and, in Pattison's view, malign influence behind the scenes.

Kettle was neither politically nor academically drawn to the conservative faction; but he did not much like Pattison either. At first, unable to put Michell forward, he promised to vote for Pattison, respecting him as a scholar and reformer. 'Well, Kettle,' Pattison told him, 'you see I have four votes already, so your's gives it me.' The news of Kettle's promise to vote for Pattison reached Michell and outraged him so much that he tried to make Kettle change his mind, suggesting that both Pattison's uncertain temper and dubious religious views made him a very unsuitable candidate. Pattison told A. P. Stanley, the future Dean of Westminster, on 10 November 1851:

> Michell I believe, favours Kay [senior] but his effort is rather directed against me, than for anyone. I think I should tell you that the topic that is urged against me is defect of judgement and temper, a topic which directs its force, from, I am sorry to say, the great proportion of truth contained in it . . . everything I have said or done during the last three weeks has been so fastened upon and misconstrued as to give it an appearance of confirming the argument that is found so effective against me.

His sister Eleanor wrote indignantly to him:

> I cannot imagine how it is that such a man as Mr M[ichell] appears to be should dare to take the field and the lead against one whom

everyone acknowledged to be so immeasurably superior and to have been the maker of Lincoln College.

In pursuit of his campaign, Michell persuaded Kay, Pattison's rival, to write two letters: one to the ultra-conservative Calcott, reassuring him of his adherence to traditional values, which Calcott was to show his friends; the other to Michell, indicating his comparative sympathy with reforms in the university, which Michell could show to Kettle. After reading it, Kettle hesitated but was swayed increasingly by the arguments against Pattison. 'I am unable,' he told Pattison the day before the election, 'to say whether my vote will be given to you or not', adding, for he had by now decided to vote for Kay, 'I feel bound ... to add that I consider the probabilities considerably in my favour of not voting for you.'

The election was timed for 13 November and was to take place, as was the custom, in the college chapel. At West's suggestion, Perry was informed of Kettle's defection, in the hope that if Pattison heard of it, he would realise that he had no chance of defeating Kay and would withdraw from the conflict. He was stunned by the news and made one last, but vain, effort to persuade Kettle to keep to his original promise. When this proved fruitless, he and his supporters turned their attention to preventing Kay from being elected Rector. Their first thought was of Calcott, whose candidature Pattison had rejected with such contempt – 'Think,' he exclaimed, 'of our extremity when we were obliged to Offer the Rectorship to Johnny!' But whatever Calcott's intellectual shortcomings, he was honest enough to reply that he would keep his promise to vote for Kay. Then they turned to a former fellow, James Thompson, who had always been West's first candidate. 'As soon as his name was mentioned,' Pattison commented, 'I saw like a flash of light the deliverance which it held out', but it was lightning in a sky dark with thunder. Pattison himself had a very low view of Thompson, whom he regarded as a reactionary and boorish lowbrow, good-natured as he might appear to be. As much as, perhaps even more than, Kay he stood for the conservative clerical ascendancy. Yet, at three that dark November morning, Espin and Andrew woke up West and told him that they were seriously thinking of putting forward Thompson as a candidate. West was not unnaturally flurried by the news. Thompson had been his first choice – he had more in common with him than with Kay – and he held that his promise to Thompson took precedence over his later promise to Kay. West's change of heart was as crucial as Kettle's had been.

So, in the early morning light, the fellows gathered in the chapel. Five – Pattison, Perry, Andrew, Espin and West – voted for Thompson. Kettle and Calcott voted for Kay. Gibbs and Metcalfe abstained, confused and angry at the turn of events. Gibbs was a close friend of Thompson, but he had previously promised to vote for Kay. Only one of those who voted for Thompson, West, really wanted him to be Rector. At the very last minute, Kettle had sought to dissuade Pattison from supporting Thompson, reminding him with some justice that, while Kay was not completely unsympathetic to university reform, it was anathema to Thompson.

The election cast no credit on any of those who had taken part in it. Indeed, no sooner was it over than attempts were made to declare it invalid. The elder Kay applied for a writ of *mandamus*, on the grounds that the college's Visitor, the Bishop of Lincoln, was empowered only to interpret, not to dispense, the college statutes. This referred to an event some years earlier when Pattison had failed inadvertently to take the bachelorship of divinity within the prescribed terms laid down by the statute. The Visitor, with some justice, had restored Pattison to his fellowship. This, in the view of Kay's legal advisers, amounted to a dispensation. Legally, Pattison was no longer a fellow; if so, the election must be declared null and void. It was not an argument which found much favour, but it helped to highlight what was thought in many quarters to be a scandalous example of academic abuse. Kettle himself publicised the recent happenings in a pamphlet which a former member of the college trenchantly described as a 'violation of College *arcana*'. Even Pattison and his friends were pleased at the prospect of overturning the election, which they had manipulated, and began to canvas other possible candidates. Understandably, the new Rector was bemused and hurt by these developments. 'Your friends,' he told Pattison bluntly, 'took me up to save themselves from out[side] College influence – in other words from Michell's nominee [i.e. Kay]. Why should they now forsake me?'

Eventually the college's Visitor, in a letter expressing his grave disapproval of what had been happening, confirmed Thompson's election as Rector. The college, having made an abortive attempt to rid itself of Kettle, settled down to an uneasy peace. As the *Memoirs* makes abundantly clear, the election had an enduring, traumatic effect on Pattison. He told his sisters:

> You must estimate the crash sufficiently, which as far as my academical career is concerned is utter, complete and hopeless. The College, for my time, is extinguished – younger men, like Espin may work for its renewal, but the labour of 12 years is undone for me – the stone which I had just succeeded in rolling up the hill is just rolled back again to where I found it . . . We have all

here lost something but no one has lost what I have lost – all their earthly hopes.

If understandable in the light of events, the statement was characteristically exaggerated and pessimistic. Even when he began rewriting his diary, the torture was still evident:

Oh, what a degrading blow this has been to me . . . I returned from town on New Year's Day with an acute feeling of pain and despair. But today this has subsided into a dull, heavy ache, perceptible even through sleep, and dawning upon me as soon as consciousness returns in the morning, and having about me all day.

Even five years later, at the start of 1856, he felt 'how keenly my moral nature has suffered under my disappointment – how Love, Faith and Hope are gradually dying out in me – and how I do not make any effort to resist the death!' The ache was to persist to the very close of his life, and was not even eliminated by his election to the Rectorship in 1861. In the *Memoirs*, he relived that searing experience.

NOTES

Chapter 1

1.   Harriet Martineau (1802–76), writer and Unitarian; autobiography published posthumously in 1877. Leigh Hunt (1784–1859), English radical writer and romantic; published autobiography in 1859.

2.   Thomas Mozley (1806–93), fellow of Oriel College 1829; married Newman's sister, Harriet Elizabeth, in 1836; editor *British Critic* 1841–3; rector, Plymtree, Devon, 1868–88. Pattison admired his *Reminiscences, chiefly of Oriel and the Oxford Movement* (2 vols, 1882). 'Not even the *Apologia*,' he wrote, 'will compare with in respect of minute fulness, close personal observation and characteristic touches.'

3.   George Sand (1804–76), French writer and novelist; author of *Histoire de ma vie* (1876).

4.   'My father': The Revd Mark James Pattison (1788–1865); educated at Brasenose College, Oxford; Rector of Hauxwell, Yorkshire, 1825–65.

5.   'Sister Dora': Dorothy Pattison (1832–78) became a member of the sisterhood of the Good Samaritans at Coatham, and an excellent surgical nurse. She left the sisterhood to take charge of a hospital at Walsall (where there is a statue of her), where she died. When, in April 1875, Dora was sick, she wrote to Mark: ' "Goodbye", lest this should be the last letter you receive from me – lest the pestilence which is raging around me should smite me'. He commented that the letter was a 'piece of play-acting', nor did he go to her funeral: 'I should be sadly out of place among those "sisters" and long-coated hypocrites.'

6.   'B.N.C.': Brasenose College, Oxford.

7.   Hodson (1770–1822), fellow of Brasenose College; Principal 1809–22. Described a few lines later by the Greek adjective: haughty.

8.   'Gentlemen commoners': undergraduates of higher social status who, in return for paying higher fees, were accorded special privileges, including membership of the college senior common room.

9.   'Lord George Gordon': Pattison's memory partly played him false. This was General Thomas Gordon, who matriculated at Brasenose College in 1806, and became a general in the Greek Army.

10.   'A tuft-hunter': one who seeks the acquaintance of men of rank. Tufts were the names given to the gold tassels on the caps worn by undergraduates of noble birth.

11. 'The two Hebers': Reginald (1783–1826), Brasenose College; won many prizes including the prize for English verse, the subject 'Palestine'; later Bishop of Calcutta; hymn writer, including 'From Greenland's Icy Mountains'. Richard (1773–1833), fellow of All Souls College; friend of William Wilberforce; MP 1821–6; founder of the Athenaeum Club.

12. J. E. Tyler (1789–1851), fellow of Oriel College 1812–26; Canon of St Paul's. Richard Whately (1787–1863), fellow of Oriel College 1811–22; founder of 'Noetics'; Archbishop of Dublin 1831–63. Sir Robert Peel (1788–1850), Christ Church, took a double first; MP for Oxford University 1817; Prime Minister 1841–6. W. D. Conybeare (1787–1857), geologist; Dean of Llandaff. Baden Powell (1796–1860), Savilian Professor of Geometry, Oxford, 1827–60; contributor to *Essays and Reviews*. A. J. Valpy (1787–1854), fellow of Pembroke College, Oxford 1811; editor and publisher of classical texts and journals. It is not clear to which of the contemporary Rollestons Pattison was alluding, but probably Matthew (1788–1817), fellow of University College 1805–17.

13. 'Litt. Hum.': Literae Humaniores or Greats, the examination (since 1802) for an honours degree in classics and philosophy.

14. The textbook on logic, long in use, compiled by Henry Aldrich 1647–1710, Dean of Christ Church.

15. 'Cain and Abel': the slang name given to a stone statue in the centre of Brasenose College quad, showing a man astride a smitten foe (actually Samson slaying one of the Philistines), on which undergraduates would climb after wine parties; it was removed in 1881.

16. Aristophanes, *Clouds* 225; spoken by Socrates as he appears in a basket suspended from the stage crane: 'I am walking on air and reflecting about the sun.'

17. 'C.P.B.': commonplace book.

18. Hume's *History of England* (1754–62).

19. William Blackstone's *Commentaries on the Laws of England* (1765–9).

20. Edward Copleston (1776–1849), fellow of Oriel College 1795–1814; Provost 1814–28; promoted higher academic standards, making Oriel the foremost college in the university; Bishop of Llandaff and Dean of St Paul's 1828–49.

21. Pattison's father was Chaplain to the Duke of Leeds at Hornby Castle, the principal ducal seat since 1811. 'Today Papa went to Hornby in the carriage and Mr Paddon came up to do duty here. We had no afternoon service. Papa saw the Duke, Lady C., Mr Fox, the Duchess' (Diary, Sunday 5 June 1831). The Duke's daughter, Charlotte, married Sackville Lane Fox, who became Lord Conyers in 1859.

22. 'Oxford Calendar': the almanack published annually which listed the names of all the fellows of the colleges.

23. Edward Ellerton (1770–1851), Master of Magdalen College School, Oxford 1799; fellow of Magdalen College; founded Ellerton theological essay prize at Oxford and exhibitions at Magdalen and Richmond Schools.

24. William Glaister, fellow of University College 1821–38; Rector of Beckley, Sussex 1837–61.

25. Lord Conyers Osborne (1812–31), matriculated at Christ Church in 1829; accompanied by Mr Paddon as a private tutor; killed accidentally in a scuffle with a fellow noble student, Lord Hillsborough.

26. Thomas Churton, fellow of Brasenose College 1821–52. Harington, fellow of Brasenose College 1822–34; Principal 1842–53. Hall, fellow of Brasenose College 1812–32; Chaplain to the Duke of Clarence and Rector of Middleton Cheney 1831–51.

27. David Horndon, Exeter College 1818; JP in Pencreven, Cornwall. A life-long friend of Pattison. He wrote of his daughter, who accompanied Pattison on a trip to the Continent in 1883, that 'she was an absolute blank – can't give attention enough to anything to understand or to remember it.'

28. William Falconer, fellow of Exeter College 1827–39. J. L. Richards, fellow of Exeter College 1818–36. *Schlendrian* means unoriginal or old-fashioned.

29. William Sewell (1804–74), fellow of Exeter College 1827, of Merton College 1831–51. A high churchman, associated with the foundations of St Columba's College, Rathfarnham, and Radley College (1847). Later, he was forced to live abroad to avoid his creditors.

30. It was normal for students to supplement college tuition, often then of poor quality, by employing coaches to whom they paid extra fees for tuition.

31. Charles Ogilvie (1793–1873), fellow of Balliol College 1816–34; Rector of Ross from 1839; first Regius Professor of Pastoral Theology at Oxford 1842–73. James T. Round, fellow of Balliol College 1820–35.

32. J. M. Chapman, fellow of Balliol College 1824–38; Rector of Tendring, Essex, 1838–78.

33. The Ireland University Scholarship in Classics, founded by Dean Ireland of Westminster in 1825.

34. John Henry Newman (1801–90), fellow of Oriel College 1822; Vicar of St Mary's, Oxford 1828; received into the Roman Catholic Church in 1845; cardinal 1879. A major influence in Pattison's life. Of him Pattison wrote later: 'Thin, pale, and with large lustrous eyes piercing through this veil of men and things, he hardly seemed made for this world. But his influence had in it something of magic. It was never possible to be a quarter-of-an hour in his company without a warm

feeling of being invited to take an onward step; and Newman was sure to find out in time whether that onward step was taken. One of his principles was that every man was good for something, but you must find out what it was, and set him to work accordingly. He kept a careful account of his pupils, always having his eye on the metal rather than on the dross ... Newman always tried to reach the heart and understanding of those with whom he had to do.' He was to pay Pattison a touching visit in his final illness.

35. Robert Wilberforce (1802–57), son of William Wilberforce, fellow of Oriel College 1826; Archdeacon of East Riding. Friend of H. E. Manning (later cardinal) and followed him into the Roman Catholic Church.

36. Richard Hurrell Froude (1803–36), fellow of Oriel College 1826; intimate friend of Newman and on the extreme wing of the Tractarian Movement. His *Remains* were edited by J. B. Mozley; brother of J. A. and William Froude.

37. Joseph Dornford (1794–1867), fellow of Oriel College 1819–36; Rector of Plymtree, Devon 1832–67. Of him Pattison wrote: 'a Peninsular hero ... carried off the highest honours ... ripened ultimately into a sort of Tractarian; and, going off into a country parish, lived in hot water with his parishioners. The provocation alleged was, of course, ecclesiastical innovation; but the real cause was the veteran's success in ingratiating himself with the female part of the parish ... An avenue of seventeen cypresses in his garden at Plymtree had been the monument of as many unsuccessful courtships.'

38. The Laudian statutes were promulgated by Archbishop Laud, then Chancellor of Oxford, in 1636. The university was governed by them until 1854.

39. 'No one is to reside or be taken in as a guest in private houses.'

40. Manuel Echalaz, fellow of Trinity College 1829–31; Rector of Appleby, Leicestershire 1830–77.

41. Edward Hawkins (1789–1882), fellow of Oriel College 1813–28; Vicar of St Mary's, Oxford, 1823–28 (succeeded by Newman); Provost 1828–74. A strong opponent of the Tractarians, he drew up a condemnation of Newman's Tract XC.

42. John Keble (1792–1866), fellow of Oriel College 1812–35; Professor of Poetry, 1831–41; Vicar of Hursley, Hampshire, 1836–66. Preached a sermon at St Mary's on 'National Apostasy' on 14 July 1833 which started the Oxford Movement. His *Christian Year* appeared anonymously in 1827 and became a best seller.

43. Hauxwell Hall was a short distance from the church and the rectory. It was the home of the local squire, the Dalton family.

44. Gilbert White (1720–93), naturalist; author of the *Natural History and Antiquities of Selborne* (1769–87).

45. Prideaux John Selby (1788–1878) published *Illustrations of British Ornithology* (1825–34). George Montagu (1751–1815) wrote *The Sportsman's Directory* (1792) and *Ornithological Dictionary* (1802).

46. James Rennie (1787–1867), Professor of Natural History at King's College, London; emigrated to Australia.

47. *The Prelude* by William Wordsworth, one of Pattison's favourite poets: 'that unique autobiographical epic.'

48. Pattison's sisters shared their brother's adherence to Tractarianism (for which he was largely responsible) and they failed to understand his later abandonment of Tractarian views, with the result that his own relationship with them (except with Rachel, who had died in 1874) became remote and even unfriendly. The 'one who remained (and remains) dedicated to me still' was Fanny Pattison (1821–92) who had become Mother Superior of the Holy Rood at Middlesbrough. He found her devotion embarrassing: 'she is really attached to me in a way which none of the others are ... Her icy reserve soon gets on my nerves.'

49. W. J. Copleston, fellow of Oriel College 1826–40; Rector of Cromhall, Gloucestershire 1839–74.

50. 'A little coat'. The word is cited only once in the Greek lexicon, from a lost play by Aristophanes. It is a rare type of the standard word for coat and it was very precious of Pattison to use it.

51. J. F. Christie, fellow of Oriel College 1829–48; later Vicar of Badgeworth, Gloucestershire.

52. Thomas Porter, matriculated at Oriel College in 1831.

53. John Belfield, matriculated at Oriel College in 1830. Took a fourth class in Greats but a first in maths; corresponded with Pattison. 'I cannot get quite disgusted with the law ... I hope I shall have the good sense to see the folly of it.' Later he became a JP, living at Primley Hall, Devon.

54. William Froude (1810–79), Oriel College; later engineer and naval architect; brother of Hurrell and J. A. Froude.

55. W. C. Buller took a first class in maths in 1835; fellow of Exeter College. A. Entwistle also took a first in maths and was a fellow of Brasenose College 1836–9. A. Sheppard was later Vicar of Flimby. William Phelps became a lawyer and was high sheriff of Gloucester.

56. 'Far from my companions in captivity being a consolation for me, I had about as much trouble in accustoming myself to them as to other things; we had so few things in common. How difficult this first meeting with an ordered society was for me (and doubtless by my fault).'

57. 'By baring the head for the right length of time'.

58. 'Bashfulness'.

59.   'It is necessary to know how to vanquish modesty, and never to lose it.'

60.   Probably his elder sister, Eleanor Pattison.

61.   G. A. Denison (1805–96), fellow of Oriel College 1828–39; Vicar of Broadwinsor, Dorset, 1838–51; Archdeacon of Taunton 1851–3; resigned over disagreement with his bishop over eucharistic doctrine. Prosecuted in the ecclesiastical court in 1856 and deprived; but the decision was reversed. A high churchman and vigorous controversialist.

62.   *Alcestis*, line 30. 'Phoebus, you are again trespassing on the honour due to the underworld.' The metre is a common one in Greek tragedy, usually for the entrance of the chorus, but in this case the line is spoken by Death. An anapaest is a foot made up of two short syllables followed by a long one.

63.   Three colleges were in the vanguard of academic reform, Balliol, Christ Church and Oriel. Oriel, as a result of the policies followed by Provosts Eveleigh and Copleston, in opening fellowships and in insisting on higher academic standards, had by the 1830s become the leading college in Oxford.

64.   'Pre-eminence'.

65.   H. G. Liddell, Dean of Christ Church 1855–91; with Robert Scott, the compiler of the Greek-English Lexicon (1843).

66.   The majority of the fellows were clerks in holy orders of the Church of England, and entrants to the university still had to swear to the Thirty-nine Articles of the Church of England.

67.   Sir Robert Peel, future prime minister. Alexander Baring, Lord Ashburton (1774–1848), financier and statesman. William Huskisson (1770–1830), politician, run down at the opening of the Liverpool and Manchester Railway.

68.   Lord Grenville, Chancellor of Oxford 1809–24; represented the Whig interest.

69.   Lord Eldon (1751–1838), Lord Chancellor 1801–27; a high Tory in politics.

70.   College estates had not yet been affected adversely by the severe agricultural depression occurring in the 1880s.

71.   'Running out leases by not renewing the fines': It had long been the practice of Oxford colleges to pay in part the stipends of fellows by levying a fine upon college tenants at the renewal of leases and dividing the proceeds among the fellows.

72.   John Eveleigh (1748–1814), fellow of Oriel College 1770; Provost 1781–1814.

73.   The examination system, a series of oral exercises, had become a farce by the end of the eighteenth century. An honours examination,

classified in its nature, which became a written examination in classics and mathematics, was introduced in 1802. Only a minority of men took the honours; the others were passmen. It was not until after 1854 that honours examinations in other subjects, such as history, law and science, were introduced.

74.   Until 1834 members of New College could graduate without taking a university examination.

75.   Every college had a Visitor, often a bishop, who was the final court of appeal for the interpretation of college statutes and other problems.

76.   'An investigation into real quality'.

77.   The Noetics, from the Greek word meaning 'pertaining to the mind or intellect', were a group of fellows of Oriel College (Richard Whately, Edward Copleston and Edward Hawkins), mainly Whigs in politics, who believed in the comprehensiveness of the Church of England and were critical of the Tractarians.

78.   *Anyone voicing objections in public*
      In the street will be shot instantly;
      Objections voiced by gesture
      Will equally be punished.

79.   E. B. Pusey (1800–82), fellow of Oriel College 1822; Regius Professor of Hebrew and Canon of Christ Church 1828; author of many tracts. Tractarians were often called Puseyites. Pattison found him unsympathetic; he had the 'effusion of a fiery zealot who had lost his balance'.

80.   Thomas Arnold (1795–1842), fellow of Oriel College 1815; Headmaster of Rugby School 1828–42; a strong believer in the Erastian and comprehensive character of the Church of England; critical of the Tractarians.

81.   R. D. Hampden (1793–1868), fellow of Oriel College 1814; gave Bampton Lectures at Oxford; criticised for heterodox theology; appointment as Regius Professor of Divinity (1836) was opposed by the Tractarians and caused bitter controversy; Bishop of Hereford 1848.

82.   Blanco White (1775–1841), educated in Spain and ordained a Roman Catholic priest, but became an Anglican and ordained a clergyman of the Church of England (1814); studied at Oxford and made a member of the Oriel senior common room (1826). A close friend of Richard Whately, whom he accompanied to Dublin, where he later adopted Unitarian views.

Chapter 2

1.   J. W. Burgon (1813–88), fellow of Oriel College 1846–76; Vicar of St Mary's, Oxford, 1864; Dean of Chichester 1875.

2. John Conington (1825–69), fellow of Magdalen College 1848–55 and Professor of Latin.

3. University Reform Act (1854), a sequel to the Royal Commission set up in 1850, reformed the government of the university by substituting the Hebdomadal Board, consisting of the heads of the colleges, by an elected Hebdomadal Council. It increased the powers of the resident masters (in Congregation) and diminished those of all MAs (Convocation). It required colleges to revise their statutes, and put in train the machinery which led to the setting up of new honours schools.

4. Goldwin Smith (1823–1910), fellow of University College 1850–67; Secretary of the Oxford University Commission; Regius Professor of History 1858–66; emigrated to North America, where he was involved in the foundation of Cornell University before moving to Toronto. A strong liberal and controversialist.

5. Pattison stated some of his criticisms of the contemporary university vigorously in his book *Academical Organization* (1868).

6. 'Putting in motion the appearance of conflict'.

7. In 1854 Newman went to Dublin as Rector of the Catholic university recently established there. The scheme turned out to be a failure, but it led to his important book *The Idea of a University* (1852), in which he considered what he believed to be the aims and principles of a Christian education.

8. 'The complete circle', i.e. education in the round.

9. 'Nonchalant'.

Chapter 3

1. Richard G. Young, matriculated at Oriel College in 1832; a close friend but suffered from ill-health and died in 1843.

2. Caspar Hauser (1812–33), a German youth said by some to be the son of the Grand Duke of Baden who had been supplanted in favour of a cadet branch; but this was denied. The wounds he received, either from a stranger or self-afflicted, publicised his case, which became the theme of many plays, novels and poems.

3. Commemoration, incorporating festivities and the giving of honorary degrees, marked the end of the academic year; sometimes called Encaenia.

4. 'Parker's': the well-known Oxford bookshop.

5. 'Carefree repose and a life that cannot disappoint', Vergil, *Georgic* 2, 467.

6. Charles Daubeny (1795–1867), fellow of Magdalen College 1815–67; Professor of Chemistry 1820–55; of Botany 1834; of Rural Economy

1840. He wrote *A Description of Active and Extinct Volcanoes* (1826) and *Introduction to the Atomic Theory* (1831).

7. 'Responsions': a university examination. Its name was originally given to one of the scholastic exercises; but from 1808 it was an elementary examination in Greek and Latin, logic and geometry, to be passed generally in the second year.

8. The *Ephemerides* was a journal, kept from 1597 till his death in 1614, by the classical scholar, Isaac Casaubon, whose life Pattison was to write; for a description of him, see M. Pattison, *Casaubon*, 2nd edn, 1892, 87–91.

9. His companion was probably his friend David Horndon. On 5 September 1883, Pattison told Meta Bradley that he had heard from Horndon 'reminding me of a tour we made together to the Lakes in 1833'.

10. J. E. Giles, matriculated at Queen's College, Oxford; Magdalen Hall barrister.

11. J. D. Collis (1816–79), fellow of Worcester College 1829–47; Headmaster of Bromsgrove School 1842–67.

12. J. T. Landon, scholar of Worcester College 1835; fellow of Magdalen College 1843–47.

13. Dugald Stewart (1753–1828), author of many philosophical works.

14. Edward Gibbon, classical historian; author of *Decline and Fall of the Roman Empire*. His *Autobiography* was published posthumously in his *Miscellaneous Works* (1796), edited by his friend Lord Sheffield.

15. E. C. Philpotts, son of Bishop Philpotts of Exeter; matriculated at Oriel College in 1832; held livings in Devon and Cornwall. C. Y. Crawley, matriculated at Oriel College in 1831; Rector of Taynton, Gloucestershire, 1864–76.

16. *Essays and Reviews* (1860), a collection of essays by seven authors, upholding free enquiry into religious matters, which caused bitter controversy and was condemned by the bishops and Convocation. Pattison had contributed a theologically innocuous essay on 'Tendencies in religious thought 1688–1750'.

Chapter 4

1. His father had recently had a nervous breakdown and was confined to a mental hospital at Acomb, near York.

2. C. P. Eden (1807–85), fellow of Oriel College 1832; Vicar of St Mary's, Oxford, 1843–50.

3. Richard Michell, Wells fellow of Lincoln College 1830–42; Vice-

Principal of Magdalen Hall 1848–68; Principal 1868–74, of Hertford College 1874–7. A man of powerful intelligence and good reputation as a tutor and an excellent Latinist; public orator 1848–77. A strong Evangelical, he distrusted and disliked Pattison; Pattison returned the compliment.

4. Hayward Cox, fellow of Queen's College, Oxford 1828–33; Vice-Principal of St Mary Hall.

5. Henry Wall, fellow of Balliol College; Vice-Principal of St Alban Hall and Wykeham Professor of Logic.

6. 'I soon observed that all these authors were almost perpetually at variance with one another, and I conceived the fanciful notion of reconciling them, which cost me much labour and waste of time. I muddled my head, and made not the least progress. Finally, I gave up this plan, and adopted an infinitely better one, to which I attribute all the progress that I have made, notwithstanding my lack of talents, for there is no doubt that I never possessed much capacity for study. As I read each author, I made a rule of adopting and following all his ideas without adding any of my own or of anyone else's, and without ever arguing with him. 'Let us begin,' I said to myself, 'by collecting a store of ideas, true and false but all of them clear, until my mind is sufficiently equipped to be able to compare them and choose between them.' . . . After I had spent some years never thinking independently, . . . I found myself equipped with a great enough fund of learning to be self-sufficient and to think without the help of another.' (*Confessions*, trans. J. M. Cohen, 226)

7. Orlando Hyman, fellow of Wadham College, Ireland Scholar 1834. He wrote to Pattison: 'I am now with a pupil at 58 Horn Street, Reading, where I shall stay till the 17th of September, on which day I return to Oxford, and will be ready for you against the 20th.' (26.8.1835)

8. James Burn, *The Autobiography of a Beggar Boy* (1855)

9. Edward Woollcombe, Oriel College 1833; fellow of Balliol College 1838–80; Rector of Tendring, Essex, 1879–80.

10. J. S. Utterton, matriculated at Oriel College in 1832, first class 1836; Suffragan Bishop of Guildford, 1874. He was writing to Pattison: 'My vacation seems to have been of much the same cast as your's, pleasant, quiet but not so profitable as it should have been . . . but now having its horizon overhung with the dark clouds of a dull Oxonian term, tho I trust the chearful (*sic*) welcome of a few old friends will cast even a bright beam over that. But, alas, why is it, my dear friend, that we are always viewing the past with remorse and the future with despondency or melancholy?' (23.9.1834)

11. James Hatsell, second class at Oriel College in 1837. 'Walk with Hatsell and wine with him after din. To Newman's party' (26.2.1839).

On 2 May following, Woollcombe told Pattison that Hatsell had shot himself.

12. William Lonsdale, matriculated at Oriel College in 1833; barrister.

13. James Mozley (1813–78), Oriel College; failed to get elected to a fellowship at Lincoln College because of his supposed Tractarian sympathies; fellow of Magdalen College 1840; Regius Professor of Divinity 1871.

14. Arthur Kensington, first class at Oriel College in 1836; fellow of Trinity College. A close friend of Pattison, whose name appears constantly in his diary; e.g. 13 April 1839: 'To Kensington; sate and walked with him till 5. He dined with me. Went and sate with him till X'; 1 May: 'Went to K. On water with him . . . did not get back till 5.'

15. Leonard Montefiore, a promising young man who died aged 26 in 1879; his unpublished writings were published privately in 1881.

Chapter 5

1. Richard Mant (1776–1848), fellow of Oriel College; Bishop of Down; edited the Bible, with notes selected from other Anglican divines (1814).

2. B. G. Niebuhr (1776–1831). His *Roman History* (1811–32) was remarkable for the employment of inferences deduced from a scientific study of evidence.

3. Eleanor Pattison (1817–96), Pattison's principal correspondent at home; a highly intelligent and well-read woman, enthusiastically attracted to Tractarianism, so drawing upon herself her father's wrath. In 1853 she married a local clergyman. Her father tried to prevent the marriage by suggesting that there was insanity in her family. In later life her relations with her brother became strained.

4. H. H. Vaughan (1811–85), fellow of Oriel College 1835–42; Regius Professor of Modern History 1845–58; a strong supporter of radical university reform.

5. Henry Shepheard, fellow of Oriel College 1836–44. Pattison expressed his disgust at his appointment to the living of Thornton Steward, near Hauxwell: 'not only an opponent of the Oxford movement, but a thorough Evangelical of the old Calvinistic school.'

6. W. F. Donkin (1814–69), astronomer; fellow of University College 1836–43; Savilian Professor of Astronomy 1842–63.

7. F. W. Faber (1814–63), fellow of University College 1836–44; joined the Roman Catholic Church; formed the community of the Brothers of the Will of God (1845) and the Oratory of St Philip Neri (1848); founder of the London Oratorians.

8. R. W. Church (1815–90), fellow of Oriel College; Dean of St Paul's 1871–90; wrote the classic *History of the Oxford Movement*. J. C. Prichard, fellow of Oriel College 1838–42; Vicar of Mitcham, Surrey.

9. Samuel Taylor Coleridge (1772–1834), poet and literary critic; student of Shakespeare; as a philosopher, much influenced by German writers, and a critic of Utilitarianism.

10. August von Schlegel (1767–1845), Shakespearean scholar and translator; literary critic. '2nd Jan 1839 12–2 Schlegel. Dramatic lectures. Read indolently and cursorily'; '3rd Jan. 10–1–0, read Schlegel'; '8th Jan. Wrote out Schlegel's view of Greek drama.'

11. Sir William Hamilton (1788–1856), Professor of History and Logic at Edinburgh University; contributed articles to *Edinburgh Review*; highly critical of Oxford.

12. H. L. Mansel (1820–71), fellow of St John's College; high churchman and strong Tory, who propagated his views at Oxford, where he was Reader in Theology at Magdalen College from 1855; and Professor of Ecclesiastical History from 1866–8.

13. John Stuart Mill (1806–73), Utilitarian philosopher, economist and radical politician; author of *System of Logic* (1843), *Principles of Political Economy* (1848) and *On Liberty* (1859).

14. 'Forms of perception'.

15. 'Poetry or poems of concept'.

16. T. H. Green (1836–82), fellow of Balliol College; Whyte Professor of Moral Philosophy 1878–82; idealist philosopher.

Chapter 6

1. William Palmer (1811–79), fellow of Magdalen College; an extreme high churchman who advocated intercommunion with Greek and Roman churches; joined the Roman Catholic Church in 1855; brother of Roundell Palmer, Lord Chancellor.

2. Thomas Scott (1747–1821), Rector of Aston Sandford, Buckinghamshire; wrote *Force of Truth* (1779) in which he showed how his beliefs had developed from Unitarian rationalism to a fervent Calvinism. His works had much influence on Newman in his early years.

3. A. P. Stanley (1815–81), fellow of University College; Secretary of Oxford University Commission 1850–2; Canon of Canterbury 1851; Professor of Ecclesiastical History 1856; Dean of Westminster 1864–81; a broad churchman.

4. Sir Travers Twiss (1809–97), fellow of University College; Drummond Professor of Political Economy 1842–7; Regius Professor of Civil Law 1855–70.

5. 'The stepmother of her own children'.

6. 'We took the house in St Aldate's,' Newman wrote, 'from June 24, 1838, and the agreement I made with J. M[ozley] was, that I would supply Rent, Taxes, Rates, and two servants at £30 a year etc, and those who occupied the house their board ... In the house were Mozley, M. Pattison, H. J. Christie, his brother, P. M. Barker and C. Seager.'

7. William Jacobson (1803–84), fellow of Exeter College 1829; Regius Professor of Divinity 1848; Bishop of Chester 1815–84; author of *Patres Apostolici*.

8. In his diary he gives details of the fellowship examination: 'Tues.5.Nov. Read over some Cicero and my MS books and at 10 went into hall to the examination. Latin trans. Out at XII½, and in again I–IV, English Essay. Walk with Neville round Parks. Din. and Chapel. Home and got up Hist. of Fall of W. Empire and Ital. Republics. Weds 6 Nov. In again at X – Latin Essay X–I½. English Essay II–IV½. In the evening got up Eastern Hist. and many other things. Thurs. 7 Nov. In again at X. Historical and Miscells questions and Viva Voce till II. To Kensington and walk with him round N[ew] Coll. Din. in Hall. C. R. Chapel. To Union to vote for Rawlinson. Ryder and Mozley had tea with me. Read Boz's Sketches (by Dickens) till 1.0. Fri. 8 Nov. To Chapel. At IX½ Mozley came up to tell me I was elected at Lincoln.'

9. John Calcott, fellow of Lincoln College 1815–64, described as a 'man of almost childish naivete' whose lectures turned on three great questions, the nature of wild honey, the relative situation of Galilee and Judaea and the titles of the Lord. He had a great dislike of cats and during the Greek Testament Lecture, undergraduates would murmur that they could hear cats in the cellar beneath the hall, causing Calcott to cut short his lecture.

10. James Thompson, fellow of Lincoln College 1823–46; Rector of Cublington, Buckinghamshire, a college living 1845–52; Rector of Lincoln College 1851–60. 'Thompson,' Pattison noted in his diary, 'getting openly offensive, in his manner of reading [in chapel] he seems to set decency at defiance.'

11. William Kay senior, fellow of Lincoln College 1823–40; incumbent of Kirkdale, Yorkshire, until his death in 1866; rival candidate to Pattison in the Rectorial election of 1851.

12. John Radford, fellow of Lincoln College 1804–34; Rector 1834–51; a benign but old-fashioned cleric, known for the excellence of his wine cellar and collection of engravings. He was not an intellectual. Pattison described a sermon which he preached in All Saints Church in 1843 as 'inappropriate and unmeaning verbiage'. A strong Tory antipathetic to college and university reform.

13. 'We set course for Rome', Vergil, *Aeneid*, I, 205. Jack Morris (1812–80), fellow of Exeter College 1837; joined the Roman Catholic Church in 1846 and strongly pressed Pattison to follow his example.

14. He wrote to his sister, Eleanor: 'I may tell you of a scheme which has been in agitation some time and is now in a fair way of being set on foot. It is to publish a series of Lives of the Saints of the British Isles. I went with Church to Littlemore and saw J. H. N[ewman] about it . . . I had my choice and, as you may suppose, seized on the XIIIth century . . .' He wrote the lives of Archbishops Stephen Langton and Edmund of Abingdon.

15. In 1846, Pattison consulted Pusey about his religious doubts, but Pusey could not understand or sympathise: 'I am persuaded,' Pusey wrote, 'that yours is only a temptation not uncommon in which everything of this world comes before the mind as real, everything spiritual as unreal . . . What I wished to say to this (1) that it is a known fact that Satan has power to vest doubts with the mind (2) that faith, being the gift of God, was upheld by him and so, . . . was not a question at all of argument, but of a moral probation.' Pattison was not persuaded.

16. Littlemore was a village three miles east of Oxford, where Newman retreated, after leaving St Mary's, to a cottage which later became the George Inn until a new parsonage house, the so-called 'monastery' was built.

17. B. P. Symons (1785–1878), fellow of Wadham College 1812; Warden 1831–71; a leading Evangelical and opponent of Tractarians. Changed the hour of dinner at his college to dissuade undergraduates from attending Newman's sermons at St Mary's.

18. Ambrose St John, Christ Church 1834; Student 1834–45; went over to Rome 1845.

19. Edward Churton (1800–74), theologian; Rector of Crayke, Yorkshire, 1835; Archdeacon of Cleveland 1846–74.

20. *The British Critic*: theological quarterly which ran from 1827 to 1843; supported Tractarianism. Newman was editor from 1838 to 1841, when he was succeeded by Thomas Mozley.

21. Nicholas Wiseman (1802–65), Roman Catholic priest who reorganised the Roman Catholic Church in England; became Archbishop of Westminster and cardinal (1850); writings influenced the Tractarians.

22. St Remigius, apostle of the Franks, who baptised the Frankish king, Clovis I; Archbishop of Rheims. His Feast day was celebrated by the English Benedictines on 1 October.

23. William Lockhart (1820–92), follower of Newman who became a Roman Catholic in 1843 and entered the Rosminian Order.

24. Richard Sibthorpe (1792–1879), fellow of Magdalen College 1818;

became a Roman Catholic in 1841 and ordained priest, but reverted to Church of England in 1843; returned to Roman Catholicism in 1865.

25. Robert Coffin (1818–65), student of Christ Church 1835–45; Vicar of St Mary Magdalene, Oxford, 1843; became a Roman Catholic, later Roman Catholic Bishop of Southwark.

26. J. R. Bloxam (1807–91), fellow of Magdalen College 1836–68; Vicar of Upper Beeding, Sussex, 1862–91; sympathetic to Tractarianism.

27. Bernard Smith, fellow of Magdalen College 1836–9; became a Roman Catholic.

28. St Faith (d. c 287), popular medieval cult. Sarum rite: modification of the Roman rite, used at Salisbury Cathedral, imposed with modifications on the English Church in 1543 and later, in part, incorporated in the *Book of Common Prayer*.

29. Carthusians: contemplative religious order founded at the Grande Chartreuse in 1084.

30. Bollandists: Jesuit editors of the *Acta Sanctorum* (Lives of the Saints), so-called after their founder John van Bolland (d. 1615).

31. St John of Beverley (d. 721), Bishop of York. A monk of Whitby who retired before his death to the abbey at Whitby.

32. Giovanni Mansi (1692–1769), Canonist and Bishop of Lucca, who edited the early councils of the church.

33. The Greek word means 'traditional doctrine' (of the Church). William Goode (1801–68) was an evangelical clergyman and a stern critic of the Tractarians. He had recently (1842) written a book entitled *The divine rule of faith and practice; or a defence of the doctrine that Scripture has been since the time of the Apostles the sole rule of faith and practice*. Johann Suicer (1620–84) was a distinguished patristic scholar, author of a famous book *Thesaurus Ecclesiasticus* (1682). Newman was himself translating St Athanasius' condemnation of the Arian heresy (1842–4).

34. John Bull (1798–1858), Canon and Treasurer of Christ Church: 'an ornamental figure, portly, handsome, well-provided with canonries at Oxford and at Exeter, a Prebend at York and a comfortable living.' Cf a contemporary set of verse:

> On the Box with Will Whip, ere the use of the Rail,
> To London I travelled: and inside the mail
> Sat a Canon of Exeter: on the same perch
> Sat a Canon of Oxford's Episcopal Church:
> In the Minster of York a prebendal stall.
> And there sat a Parson, all pursy and fair,
> With a vicarage fat and three hundred a year.
> Now, good reader, perhaps you will deem the coach full:
> No, there was but one traveller – Dr John Bull.

35. Cistercians: religious order (White Monks) founded at Citeaux in 1098. St Bernard of Clairvaux was their most illustrious member.

36. In April 1833, Newman returned to Sicily, which he had visited early with Hurrell Froude and his father, 'drawn by a strange love to gaze upon its cities and mountains'. On his return, he fell dangerously ill of a fever at Leonforte, exclaiming, however, at the height of his illness, 'I shall not die. I have a work to do.' He suffered a relapse and was for a time delirious, but eventually he sailed from Palermo to Marseilles in an orange-boat. During the voyage the boat was becalmed for a whole week in the Straits of Bonifacio and he wrote the poem 'The Pillar of the Cloud', better known as the hymn 'Lead Kindly Light'. He arrived back at Oxford on 9 July 1833, five days before Keble preached his historic assize sermon at St Mary's.

37. S. R. Maitland (1792–1866), historian, librarian and keeper of the manuscripts at Lambeth 1838.

38. Lord Ashley, later Earl of Shaftesbury, was a fervent Evangelical. In 1840, he was president of the Parker Society, formed to reprint the works of the English reformers. He was strongly opposed to the election of the Tractarian candidate, Isaac Williams, to the Oxford chair of poetry in 1841–2, stating that 'no power on earth' would induce him to help in elevating Williams, the author of Tract 80, 'to the station of a public teacher'.

39. Charles Lloyd (1784–1829), Regius Professor of Divinity 1822–29; Bishop of Oxford 1827–9.

40. 'Clarity of style'.

41. 'The Oriel men, brimming over with intelligence, are barbarously denied St Mary's Hall.' St Mary's Hall was originally an academic hall supervised by Oriel but became independent of the College in 1656. It was reunited with Oriel in 1902. J. Dean, Principal of St Mary Hall, 1815–33.

42. Henry Wilberforce (1807–73), son of William Wilberforce. Took holy orders for the Church of England but became a Roman Catholic in 1850.

43. 'Non-jurors': members of the Church of England who, after 1688, were unready to take the oath of allegiance to William III, as this would break their previous oath to James II. They held a high conception of the church and priesthood, and their views influenced the Tractarians.

44. William Laud, Archbishop of Canterbury 1633–45; Chancellor of Oxford 1629–45; executed 1645.

45. H. O. Coxe (1811–81), sub-librarian (1838) and later librarian of the Bodleian Library at Oxford.

46. Pattison made several visits to France and was much impressed

by some aspects of the Roman Catholic Church there. In 1843 he visited the Sulpician seminary at Issy and wrote: 'What a contrast between this seminary and one of our Colleges ... between our short and badly attended Prayers and their almost hourly solemn and serious worship.'

47.   Kenelm Digby (1800–80), Trinity College, Cambridge; writer and Roman Catholic convert, whom Pattison met in 1845, *not* 1843.

48.   W. G. Ward (1812–82), fellow of Balliol College; wrote in defence of Newman's *Tract XC*; author of *The Ideal of the Christian Church* (1844), thought to be Romanist in its teaching; so deprived of his degree for holding heretical views. Became a Roman Catholic.

49.   Frederick Oakeley (1802–60), fellow of Balliol College 1827; became a Roman Catholic in 1845; later Canon of Roman Catholic diocese of Westminster.

50.   Manuel Johnson (1805–59), astronomer; keeper of the Radcliffe Observatory, Oxford. Of him Pattison wrote, a man 'who, at the age of thirty-five, and after some military service ... put himself to school to learn Latin and Greek, became a Radcliffe Observer, and a Gaius mine host to younger Tractarians ... None who have seen it can forget the beaming countenance, the laughing eye and the genial presence which thawed the sternest.'

51.   Charles Marriott (1811–58), fellow of Oriel College 1833; Principal of the Theological College, Chichester, 1839; Vicar of St Mary's, Oxford, 1850–58.

52.   W. J. Copeland (1804–85), fellow of Trinity College 1832–49; Vicar of Farnham, Essex, 1849–85.

53.   'Decamping'.

54.   J. A. Froude (1818–94), historian; fellow of Exeter College 1842. Wrote life of St Neot for Newman's 'Lives of the Saints': 'one which', as Pattison wrote, 'made the heaviest demands on credulity'. Subsequently broke with Tractarianism and orthodoxy. Author of *Nemesis of Faith* (1849), which was burned publicly by his colleague, William Sewell. Resigned fellowship; later Regius Professor of Modern History 1892–4.

55.   Charles Rose, fellow of Lincoln College 1812–36; Rector of Cublington, Buckinghamshire, a college living 1835–45. A haughty and indolent man who, as Curate of Combe, near Oxford, had upset his parishioners by strongly criticising the girls who came up the aisles, wearing pattens. At Cublington he held the service at whatever time he chose and was so long getting through it that no one came to it. Kept eight servants. A violent man who once threw a piece of bacon at his wife 'and the mark left on the wall yet'.

56.   Cf the letter which Pattison wrote to his sister, Eleanor, immediate-

ly after his election, 10 November 1839: 'The corporeal stature of the fellows is large, their intellectual small, the studies and thoughts of the older ones rather of the good old days of "Tory ascendancy" than of the reform era . . . They are of the Port and Prejudice School, better read in Hawker on Shooting, Burn's Justice or "Every Man his own Butler" than in Hooker or St Augustine. To explain the Gilbert Act, to get near partridges in January, to effect a Tithe Composition, and to choose a pipe of wine, to anathematize Ld. Melbourne and Co, none surpass them.'

57.   C. J. Meredith, fellow of Lincoln College 1826–49; Rector of Waddington, Lincolnshire, a college living.

58.   M. J. Green, fellow of Lincoln College 1837–49; Rector of Winterborne, Dorset, a college living 1848–89.

59.   William Kay junior, fellow of Lincoln College 1840–67; Principal of Bishop's College, Calcutta 1849–65; Rector of Great Leighs, Essex, 1866–86, a college living. A Hebrew scholar, he was later involved in the revised version of the Bible. He was also a strong Evangelical who supported Pattison on university reform, but Pattison found him personally disagreeable. A contemporary described him as 'narrow, intense with the temperament of a Torquemada but withal a good Hebraist of the old school'.

60.   Haynes Gibbs, fellow of Lincoln College 1824–56. Pattison's description seems somewhat unjust. Another fellow called him an 'inoffensive man of a sociable disposition who enjoyed his glass of wine'.

61.   The 'female cousin' was Philippa Meadows who, with her mother, Mary (1789–1860), Mark's father's sister, lived at Ainderby, near Hauxwell. An intelligent woman of great, if indiscriminate, learning, she became so obsessed with Tractarianism that she and her mother followed the Tractarian, John Keble, to his parish at Hursley. But Philippa became a fervent convert to the Church of Rome. Much as he admired his cousin's intellectual vigour, Pattison was repelled by what he came to regard as her closed mind on religious matters and her obscurantist ultramontanism.

62.   Anne Dacier (1654–1720), French female 'savant' highly reputed for her scholarship.

Chapter 7

1.   Pattison had become alienated from Tractarianism and was afflicted by religious doubts, which were not resolved by his correspondence with E. B. Pusey.

2. Rowland Muckleston, fellow of Worcester College 1837–56; classical examiner 1847.

3. J. E. Bode, Student of Christ Church 1841–7; classical examiner 1846–8.

4. George Hudson (1800–71), the 'railway king', manager of the York and North Midland Railway Co, etc. As a result of over-speculation, the railway boom collapsed and Hudson retired to the continent.

5. C. P. Golightly (1807–85), a 'clerical gadfly'; opposed Hampden's appointment as professor, but was strongly hostile to the Tractarians; a strong supporter of the scheme for erecting a Martyrs' Memorial at Oxford.

6. 'Two government commissions': one set up in 1850, which reported in 1852, and one in 1872, which reported in 1877.

7. These criticisms had already appeared in Pattison's book *Academical Organization* (1868).

8. 'Rhapsodic visions', implying intense mystical experience expressed in highly poetic language.

9. 'Diverted by witticisms about belief which the reasoning of a Pascal could not have succeeded in dispelling.' Ernest Renan (1823–92), historian and Hebrew scholar; wrote a heterodox life of Jesus (1863) which attracted much attention.

10. Arthur Haddan, fellow of Trinity College 1840–58; Rector of Boston on the Heath 1857–73; ecclesiastical historian.

11. The annual ceremony at the close of the academic year, when honorary degrees are conferred.

12. 'What a tiny wound, and what a huge man it overpowers'.

13. Coombe or Combe, a village seven miles from Oxford. The living had been appropriated to the college to supplement the Rector's stipend in 1479, and technically the Rector of Lincoln was the incumbent. The villagers were usually looked after by a curate, but the Rector lived a part of the time at Combe rectory.

14. 'Whatever the result, it is regrettable'.

15. Francis Jeune (1806–68), fellow of Pembroke College 1830–37; Master 1843–64; active as a supporter of university reform; Dean of Lincoln 1864; Bishop of Peterborough 1864.

16. A. C. Tait (1811–82), fellow of Balliol College 1834; Headmaster of Rugby School 1842; Bishop of London 1856; Archbishop of Canterbury 1869.

17. W. C. Lake (1817–97), fellow of Balliol College 1838–59; Dean of Durham 1869–94.

18. Two articles on the 'State of the English Universities with Special Reference to Oxford' (1831) and two on the 'Right of Dissenters to

Admission' (1834–5) in the *Edinburgh Review*, reprinted in Hamilton's *Discussions on Philosophy and Literature, Education and University Reform* (1852).

19.   The Great Western Railway was opened to Steventon near Didcot in 1840, but the branch line to Oxford was only opened in 1844. The university was opposed to the bringing of the railway to Oxford and sought, successfully, to keep the station as far away as possible from the colleges.

20.   *Suggestions on Academical Organization* (1868) was a radical book, far ahead of its time. In it Pattison stressed the accountability of universities to the nation, argued further for the endowment of research, for higher academic standards for entry, the creation of a strong professoriate and greater attention to science. He deplored the emphasis placed on athletics, the continued predominance of clerical influence and the restricted social entry.

21.   George Stilwell, of whom Pattison wrote at the time: 'The stillness that pervaded the college during the three days that the body was lying in Chapel I shall not soon forget.' Pattison's sermon in chapel was printed in *Sermons* (1885), 229–243.

22.   R. C. Christie (1830–1901), a Lincoln undergraduate, later Professor at Owen's College, Manchester. William Stebbing, another Lincoln undergraduate (1850), fellow of Worcester College 1856–71; barrister.

23.   'The old fogies do not quite like our cutting them so dead, but it is so much nicer to dine early'; 'Din. in hall for 2nd time this term. Very disagreeable to me'; 'I have eschewed C[ommon] R[oom] except during the audit and Christmas week.'

24.   'Thoughtlessness'.

25.   G. G. Perry, Wells Fellow of Lincoln College 1842–52; Rector of Waddington, Lincolnshire, a college living 1852–97

26.   A college feast, from the Latin *gaudeamus* (let us rejoice).

27.   'Necessary regency': By the Laudian statutes, the bachelor of arts might proceed to a master's degree after a series of further exercises, including the delivery of six lectures. He was then allowed to supplicate for a master's degree, which was granted by the Vice-Chancellor after a year of further disputations, etc. When he became a master, he was made a necessary regent and could attend meetings of congregation, lecture and so forth. While the concept of necessary regency (i.e. becoming an MA) survived, in the nineteenth century it had ceased to entail residence in the university.

28.   Philip Bliss, fellow of Lincoln College (1787–1857), university registrar 1824–57.

29.   J. C. Andrew, fellow of Lincoln College 1846–56; emigrated to

New Zealand where, after sheep-farming, he became a schoolmaster. Although one of Pattison's supporters, Pattison did not much like him: 'a man of fair abilities but not anything very superior'; 'a rough tyke'.

30. T. E. Espin, fellow of Lincoln College 1849–54; Rector of Hadleigh, Essex, a college living 1853–68; Warden of Queens College, Birmingham, 1865–75; Rector of Wallasey 1875–85, of Wolsingham 1885–1912. An enthusiastic supporter of Pattison. 'You can't imagine,' he wrote in 1847, 'how very much I sometimes want to talk with you', but later Pattison's increasingly unorthodox religious views led to a breach in their relationship.

31. Frederick Metcalfe, fellow of Lincoln College 1844–85; Vicar of St Michael's Oxford, 1849–85; a graduate of Cambridge where it was rumoured that he had once killed a man in a fight; a consistent opponent of reform, academic as well as ecclesiastical. Pattison described him as a 'vulgar and conceited fellow'. An enemy of Washbourne West: he once asked in the common room for a wad of cotton wool so that he could not hear West laugh. He had some knowledge of Scandinavian folklore.

32. Washbourne West, fellow and Bursar of Lincoln College 1845–97. An ardent Tory who cast as many votes as he could by the purchase of properties in some thirty different constituencies: he cast twenty-three votes in one general election. Not an intellectual, but a shrewd business man who promoted the college's interests, as well as his own. Preaching on Judas Iscariot, he is said to have criticised him for unbusiness-like conduct in accepting such inadequate remuneration as thirty pieces of silver.

33. Richard Hutchins, Rector of Lincoln College 1755–81.

34. J. L. R. Kettle, fellow of Lincoln College 1836–72; barrister at Lincoln's Inn.

35. Richard Bethell, Lord Westbury, Lord Chancellor 1861.

36. The offending preacher was W. W. Merry, fellow of Lincoln College 1859–84 and Pattison's successor as Rector, who in a sermon at St Mary's in 1879 painted an 'impudent portrait of me, which must have been unmistakeable to everyone'.

37. Pattison refers to the novelist Rhoda Broughton (1840–1920), who wrote an unflattering portrait of Pattison as Professor Forth in her novel *Belinda* (1883). Pattison had offended her by attributing to her the authorship of an anonymous letter, questioning his relations with a young lady friend, Meta Bradley.

38. Richard Greswell (1800–81), fellow of Worcester College.

39. A number of pamphlets describing the election, partisan in character, were published, e.g. J. L. Kettle, *A Letter to the Rev. James Thomp-*

son, London, 1851; T. E. Espin, *A Letter to the Rev. James Thompson*, Oxford, 1851; J. L. Kettle, *A Letter to the Rev. T. E. Espin*, London, 1851; *A voice to the Uninitiated on the Mysteries of the Lincoln Common Room*, London, 1852.

40. Roundell Palmer (1812–95), fellow of Magdalen College 1835; Tractarian sympathiser; Lord Chancellor 1872–4, 1880–5; first Earl of Selborne.

41. Sir Fitzroy Kelly (1796–1880), Solicitor-General 1845–6 and in 1852; Lord Chief Baron 1866–80. Sir R. J. Phillimore (1810–85), jurist and classical scholar.

42. 'I passed this day pretty miserably, as always.'

43. 'Either I must by temperament be destined to lead an exceptionally miserable existence or the commonly heard saying that one day can end men's illnesses is not true.'

44. Pattison's complaint of the treatment he received from Rector Thompson was not wholly justified. Although still a fellow, he absented himself from chapel and college meetings. 'You should,' the rector told him, 'consider that you are one of a Body, and not a dictator.'

45. Benjamin Jowett (1817–93), Master of Balliol College and Regius Professor of Greek. His career had followed in some ways a markedly similar pattern to that of Pattison, but Pattison criticised his concept of a university.

46. The Museum, erected partly as a result of the enthusiasm of Dr Henry Acland, to house the university's scientific collections, then sadly neglected. In spite of heavy opposition from the university's conservatives, the foundation stone was laid in 1855. The architect was Benjamin Woodward; John Ruskin was an enthusiastic supporter.

47. Anteia, wife of Proetus, King of Argos, loved Bellerophon but he rejected her overtures, so she falsely accused him to her husband. He sent Bellerophon with a message to the King of Lycia that he should be killed, but the assassination failed. The King realised that Bellerophon was more than human and had him married to his daughter. Eventually he fell out of favour with the gods, and grief-stricken wandered over the Aleian plain.

48. i.e. Philippa Meadows.

49. 'To disaccustom oneself from half-measures. And to live resolutely amidst the whole, the good and the beautiful.'

50. H. T. Buckle's *History of Civilisation* (1857–61) criticised methods of previous historians and tried to establish a secular basis for history by arguing that unchanging phenomena have unchanging laws and that the growth of civilisation depends on a series of unrelated factors, such as food products, climate, population and wealth.

51. After prolonged controversy, the university agreed to move the examination schools from the Bodleian library, so freeing invaluable space, to a new site on the Angel Inn in the High Street. This plan was strongly opposed by Dr C. E. Appleton, a fellow of St John's College and founder of the journal *The Academy*, and by others, like Pattison, who argued that the university should endow research rather than spend money on the examination schools. Pattison had chaired a public meeting at the Freemasons' Tavern in London in November 1872, where strong support for expenditure on research was expressed.

52. 'As I came from London last July,' Newman told their mutual friend, Robert Ornsby on 8 November 1861, 'I fell in with Pattison in the train. He did not recognize me, till I spoke to him but I knew him, and had a good deal of conversation with him down to Oxford.'

53. Isaac Casaubon (1559–1614), classical scholar. Pattison's book on Casaubon was published in 1875.

54. Whitwell Elwin (1816–1900), editor of the *Quarterly Review* 1853–6.

55. Henry Hallam, *An Introduction to the Literature of Europe During the Sixteenth and Seventeenth Centuries* (1837–9).

56. J. J. Scaliger (1540–1609), classical scholar; established the modern system of chronology and edited classical texts. D. Petavius' work *De Doctrina Temporum* (1627), directed against Scaliger, actually carried on his ideas. Pattison intended to write a book on Scaliger but ill-health and a dilatory nature made this abortive.

57. Chevalier Bunsen (1791–1830), German diplomat and theologian; ambassador in London 1841–54; largely responsible for the scheme for a joint Lutheran–Anglican bishopric in Jerusalem.

58. *The Counterfeit Scaliger*, title of a book by the Jesuit Caspar Scioppius (1607), criticising Scaliger.

59. 'I did not make trial of my manhood before the due time, but even postponed it.'

60. 'The work is growing, concrescing, gradually, and slowly, like a child in its mother's womb; I do not know what came into being first, what last. I become aware of one limb, one vessel, one part after another, that is, I simply write (things down) without troubling as to how they will fit into the whole, for I know that everything is derived from the same source. This is the way an organic whole comes into being, and only that can truly live.'

61. Peter Abelard (1079–1142), philosopher and theologian who drew large numbers of students to his lectures, which were marked by original thought and radical scholastic ideas.

62. 'I have profited from the days and years which have given me the

opportunity to live in intimacy with the great minds of the past. These good spirits who have given lustre to the world have not disdained me. Without asking for my credentials, who I was or where I came from, they have admitted me to their company. They have made their works available to me; they have allowed me to read into their thoughts, into their secrets; they have let me soak myself in their sweet learning. I have forgotten in this occupation the bad days which engulfed me. I have ventured also to share in their life, of that winged life, all powerful, omnipotent by which they rule as sovereigns of reality. Like them I have dared to make a profession of thinking. I have enjoyed plumbing the depths of things. I have conversed with ideas, embraced the possible; for, in such moments, I have managed to forget myself, and in following the beautiful procession of intelligences which have gone before I have enjoyed like them the truths of that moral universe of which they have given me the entry.'

63. Macmillan's had agreed with Mark Pattison to publish his *Memoirs* on 27 December 1883. 'It is a book', George Macmillan wrote, 'that cannot fail to excite keen interest.' After Pattison's death, Mrs Pattison prepared the book for publication, advised by Pattison's friend, the classical scholar, Ingram Bywater. She told the publisher (11 November 1884) that she had made some 'large omissions', more especially 'the detailed account of an outbreak of "mania" in his father' as well as 'some strictures on living people'. The original manuscript has not survived. The *Memoirs* was published on 4 March 1885 and subsequently reprinted, a run of 4,000 copies in all.

INDEX